THE FATE OF HONG KONG

THE FATE
OF
HONG KONG

Gerald Segal

St. Martin's Press
New York

ISBN 0-312-09805-7

Originally published in England by Simon & Schuster Ltd.

First U.S. Edition: September 1993
10 9 8 7 6 5 4 3 2 1

Contents

Preface to the American Edition

Why does the fate of Hong Kong matter to Americans? The destiny of nearly six million people is not merely a matter of a fading Britain disposing of the remnants of its colonies. Nor is the fate of Hong Kong just an unusual faltering step on the East Asian relentless climb to prosperity. As we rapidly approach 1997, when Hong Kong will be handed over to the Chinese government, the way in which the United States handles the issue will be a key test of how it handles the single most important issue in East Asia—the fate of China.

The fortune of Hong Kong has always been tied up with the fortune of China. When China was weak in the heyday of European imperialism, Britain was able to force China to surrender the land that eventually became Hong Kong. When China was divided and in decay, the United States joined with other powers in using the colony as a trading base. When China finally began to reform in the 1980s, Hong Kong boomed because it was a vital entrepôt for the China trade. In the immediate aftermath of the Peking massacre in June 1989, the United States joined with Britain in expressing concern about whether the people of Hong Kong would be dealt the same brutal treatment by Chinese troops. But as optimism about the Chinese economy returned in the 1990s, Hong Kong was increasingly seen as an engine of economic growth for China as a whole.

The very success of Hong Kong and China is the basis of the new American attention to this colony in the dying days of British rule. The crux of the problem is that China's economic growth has been so rapid that it looks set to become the world's largest economy soon after the year 2010. Thus China will finally live up to its historical promise of dominating East Asia—a region of increasing importance to the United States in the twenty-first century. Because the reason for China's success has a great deal to do with Hong Kong, the importance of American attitudes to the colony become tied up with broader problems with China as a whole.

China's success is built on a strategy of regional economic development, which in turn is built on the role of Hong Kong in helping develop Guangdong province, which surrounds Hong Kong. Deng Xiaoping has decided that the best way to avoid the fate of the Soviet Union is to put economic growth first, and in order to do so he has allowed China's regions to develop their own trading links with the outside world. The fastest growth and the best evidence that Deng's strategy is working comes from Guangdong and depends to a great extent on the lead and prosperity of Hong Kong. It is no exaggeration to say that China now relies more on Hong Kong than ever before, and this despite China having developed a far wider range of contacts with the outside world. As a result, the United States is coming to realize that by encouraging Hong Kong to stand up for its own interests, it is more possible to encourage and even help shape reform in China as a whole. The stakes in Hong Kong are about the 1.2 billion people of China as well as the nearly 6 million people in the colony.

As China grows strong, the United States will increasingly have to find ways to cope with the Chinese challenge. Helping Hong Kong to develop a more democratic form of government and to stand up to pressure from Peking is in essence a struggle to change all of China. As China's economy grows stronger, it becomes all the more important to make sure that different regions in China are given greater independence. A China that is more divided (although not necessarily formally divided) will be easier to handle than a monolithic power. If China's regions, such as Shanghai and Guangdong, can be encouraged to bargain for the favors of the global market economy and American corporations, then foreigners' bargaining positions will be enhanced. If Americans worry about managing trade with a Japan of some 120 million people, the process will appear to be a picnic compared to having to deal with a China ten times larger.

Of course, the United States and the West face difficult choices in dealing with the Hong Kong problem and the Chinese challenge. An important consideration is the level of American investment in Hong Kong and what is best for American corporations. When it was difficult to do business directly with China, American companies found it necessary to invest in and work through Hong Kong as a means of keeping in touch with the Chinese market. When direct trade with China became possible, American firms still found it useful to use a Hong Kong base for the China trade. And as Hong Kong itself prospered, it was simply good business sense to be involved in the booming Chinese market. But as Sino-American relations deteriorated after the Peking massacre and Chinese exports to the United States reached their present very high levels, support developed in Congress to punish China for human rights violations and the administration became anxious to reduce China's trade surplus. Both branches of government threatened trade sanctions of various sorts and the issue even became a feature of the 1992 election campaign. Needless to say, those with trading interests with China, and especially those with investments in Hong Kong, worried about a tougher line toward China.

The worry was derived from the fact that as the Hong Kong and Chinese economies converged, it became clear that most restrictions on Chinese trade that might be imposed by Washington would hit the Hong Kong economy especially hard. By knocking a few percentage points off Hong Kong's growth rate, albeit inadvertently, the United States would undermine confidence in the colony and perhaps even help increase the pace of migration. America's close ally, Britain, was certainly opposed to any policy that would harm Hong Kong's economy and increase migration.

The migration issue was also a problem in Washington. As the United States modernized its immigration rules (see the chapter on the United States) the Congress and administration were sympathetic to the British desire to see more places provided for people from Hong Kong. As 1997 approaches, and especially after the Peking massacre, the level of emigration from Hong Kong is increasing. Britain sought help from its allies in the form of a promise to provide immigration places, but ones that need not be taken up immediately. By arranging for such deferred migration, the United States made it possible for the jittery people of Hong Kong to prepare a bolt hole in case of emergency, but otherwise to stay in Hong Kong and make the transition to 1997.

The fact that the United States was so helpful to Britain and Hong Kong was due to a good measure of self-interest. By allowing a larger number of rich and educated people from Hong Kong to obtain American papers, the United States was draining off those who might otherwise have fled earlier to Canada and Australia. By boosting the numbers of Hong Kong Chinese with American citizenship, the United States was even better placed to prosper if the Hong Kong and Chinese economies continued to boom. But by undertaking such reform of American immigration policy, the United States was acknowledging the fact that the fate of Hong Kong had become an international problem. Although China was not displeased to see confidence reinforced in Hong Kong by the immigration scheme, its officials did worry that Britain was managing to involve the United States in an issue that had once been more or less contained to Sino-British relations.

From the Chinese point of view, being able to keep Hong Kong as a bilateral issue meant Peking had greater leverage. As the United States began cooperating in the internationalization of the Hong Kong problem, it was also taking a tougher line on Chinese abuses of human rights. With the end of the Cold War, China correctly understood that its human rights policies were under far closer scrutiny. The result was deteriorating Sino-American relations, with the fate of Hong Kong tied up in the knot of relations.

Chinese sensitivity to the matter of internationalization became acute in 1992 when Hong Kong's new Governor, Chris Patten, proposed reforms to the way in which Hong Kong would be governed. Although not in violation of the previous accords with China, Patten's proposals marked a change in tone and negotiating practice. Britain was now prepared to propose reforms without prior agreement by China, and negotiations were undertaken in somewhat more of a public glare. Although Chris Patten did not explicitly seek American help in getting China to accept his proposals, in practice there was much talk of seeking international and above all American support.

Britain knew that to seek American support directly would make China all the more jittery about an international conspiracy to democratize China via Hong Kong. Although in essence China was correct that the West and the United States were seeking the "peaceful evolution" of the Chinese system, a charade of noninterference in internal Chinese affairs was played out. Thus when Chris Patten visited the United States and told China that he could help them in their common interest in avoiding American trade sanctions, he was also implicitly saying that Britain had influence in Washington. He was, in effect, warning China that if he was humiliated by Chinese opposition to his reforms and if the economy of, and confidence in, Hong Kong was damaged, then the United States would not stay aloof from the dispute. If China did not help Chris Patten and Hong

Kong, then the American Congress, and the new Clinton administration, would be more likely to take a tougher line on China.

As the American edition of *The Fate of Hong Kong* goes to press, it is still unclear just how much tougher the Clinton administration will be on China than was the preceding administration under George Bush. It is certainly clear that Chinese fears about the new administration have encouraged them to moderate their tactics in response to the Patten proposals, even if they have not muted their rhetoric. In practice, China has come to accept that the United States is a major player in deciding the fate of Hong Kong. An American administration that wants to support the Patten proposals in the hope that it will teach China some moderation and even help democratize the country will find that Britain is willing to cooperate in the de facto internationalization of the Hong Kong question.

The key question remains whether it is wise for the United States to become more involved in the fate of Hong Kong. There is a cautious school of thought that sees China as too strong and important to be pressed into moderating its policies and therefore little attempt should be made to browbeat China to reform either its domestic policies or its attitudes to Hong Kong. Those with strong trading interests in China and Hong Kong tend to support this view.

On the other hand, the voices seem to be growing in favor of a more robust attitude. Even under the Bush administration it was demonstrated that China could be forced to compromise on trade issues when the United States held many cards and was prepared to play them. The fear of damaging American exports was overcome as part of a larger and longer-term calculus. The end of the Cold War also made Americans less fearful of upsetting a China that was once needed for its anti-Soviet capacity. The defeat of European communism also made Americans more prepared to punish a Communist party regime in Peking that was seen to be vulnerable. In general, the end of the Cold War demonstrated that appeasement of great power rivals did not work. When a British Governor proposes to challenge China with reasonable proposals enhancing democracy in Hong Kong and possibly even affecting China as a whole, it is not surprising that he should win support in the United States.

And yet it is clear that the United States has yet to have a full-fledged debate about its policy toward China. In the early post–Cold War days, the United States has focused on how to manage the decay of the Soviet empire and the new wars in Europe. What ever happened to all that talk of the "Pacific Century" and the supposed turning of the United States from the Atlantic to the Pacific? Of course, the roots of interest in the Pacific are still present as the economies of East Asia continue to flourish. When the United States eventually does pay more attention to the Pacific, it will see a different configuration than it last saw in the 1980s. By the mid-1990s, it will become increasingly clear that China is the major challenge to the states of East Asia and the United States across the water. How will the United States react?

While one can envisage a range of scenarios, including much closer United States–Japanese relations in order to cope with a China set to surpass Japan as the region's largest economy, it will be clear that the United States will need to formulate a more coherent strategy for coping with China. If China is still achieving its growth by allowing its coastal regions greater independence, then the fate of Hong Kong as the engine of growth in Guangdong will be vital. As we approach 1997, there may be the potential to help Hong Kong and southern China evolve distinct policies that are not necessarily those desired in Peking. For example, a regime anxious to pursue territorial claims in the disputed waters of the South China Sea may find that the authorities in Guangdong and Hong Kong would wish for a quieter life in order to develop their regional economy.

No one doubts that undertaking such a differentiated policy toward China will be more difficult in its early stages. But the choice for the United States is whether it wishes to help shape a more malleable China while it still has a chance to do so, or whether it will be more passive and face a stronger and more difficult China in the twenty-first century. In essence, the choice that the United States faces about Hong Kong and China is part of a broader choice about how active the United States should be in the post–Cold War world.

—GERALD SEGAL
London, February 1993

THE FATE OF HONG KONG

Introduction

Hong Kong is a place unlike any other and its fate, too, is likely to be unique. Could it be that the nearly six million people living in Hong Kong's thriving capitalist economy under British colonial rule will be handed to the rulers of communist China in 1997? Unusually for observers of current affairs, we already know the outcome of a major international issue: Hong Kong will be returned to China. However, we do not know what shape Hong Kong will be in when it is delivered to China, what kind of China will be there to receive it, or what will be the reactions of the major interested parties.

The fate of Hong Kong is not 'merely' important for the millions of people being handed back to communist rule. It may also be part of a major transformation in the way China is governed and, in particular, in the extent of the power held by China's regions. As these major changes take place, the vital East Asian region will be affected and therefore the wider world will watch with a great deal of concern. As Hong Kong and southern China converge, there is a risk of major upheavals in the region and the already significant brain drain from the colony may turn into a flood of refugees, which eventually would be a challenge not only to British policy but also to the United States, Canada, Australia and many in East Asia. A major flight of capital from Hong Kong and a decay of its economy would also be of significant importance for a global market economy that has grown used to Hong Kong as an important player. What is more, a crisis concerning Hong Kong might help de-stabilize the vital regional economy in East Asia and therefore de-stabilize international trade and finance.

Even if the transition to Chinese rule is less catastrophic for the people of Hong Kong, it may well take place as part of major shifts of power and policy in China. Should the convergence of Hong Kong with China encourage a trend to greater regionalism

1

in China, East Asians may find that a series of new Natural Economic Territories (NETs) are created around China, with major consequences for regional and global patterns of trade, politics and even security. The fate of Hong Kong, like the place itself, has ceased to be a concern for Britain alone: it is now an important international issue. As a result, we need to see the problem of Hong Kong not just in relation to British and Chinese policies but also in its international context.

Of course, there are other studies which have already explained how Hong Kong found itself in such a predicament.[1] But this is a book about where Hong Kong might go from here, the importance of international affairs and what the role of the international community might be in Hong Kong's future. Hong Kong could be described as a small but fast-whirling cog that will have to click into place with a much more slowly moving and far larger cog called China. The speed of the Hong Kong cog has allowed it to operate smoothly as part of the international community, but it will have to slow down if it is to mesh with China. Optimists about the fate of Hong Kong claim that China is already speeding up sufficiently so that the connection can be made without a crippling jolt and that, once the two are joined, Hong Kong will help speed up China's own pace. The more pessimistically inclined worry that the convergence of Hong Kong with China will end in serious damage to the smaller cog. Both optimists and pessimists also contemplate that contact between the two cogs might even cause a larger area of southern China to pull away and thereby encourage a wider process of regionalization and perhaps even a degree of disintegration of a once united China.

The fate of Hong Kong involves a bewildering range of factors. At the core is an understanding of the unique power that makes Hong Kong spin. Seen in broad perspective, there is the role played by Britain in fostering its colony and then negotiating its fate. But by far the most important factor in this wider focus is China, whose actions have always been the single most important determinant of the fate of Hong Kong. The triangle of interests between China, Britain and Hong Kong is assessed in chapters 1–5.

Because so much of the success of Hong Kong has been based on Britain's decision to let Hong Kong more or less find its own way in the wider international system, it is impossible to assess the fate of Hong Kong without understanding the international interests and policies at work. Indeed, it is precisely this international context which has been absent in most previous analyses of Hong Kong and is the focus of chapters 6–10. Particular stress is placed on the risks of migration from Hong Kong because one of the greatest threats to the future prosperity of Hong Kong is that so many of its people will leave in fear of a China-dominated future. As a result the colony will begin to spin at a dangerously slower speed, even before 1997.

The sharp differences between optimists and pessimists derive in part from the relative emphasis placed on the responsibility of the key actors. Without pre-empting the analysis that follows, it might as well be stated at the outset that this study sees China as the primary determinant of the fate of Hong Kong. If China, whether in reforming mode or not, feels that Hong Kong can only be safely incorporated into China if it is sufficiently slowed down to a pace where it can converge with the mainland, then there is little that the people of Hong Kong, the government of Britain or, indeed, the government of any other state can do about it. If China allows convergence with Hong Kong on the basis of a more general policy of encouraging regionalism, then the emergence of a distinctive and larger unit in southern China will be part of a more complex process where attitudes in the international community will be of great importance. Thus in almost all eventualities, this analysis tends to apportion less 'blame' to Britain for the fate of Hong Kong than do most earlier studies.[2] Yet it is a central theme of the analysis that follows that there is much that Britain, when acting with other states, can do to help give Hong Kong a better chance of surviving in decent shape. The initial success achieved by Chris Patten in April 1993 in forcing China to negotiate about his proposals for greater democracy in Hong Kong was in part due to his ability to mobilize international, and especially American support.

Final material was written, as well as that for the paperback edition, while the author was a Senior Fellow at the International Institute for Strategic Studies. Throughout all these phases the research has been done in several countries. Interviews with officials were guaranteed to be off the record and so there will be no references to "informed (and untraceable) sources". It would be pompous to put such material in inverted commas in the text, and so it is integrated to make for easier reading. Research and interviews were begun in 1989 and often people were revisited to update for newer events. The relatively large body of endnotes covers open sources and should meet the needs of more academically-inclined readers. The remarkable staff in the RIIA press and book libraries have also made sure that I read as much of the primary and secondary source material as possible. Anne Jewel was a vital assistant in sifting the material in the press files. I am also grateful to the Canadian government's academic support scheme for financial assistance in 1990–92 with some of the research trips. Various people read all or part of the text, and in the belief that they would rather have a free copy than their name in a long list I offer here a collective thank-you. Carol O'Brien, my editor at Simon & Schuster, had the courage to commission a book on Hong Kong before it was fashionable to do so, and then had the energy to move her colleagues into higher gear when the book was launched into the tense political atmosphere surrounding Hong Kong in 1992–93.

PART I

Hong Kong to the 1990s

1

Hong Kong to 1949

Hong Kong was both a product and a pawn of empire. Before Western empires arrived along China's Pacific coast, Hong Kong island was little more than the 'barren island' so disparagingly described by British foreign secretary Lord Palmerston in 1841. During the nineteenth century, when Hong Kong was detached from the underbelly of China, both Western and Asian empires were engaged in their long-practised games of manoeuvring for advantage. To be sure, the territory that Britain would eventually seize was long part of the Chinese empire; but the process by which Hong Kong became a part of the British empire was a tale of unsavoury imperialism in the East and West.

Modern China, like the former Soviet Union, is a continental empire created through centuries of expansion into neighbouring lands. But China is unique among empires because of the length of time it has managed to hold on to its acquisitions. While empires in the Arab or European worlds have all contracted, and in the late twentieth century even the Russian empire shrank, the Chinese empire has waxed far more than it has waned over the past 2,000 years. For centuries China was the most glorious of civilisations, outlasting all of its rivals. Arabs and then Europeans came to trade with China, but none of the commerce was vital to the existence of the Chinese empire. In the 1990s, when international commerce had become vital to the prosperity of the modern Chinese empire, it seemed at least possible that reform in China's south coast off which Hong Kong lies might be the start of the loosening of the Chinese empire. As the history of Hong Kong demonstrates, this is a story of conflicts over commerce and empire.

To the Nanjing Treaty

Europeans first came to East Asia in significant numbers in the sixteenth century, and, unlike their predecessors, they came by sea. Their primary objective was to obtain the expected benefits of trade with China, but the first obstacles came from the Arab traders who were long established in the region.[1] As Portugal and Spain brazened their way into the regional trade in Southeast Asia, the Chinese at first saw these Europeans as yet another minor player in a world long dominated by the looming Chinese empire. Even as Spanish galleons became the first to span the Pacific in regular commerce, Chinese traders in Southeast Asia profited from the flow of Spanish silver.

But it was Spain's great Iberian rival, Portugal, that established the first colony in China. The base in Macao, established in 1557, was tacitly tolerated by China as part of the developing trade with the far more important Pearl river city of Canton. But valuable as these contacts were later to become, Chinese leaders in the fading Ming dynasty had their eyes on the battles taking place in northern China.

By the eighteenth century, the gaze of China's new Qing empire was still focused on its continental frontiers, but now in the cause of territorial expansion. While Europeans knocked increasingly persistently on China's Pacific doors, the Qing were busy doubling the territory of their empire in the West.[2] By the end of the eighteenth century more than half of China's land was inhabited by a population with a non-Chinese majority. Clearly by the time the Europeans arrived in force, China was not simply waiting passively in dread of the next blow from Western imperialism.

Because of its imperial distractions, and a long-standing disdain of international trade, China was far from prepared for the demands and strategies of the Europeans who came by sea. By the late eighteenth century Britain had emerged as the leading European power and, if only by virtue of its control of India, was taking an increasing interest in Asian affairs. In the 1790s Lord Macartney led a diplomatic mission to the Qing court seeking official trade relations. China saw no need for such ties and felt it highly impertinent that other sovereigns should feel they had the right to demand 'the right to trade'. In the Chinese perspective, trade rights might be bestowed or tolerated, but they were not a subject for international negotiation.

That other great north European sea-borne trader, Holland, also came to China seeking trade rights. But it, like the Russian empire, found no satisfaction in its missions to the Qing court. Yet China's haughty rejection of trade rights for Europeans soon gave way to a more pragmatic reality, with fruitful trade carried on with Europeans in Canton – far from the capital in Peking. But this trade was conducted on terms unfavourable to the Europeans: the Chinese superintendent of customs and Chinese merchants squeezed the foreigners with all manner of tariffs and fees.

With nominally thirteen foreign 'factories' squashed into Canton, the 'factory' established by the British East India Company was larger than all the others combined. Because trade was confined to the months from October to May and because no women were allowed in the Canton factories, Macao became a vital base for Europeans. Although this trade pattern was far from satisfactory for the Europeans, the issue was still small enough to be kept off the main agenda of the great powers. China ran a huge trade surplus as it exported silk and tea and imported little in return. The flow of silver into the pockets of local Chinese and the exchequer in Peking was sufficient to keep the trade door ajar.

The jolt to the trading system came from across the Pacific. The defeat of Britain in the American war of independence did serious damage to British trade. London then reduced the import duties on Chinese tea in order to legalise the trade and therefore earn more revenue from taxes when the smuggling of teas ceased. The strategy worked and, with a far lower price, tea became Britain's national beverage. But the vastly increased imports also required vastly increased exports to stem the loss of silver.

The solution was soon found in the export of opium to China from India. Of course, opium had been grown in China from as early as at least the ninth century and in both Europe and China it was a vital part of the medicine of the time. Consumption was regulated but not prohibited, much like alcohol. In 1729 the consumption and sale of opium was made illegal in China and in 1796 its import was also banned. Until that time, the problem was literally home-grown, for China produced more opium than it imported. Even as late as the 1830s, China's imports of opium were less than that of Britain on a per-capita basis. The British

East India Company connived in keeping prices high and supply low until the early nineteenth century. It was only when private growers in western India sought a piece of the market and prices fell that mass consumption in China became possible.[3]

This is not to suggest that Britain was blameless in the opium trade, for in 1821, when the Chinese finally began to implement their anti-opium regulations, the extent of British dependence on the opium trade became glaringly clear. But it is also true that the devious ways in which the opium trade was managed ensured that the local Chinese traders developed a lucrative stake in the trade and frustrated attempts by Peking to limit the transactions. Indeed, a key feature of the run-up to the Opium War, and a theme throughout the course of Hong Kong's history, has been the rivalry between north and south China and Peking's suspicions about the intentions of Chinese along the south coast. What is more, other British traders resented the East India Company's monopoly and began ingeniously evading the regulations. Americans also played an important part in the opium trade as they shipped opium from Turkey into China.[4]

Indeed, the desire for free trade that forced the abolition of the East India Company's monopoly in 1834 was part of a much larger pressure that led to vastly increased demands for access to the Chinese market. This international pressure developed in large part from the Industrial Revolution which was led by Britain, but it also was part of broader trends in the developing international economy. With the shattering of the British East India Company's monopoly, it became harder to control the activity of foreigners and the question of judicial jurisdiction became even more acute. The fact that the Chinese authorities still refused official communication with the traders and their national governments meant that the trade was always likely to be a source of friction. China's tribute system of international relations – often more a fiction than a fact – was failing to meet the new realities of the European-dominated international trading system. The forces facing China were part of the broader challenge of industrialisation and modernisation which China had so far refused to meet.

Britain was playing a leading role in this new international system. The British empire-building was just getting into its stride, adding Singapore in 1819, Aden in 1839, New Zealand in 1840, and Sind and Natal in 1843. Indeed, from Britain's point of view, the decay of Chinese authority and the increasing chaos in trade relations bore alarming similiarities to the forces in the Asian sub-continent that led to Britain's reluctant assumption of control in India. British views of the Hong Kong region were distinctly unenthusiastic and London certainly did not want to take over China. Yet it wanted unpredictability in its trade even less.[5] In 1834 Foreign Secretary Palmerston sent Lord Napier to negotiate new arrangements but he soon had to retreat ignominiously from Canton. In 1838 Lin Zexu was appointed by the Qing court to take a tough line with the foreign traders as a whole in order to deal with the opium problem. Opium supplies were destroyed but, in keeping with market principles, prices rose, thereby feeding the desire of Europeans to profit from the trade.

While Portuguese Macao was reluctant to become involved in the growing conflict, in 1839 ships found safety off the tiny island of Hong Kong, less than one hundred miles from Canton. In military engagements in the autumn of that year, the weakness of China's position in limiting the European presence was vividly demonstrated. Although Lin continued to mislead his superiors in Peking about his progress in dealing with the foreigners, the reality – that the opium trade was flourishing – was soon apparent. In February 1840 Palmerston ordered a larger British force be sent to enforce trading rights (this was the age of gunboat diplomacy and Britain had the best fleet in the world). After an abortive agreement on 20 January 1841, in the summer of that year Sir Henry Pottinger arrived in China determined not to put up with any refusal to trade from the Peking authorities. Attacks on Shanghai and even Nanjing led to the Treaty of Nanjing on 29 August 1842. Hong Kong was surrendered to Britain and five treaty ports, including Shanghai and Canton, were opened to British trade. A supplement to the main treaty (Treaty of Humen, October 1843) granted foreigners exemption from the laws of China, a concession far more worrying to the Qing court than the loss of Hong Kong, even though some degree of extraterritoriality had already been in operation in China. Opium was not mentioned anywhere in the Treaty and the Chinese even offered to legalise the trade if Britain would guarantee the payment of a regular tax. Indeed, in subsequent years the Chinese were to earn significant revenue from the opium trade.

Britain and its traders had obtained the base they wanted in order to be free of Chinese restraints. Except for Macao, which had never been formally ceded, and a few relatively empty spaces on the border with Russia, Hong Kong was the first parcel of Chinese territory to be formally handed over to Europeans. Although the British government was initially uncertain about whether to establish a permanent base on the island, the local traders moved faster than London.[6] As was to become common in Hong Kong's history, market forces were often far more important than government dictate. It was also true, even at this stage, that Hong Kong was of little intrinsic interest to Britain and policies soon came to be set more by the force of circumstances than as the result of any grandiose plan.[7]

The thirty-five square miles of rock that constituted Hong Kong was a tiny part of China, but its loss, not to mention the loss of sovereignty in the treaty ports, was a powerful symbol of the weakness of the Chinese empire. Although China was to lose far more territory to Russia in the northeast, the other European powers that pressed in along the coast were a special challenge because the coastal regions were some of the most developed parts of China and China's weakness demonstrated the fatal flaws in the sinocentrism of the Qing dynasty. Britain was merely the cutting edge of European power, but as such it was also the most painful evidence that China was no longer superior to the world outside and would have to change its approach to international affairs.

The creation of Hong Kong as a foreign enclave also constituted a break with Chinese tradition. Despite the fact that the vast majority of the population was Chinese, this new British colony was established as a haven from the rules of China. It was at this point, as one perceptive observer noted in a different context, 'history became a luxury in Hong Kong', while in China the weight of tradition prevented much of the necessary innovation.[8]

In 1845 France and the United States negotiated a similar treaty with China and other powers began looking for new advantages in the China trade. Peking, seeing the potential for playing off one foreigner against another, felt it was not yet necessary to capitulate to the Western notion of international relations. Indeed it was a central feature of the era when Hong Kong was established as a British colony that the Western powers were an unstable mix of competitors and co-operators in the opening of China. French interests in the region of Indochina were of particular concern to Britain.[9]

Yet the Nanjing treaty was only the first of the 'Unequal Treaties' imposed on China. Had this challenge to Chinese imperialism been met with wisdom, the humiliation of China might have been less complete.[10] Unlike Japan, China was reluctant to reform and therefore likely to suffer further indignities. From the Chinese perspective there was little reason to acquiesce in opening its doors to the Europeans, except that to have the doors prised open by force would be far worse. The curious over-confidence on the part of the Chinese ensured that the struggle with the West would continue and, as a main base for the leading imperial power, Hong Kong would remain a pawn in the game of empires.

To the 1911 revolution

On 26 January 1841, Hong Kong was officially claimed by the Royal Navy and by October some 15,000 people lived on the rocks. This free port was already well established as a rambunctious sort of place by 26 June 1843, when the Treaty of Nanjing was ratified and Hong Kong was declared a crown colony. Even at this stage the distinctiveness of Hong Kong was manifest. As a crown colony, unlike for example the French colony in Algeria, British laws did not apply automatically to Hong Kong and money was not remitted to the British exchequer, except in payment for such services as military protection.[11]

It was not long before the basic instabilities in the relationship between China and the West again emerged into open conflict. A Sino-American treaty following the Nanjing Treaty had allowed for a revision of the treaty in twelve years and Britain now claimed the same right for the Nanjing pact. But after a frustrating attempt to negotiate with China, the Qing court refused both American and British requests to revise the treaties. Peking was clearly attempting as much as possible to nullify the effect of the treaties. China had still not learned that it had to deal with the foreigners on a regular and equal basis. The Crimean war distracted some of the Europeans for a while, so that the Chinese were led to believe that they need not change policy. But the reality of Western power and China's weakness had not really been erased. Had China been more willing to take part in the extension of the European game of rival great powers, it might have seen that the Crimean war offered opportunities to play off suspicious powers. Britain was certainly concerned that the Crimean war might lead Russia to send its Pacific fleet and, for a time, panic was rife in Hong Kong.[12]

The specific trigger for the second Anglo-Chinese war was a combination of the long-standing disputes over the interpretation of the earlier treaties and the boarding of a Chinese-owned (but Hong Kong-registered and under the command of a British captain) boat, the *Arrow*, by Chinese in search of pirates. After uproar in Parliament in London, Palmerston called an election and returned with a mandate to send in the navy. Action was delayed by the mutiny in India but Lord Elgin arrived in Hong Kong in mid-1857 seeking compensation from Peking and the right to keep an ambassador in the Chinese capital.

It was not until late 1857 that the troops were ready to move into China, and, when they did, they had the support of 1,000 French soldiers anxious to pursue their own cause in China. Tianjin was occupied and a treaty quickly agreed. Ten more treaty ports were to be opened and foreigners would be allowed to travel anywhere in China with a passport. Four of the treaty ports would be on the Yangtze river, extending upstream to Nanjing and therefore raising the acute fear of foreign penetration into the heart of China. France and the United States quickly obtained similar treaties and the three were linked through the 'most favoured nation' clause in each.

But the Chinese reneged on the deal, which allowed time for other powers, notably the Russians, to seek a piece of the action intended to teach the Chinese how to operate in the modern international world. When the next expeditionary force moved up to Shanghai from Hong Kong in May 1860, the French and British moved on to plunder the Summer Palace outside Peking.

The vacillating Chinese reaction was the result of basic uncertainty about the Western challenge and deep concern with the Taiping rebellion begun in 1851. When faced with a choice between compromise with the foreigners and capitulation to the Taiping, the Qing chose the lesser evil of seeking Western aid against the internal threat. Most foreigners (apart from some missionaries) were not very keen on supporting the Taiping and many Western merchants preferred to trade with the Qing rulers. In short, there was a raw pragmatism about the relationship with China that had little to do with the specific ideology of the regime in power in Peking. Uncertainty in the relations among the Europeans and in their attitudes to China only encouraged the Chinese to believe that they could somehow escape from the threat posed by European imperialism.[13]

The convention of Peking in October 1860 brought the formal ratification of the Treaty of Tianjin. The revisions of the treaty agreed in Peking provided for the inclusion of a sixteenth treaty port – Tianjin – and the addition of the tip of Kowloon peninsula to the colony of Hong Kong. This additional snip off China was a mere three and a half square miles, but it was intended to provide additional space for warehouses and facilities for the army.

The demands of international commerce were also a large part of the motive for establishing foreign concessions in the treaty ports. Shanghai was the first to develop these areas of foreign settlement which were governed by foreign regulation. But because of the more general decay of the authority of the Chinese government, many concessions made to the European powers, and especially in the case of Hong Kong at this time, had as much to do with such practical considerations as the need for more space. They were not always intended as a deliberate snub to Chinese sovereignty. But with foreign gunboats used to defend foreign interests on Chinese soil, the message was loud and clear that the Qing dynasty was dying and China was vulnerable to plunder.

The decay of the Qing dynasty was not inevitable. China, like Japan, had an opportunity to take Western advice and strengthen itself. To the extent that a self-strengthening movement was begun, it was usually half-hearted and patchy. In general, the Chinese were far too proud of their own past to admit the necessity to learn such lessons and so fought shy of accepting foreign help and guidance. It was the past greatness of China that ensured present vulnerability. Hong Kong, having been taken out of Chinese influence, was set on another course. In fact, in the closing decades of the nineteenth century, Hong Kong had become the main port for the large-scale exodus of Chinese migrants across the Pacific and to Europe. As such, Hong Kong was the most vivid symbol of the failure of the Chinese empire and the link to the outside world.[14]

By the last decades of the nineteenth century, the pace of events around Hong Kong was determined by the rivalries of empires. The war between France and China over Vietnam, which ended in 1884, led not only to greater Chinese insecurity but also to a British concern about reinforcing Hong Kong. In the following year, Russian action in Korea also caused worries in Hong Kong and London. The decay of the Qing dynasty, the rise of the Japanese empire just offshore and the predatory policies of the expanding Russian empire led to concern on the part of the United States and the European empires that they had to scramble for their piece of China before someone else took it. The American preparation to seize the Philippines also increased worries in some quarters that Hong Kong might be vulnerable to an expanding American empire. This whirl of self-interest was felt most intensely when Japan defeated China in 1895 and demanded a range of concessions. Germany, France and Russia rescued China from the worst of the Japanese demands, but these 'saviours' were primarily interested in the fate of their own claims rather than intrinsically concerned about the fate of China.

For China, the threat in the northeast was far more serious than anything taking place in the southeast. But from Britain's point of view, the growing interest of other empires made it all the more important that its base in Hong Kong be reinforced. To that end, a convention was signed in Peking on 9 June 1898 for the acquisition of the New Territories – compromising the area north of Kowloon up to the Shenzhen river, and 235 islands – under a 99-year lease. As if to demonstrate the real target of the treaty, Chinese ships were not banned from using the Kowloon harbour, but those from France and Russia were prohibited. The negotiations were remarkably haphazard considering that what was at stake was 365 square miles of additional territory. The acceptance of a finite agreement to return the New Territories in 1997 was unique in British imperial history. For an empire that then ruled nearly a quarter of the world's landmass, governed a quarter of the world's population and commanded all of its seas, this was a peculiar oversight. But it was a finely balanced argument in London whether, by seeking a permanent grip instead of a lease, British would merely stimulate its imperial rivals to seek similar status for their leases of more valuable territory.[15] Considering the importance that the 99-year lease would assume in the 1980s, this crucial decision in Hong Kong's history was taken with surprisingly little consideration of its possible impact.

China too had other things on its mind. While in rapid decay,

China was in full knowledge that Britain was far from the most rapacious of the foreign threats. This was the heyday of imperialism, the time when various other great powers were grabbing what they could. Japan took Taiwan, and Britain also picked up Weihaiwei, to be held as long as the Russians held Port Arthur. The only hope for the Qing was that somehow these rival foreigners would keep each other sufficiently at bay to stave off complete collapse.

The revolutionary forces building in China were far too advanced to be blocked by foreigners. Sun Yat-sen, the father of the 1911 revolution that overthrew the Qing dynasty, had been banned from Hong Kong in 1897 as a troublemaker. Although Hong Kong was not the primary base for the movement that brought down the Qing dynasty, the colony did serve as a place where ideas were developed and even money was raised for the cause. Perhaps above all, Hong Kong was one of the most important symbols of the decay of the Qing dynasty and the desperate need for change in China. In this respect, as was to be the case at the end of the twentieth century, Hong Kong and the neighbouring parts of southern China were on a different wave length from that of the court in Peking.

To the Communist revolution

The population of Hong Kong had risen from some 33,000 in 1851 to nearly 880,000 eighty years later. This region had long seen regular movements of population and the migrations were very much in line with those in southeast Asia as a whole.[16] Although all but 20,000 of the population in 1931 was Chinese, Hong Kong itself was clearly on a different course from that of most of China, even though it was handling some 40 per cent of all China's foreign trade at the turn of the century.[17] Yet Hong Kong was also very much tied to the fate of China, relying for most of its prosperity on the China trade and the immigration of Chinese from the mainland. Even Hong Kong's currency, the silver dollar, was otherwise used only on the mainland, and when China shifted to the 'managed dollar' in 1935 Hong Kong followed suit. Of course, in Hong Kong's typically pragmatic form, various currencies were circulating in the colony and in the 1930s Hong Kong found that its trading ties were stronger with other countries than with China. As Japanese control of China was extended, Hong Kong returned to playing the part of the vital export outlet for China, at least until Japanese troops moved into Hong Kong itself.[18]

In the period before the war, in some important respects the domestic politics of Hong Kong followed a normal pattern for a British overseas territory, with a governor nominated by Whitehall. The British residents of the colony regularly demanded self-rule, but London was strongly opposed to so few Westerners governing the vast majority of Chinese. The British authorities were far happier simply to allow Hong Kong to be governed in as *laissez-faire* a manner as possible. As a key coaling station for the British empire, there was a serious risk that popular representation might mean the end of British rule and British control of a strategic asset.

Given the unrest next door in China, it is remarkable that Hong Kong managed to remain relatively untouched. With the regular wars and the poor government on the mainland, there was an equally regular stream of refuges into the colony. But with the end of the Qing dynasty and then the shabby treatment of China at the Versailles peace conference that ended the First World War, nationalist unrest also spread to Hong Kong. China's desire to regain the former German holding in Shandong raised the basic question of foreign occupation of Chinese territory, a problem that obviously touched on the fate of Hong Kong. Britain had the largest foreign investment stake in China at the time and therefore was often the target of Chinese nationalist demands. A seamen's strike in Hong Kong in 1922 was called for from China and was followed by a general strike in 1925/6 which spread to Hong Kong from Canton. The risk, as always, was that the revolutionary trends in China could not be kept out of the Western enclave of Hong Kong.

The fate of Hong Kong also depended on its ability to develop a distinctive international economic role. However, in the heady days of the 1930s, Hong Kong was a conspicuous failure. Its great rival was Shanghai, a city far more genuinely cosmopolitan and more directly plugged in to the heart of the China trade. Chaotic as China may have been at the time, Shanghai was a more Chinese city and its opportunities were more typical of those on the mainland. Hong Kong languished, although its relative obscurity was later to be part of its protection when the communist revolution swept the mainland.

In comparison with Shanghai, Hong Kong was very much a British colony. With its social distinctions that only the British at their worst can manage, Hong Kong was divided by its British and Chinese communities.[19] The standard of living of the two communities could not have been more different. The labour unrest on the mainland did spread to Hong Kong, but it eventually petered out as much larger political forces – both internal and external – took hold of China. Britain and its colony were saved from further attention by the rise of a far more serious threat to Chinese nationalism – Japanese imperialism.

With Japan seeking the 'fruits' of empire that Western powers had long obtained, China was always likely to be a prime target. As we have already seen, Japan had defeated China in war in the last decade of the nineteenth century and during the First World War presented its list of twenty-one demands. By 1931 Japan had invaded Manchuria and in 1937 launched a full-scale attack on Guomindang-governed China. Canton fell to the Japanese in 1938, resulting in mass immigration to Hong Kong. Some 100,000 refugees had entered in 1937, five times that figure entered in 1938 and then 150,000 in 1939. By the end of 1939 the population of Hong Kong had reached 1.6 million and at the height of the influx some half a million people were sleeping in the streets.

An immigration department was set up in Hong Kong in 1940 in order to cope with the flood of refugees. But the colonial administration, fearing a Japanese attack, also evacuated some 3,400 expatriate women and children to Australia, an unpopular move leading to accusations of racism.[20]

The fate of Hong Kong, with the Japanese sitting close by, depended on the fate of Japan's relations with the Europeans. Hong Kong was clearly treated more as a part of the West than as a part of China. Thus when the Japanese attacked Pearl Harbor on 7 December 1941, Hong Kong was also on the Japanese target list. After less than two weeks of resistance, the colony surrendered to the Japanese on Christmas Day 1941 and was to remain under occupation for three years and eight months. Thus Hong Kong and much of China suffered a similar fate – occupation by Japan – but for very different reasons.

At a time of war, not surprisingly trade faded into insignificance and Hong Kong deteriorated. Hong Kong was no longer defendable by Europeans and, even when the Americans battled their way up the Pacific towards Japan, Hong Kong was not an objective worth fighting for. The surrender of Japanese forces was taken on 14 August 1945 and units of the British Pacific fleet arrived in Hong Kong on 30 August to establish a temporary military government. Formal civil government was only restored on 1 May 1946. Although the British were back, the Japanese occupation was to help shatter many of the old social structures and the influx of new immigrants was to help boost the role of the Chinese in running the local economy.

The Guomindang clearly wanted to take over control of Hong Kong and for a time there was even some support from the United States for applying the principles of the Atlantic charter of March 1943.[21] President Roosevelt never pushed very hard for the return of the colony to China, if only because it was far from clear whether the principle of self-determination would be better suited by British or by Chinese rule. While it is true that other foreign concessions in China were abolished, Britain had ruled Hong Kong longer than any other Chinese territory apart from Macao, and Hong Kong had developed as a refuge from the persistent chaos of China. Britain was prepared to surrender treaty port rights, but not its colony.[22] In any case, despite the British humiliation of having been defeated in the initial stages of the war, the obvious division on the mainland between communist and Guomindang forces made the fate of Hong Kong a far from central issue.

The people and government of Hong Kong were more concerned with the fact that the fighting in China was far from over. Even though Japanese troops had been defeated, China's own civil war was then free to resume in full force. During the Japanese occupation many Chinese had moved back into China but, with the ensuing civil war, some 100,000 a month returned to Hong Kong. The population in August 1945 had been reduced to 600,000, but by the end of 1947 it had risen to around 1.8 million. Yet this was only the beginning of the flood. As the Guomindang crumbled, hundreds of thousands of refugees swept into Hong Kong, mainly from Guangdong province and more distant Shanghai and other major cities. By mid-1950 the population was estimated to be 2.2 million.

The People's Republic of China was proclaimed by Mao Zedong in Peking on 1 October 1949. The obvious fear for the people of Hong Kong was whether they too would be swept up in the revolution.[23] The British garrison on the New Territories was reinforced, and yet there was no significant consultation with allies, either in the Commonwealth or across the Pacific in North America. This symbolic act of bravado only strengthened the view that, as in the case of the Japanese invasion, Britain could not defend Hong Kong as it had in the days of gunboat diplomacy. The fate of Hong Kong depended on the extent to which the Chinese communists recognised that the risks of taking Hong Kong were too great and it seems that the Chinese leadership did believe that the Americans had provided Britain with a guarantee that it would help defend Hong Kong. The Chinese also appeared to recognise that, in terms of international prestige, the risks of taking Hong Kong were greater than the gains to be earned from a demonstration of military power. In the event, the discipline of the communist troops held and Hong Kong remained British.

The most challenging force to cross the frontier was the masses of refugees. With hindsight it is clear that this flood of refugees was a benefit to Hong Kong. Indeed, the influx of such large numbers fleeing unrest and communism helped divide Hong Kong from the rest of China. As nearly all other foreign enclaves in China were abolished in these revolutionary times, Hong Kong stood out as unique. Given this new image, the trade orientation and thus the economic prosperity of the colony turned away from the old model of an entrepôt for the China trade, as Hong Kong searched for a more independent path. China accounted for 30 per cent of Hong Kong's trade in 1936–40, but only 20 per cent in 1948.[24] These were clearly days of uncertainty, but they were to lay the groundwork for future prosperity and distinctive development.

The distinction was particular evident when comparisons were made with that old rival of Hong Kong – Shanghai. Despite promises from the communists that Shanghai would remain a special case in order to build foreign confidence in the new regime, it soon became apparent that Shanghai would become another impoverished city in a communist-run China. Shanghai, like Hong Kong, had initially been flooded with refugees seeking escape from communist rule. The international and French settlements in Shanghai were seen as escape routes, but many foreigners had already fled. As communist troops approached in May 1949, the British community in Shanghai was halved to 2,000 in a matter of weeks and the Guomindang began taking its forces off to Taiwan. Communist troops did not interfere with the evacuation in May and the Americans ordered all their citizens to leave or face the consequences.[25]

Later in May the People's Liberation Army (PLA) did bomb the airfields and close the river to such evacuation efforts. Exit permits eventually became available, but the process often took years to complete.[26] Shanghai was always more a part of the international economy than an integrated section of the Chinese economy, and this was to be part of its weakness when the communists eventually decided that there could be no compromise between revolution and international capitalism.[27] Typhoons, floods and Guomindang attacks all led the communists to move quickly from a softly-softly approach to Shanghai and in August they adopted a tougher line demanding the abolition of the old system. Shanghai was clearly treated as part of China and the fate of the once-great city was starkly evident. Hong Kong, by virtue of its colonial status, hoped for, and received, far better treatment. Before the communist revolution, Hong Kong had lived in the shadow of Shanghai – beyond question the premier industrial and cosmopolitan city on the Chinese coast. The Chinese and the Westerners – especially those engaged in the textile industry – who escaped Shanghai took their know-how, initiative and even some of their newly ordered (but not yet delivered) equipment to Hong Kong in search of new opportunities. Shanghai's tragedy was Hong Kong's good fortune.

Hong Kong benefited not only from the flood of capital, people and expertise from Shanghai but also from the example that was set to the outside world. Hong Kong's difference from Shanghai now became the basis of its appeal as the colony absorbed some of the more cosmopolitan characteristics that had been so much a part of Shanghai's success. Hong Kong was again unique among the former trading posts along the Chinese coast for not being under communist rule. The welcome for foreign capital and the fact of British rule were vital components for future success. As it became clear that the communists would not take over the British colony, Hong Kong began to rethink its own self-definition.

2

Thirty Years of Prosperity: 1950–80

The old joke in Hong Kong wryly asks, 'How will China take Hong Kong?' and the answer comes back: 'By telephone.' Because the colony could not be defended against China after 1949, the state of relations with the new communist rulers of the mainland became the central uncertainty in ascertaining the fate of Hong Kong. As the Chinese people of Hong Kong gradually accepted that the civil war on the mainland was over, and they were still safe in Hong Kong, the concerns of the colony shifted. Britain tried to ease Hong Kong's transition into this new world by making it clear that London was prepared to establish diplomatic relations with the communist regime well before the United States was prepared to contemplate such accommodation. But as even a remote part of the West, Hong Kong became tied up in the broader problems of Chinese relations with the Western world, and the United States in particular.

The most immediate challenge for the colony, apart from the integration of the new immigrants, was adaptation to the new international system. Initially, at least, Hong Kong tried to retain its role as the entrepôt for the China trade.[1] But the outbreak, of the Korean war in June 1950 heated up the Cold War in East Asia and Hong Kong suffered as a result. The West, led by the United States and including Britain, was soon at war with China farther up the Pacific coast. By 1951, what was left of the trade with China from Hong Kong had passed into the hands of Hong Kong Chinese and Peking shut down what was left of foreigners' operations on the mainland. The Chinese authorities built a fence along the frontier with Hong Kong and relations deteriorated as the communists looked on the British colony as a base of capitalist corruption. The residents of Hong Kong soon learned via the refugees how bad life could be under communism and the flow of refugees from the mainland ensured the relationship remained uneasy. The British demanded civil obedience from the communists inside the colony, but otherwise there was no attempt to ban the influence of the new regime in Peking. The Guomindang was more of a source of political agitation as it tried to undermine the communist regime and waged part of the struggle both in and through Hong Kong.

Hong Kong also felt the direct pressure of the Korean war, for in January 1951 the United States went so far as to advise its citizens to leave Hong Kong and American firms paid 'danger money' to their employees.[2] The fear was that the hostilities with China were possibly leading to a tougher Chinese line on Hong Kong and even a complete Chinese takeover. Trade restrictions that were imposed on China were also imposed on Hong Kong at the same time and thus the local economy was in serious difficulty. One visiting American journalist in 1951 described Hong Kong as a 'dying city', even though much of the basis of Hong Kong's future success was already present.[3]

It was not until the ceasefire in Korea in 1953 that tension with China could be said to have been reduced to a satisfactory level. In the meantime, the basis for Hong Kong's development was laid by the local population, and especially its new immigrants. In an atmosphere of minimal government intervention in Hong Kong, local entrepreneurs were allowed to get on with building new enterprises. Industrial growth was rapid, although based on small-scale light industry. Many people worked in unregistered factories and most operations were small family enterprises using self-generated capital and, often, employing relatives. Working conditions were in many cases appalling, and exploitation of sweat-shop labour was rife. With the major influx of refugees, social relations between different immigrant groups deteriorated as the society adapted to the new, rapidly changing reality. The welfare net, such as it was, came from traditional Chinese family and local organisations as well as missionary relief efforts.

Nevertheless, the new economic enterprises provided a key method of improving the position of the masses of immigrants, especially as the entrepôt role of Hong Kong was shattered. In 1958 more than 75 per cent of all factories employed less than twenty workers and, in 1970, 75 per cent of all factories employed less than one hundred workers. The textile industry was dominant, employing some 30 per cent of the workers in 1954 and 40 per cent in 1970.

By 1970 plastics accounted for 12 per cent of exports and electronics took another 10 per cent.[4]

The abandonment of the role of entrepôt for the China trade was dramatic and yet successfully managed under British rule and by the sheer pressure of market forces. In establishing itself as the first of what would become known as the NICs (Newly Industrialised Countries), Hong Kong flourished at first because of low wages, and despite the absence of raw materials or even enough food to feed the population. Initial export markets were to neighbours, and the relatively poor ones at that. In 1956 Indonesia was Hong Kong's main export market.

In a pattern that would later become familiar in the other NICs, Hong Kong shifted its exports in waves to the more developed world. The United States and Europe were the main targets. The shift in policy was assisted by the creation of the Export Credit Insurance Corporation in 1956 and other bodies were set up to make Hong Kong better prepared for the global market economy rather than simply focused on its neighbours. As this trade developed, Hong Kong was one of the first to come under quota restrictions imposed by the advanced Western economies, even by Britain.

Indeed, Hong Kong was clearly developing as an independent unit, especially as Britain was increasingly concerned with managing its retreat from empire and confused about its new status in the world. The Suez crises of 1956 was graphic evidence of the uncertainty and problems in British foreign policy. But Britain was also vital as the provider of a basically stable international environment and a talented and enlightened administration for the colony. Hong Kong was one of the few places in Asia to be afforded an international business environment based on fair implementation of the rule of law.[5] The government eventually also began to tackle social problems as the general level of prosperity rose.

Thus Hong Kong developed its own status as a developing country in international organisations, albeit always as a special case. Legally Hong Kong was ruled by the British, but in reality it was an independent and fast-growing developing country. Of course, Hong Kong never entirely lost contact with China or its old status as an entrepôt. Some 20 per cent of exports still went to China and the mainland remained the major source of imports. China supplied nearly 45 per cent of total food imports and was also a vital partner in the re-export business. Hong Kong was learning that success in the international market economy did not mean it had to lose touch with China; indeed, at times, when China was shut out of that global economy, Hong Kong could play an important part in linking China to the outside world. The key to Hong Kong's success was a pragmatic adaptation to the international system.

The pressure for change in Hong Kong was relentless and yet the challenges were met with more or less unbroken success. In political terms, Hong Kong watched its Western friends gradually improve relations with China, although it would not be until the 1970s that something approaching normality in their dealings was achieved. But before the visit to China of President Nixon in 1972, there was strong evidence that the serious risks of crises with China were under control. In fact, the most serious challenges came from the internal unrest in China.

The Great Proletarian Cultural Revolution on the mainland which took a turn for the worse in 1966 revived fears that Hong Kong could be damaged by this unrest. While the rioting in April 1966 was more related to social conditions and the need to reform Hong Kong government policy, the riots in May and December 1967 were directly related to the unrest in China.[6] The political objectives fuelled by the Cultural Revolution included demands for an end to Hong Kong's colonial status and the British firmly refused to consider any change. At a time when other British colonies were being given their independence, some people in Hong Kong did reconsider their own future. But with the option of exchanging the benign colonialism of Britain for the harsher and more radical variant in China, few people were interested in challenging the existing order. However, the British did learn that more 'consultation' and improved social policies were sensible reforms that might defuse some of the political tensions.

The unrest in 1967 was not apparently initiated in Peking, although there were some signs that as a result of the general ferment generated in the Cultural Revolution the authorities on the mainland did try for a time to exploit the instability.[7] By December it was clear that the Hong Kong authorities had benefited from the unrest in the sense that the people of Hong Kong grew more sure that they preferred British rule to that from Peking. In the four years following the violence, the Hong Kong government did not simply rest on its laurels; as it began more

far-reaching reforms of the political and social system.
Yet it is also remarkable the extent to which Hong Kong's external position was relatively unaffected by the chaos next door in China. Even at the height of the unrest, trade relations were maintained. Most of the problems in commerce at the time were more related to the economic dislocation in China than anything else. To be sure, there was real damage to business confidence in Hong Kong, but as the limits were set in Peking, confidence returned to the colony. The key was the determination in China that, despite its domestic politics, Hong Kong was worth more as a stable British colony than as a ruined part of communist China. It was certainly within China's power to convey that message to Hong Kong and therefore, by building confidence, make it a reality.

Challenges to Hong Kong also came from the international system. As we have already seen, Britain had a decreasing intrinsic interest in the colony. At a time of widespread decolonisation, Hong Kong was always the exception. There were neither moves towards local democracy nor steps to return the territory to China. It was the fact that Hong Kong was nearly unique among colonies – it was claimed by a large, powerful neighbour – that made both democracy and/or independence unlikely ideas. Even though China was perceived as acting prudently (with the sole exception of the events of 1967), it was never thought that China would tolerate full independence for Hong Kong.

If independence was never on the cards, then democracy, particularly in view of the absence of it on the mainland, was also never a serious consideration. Certainly China made it clear to various British officials over the years that it did not want to see anything like a Western democratic system established in the colony. It was not as if Hong Kong was failing to grow and prosper without democracy, especially in comparison with many former colonies which had been granted both independence and democracy. So long as the system in Hong Kong was working, there was little desire to tinker. Politics was about pragmatic prosperity and not about the theory of just government. In response to the obvious inequalities in standard of living, the Hong Kong government did eventually take a more active part in providing basic services. Private developers did not find it profitable to provide low-cost housing so the government stepped in, although always a few steps behind the regularly rising immigrant population.[8] Hong Kong had retained, in Han Suyin's image, a sense of 'a borrowed place', living on 'borrowed time'. By the late 1960s there was an increasing sense of a civic culture in Hong Kong and the communist-inspired riots of the Cultural Revolution merely enhanced the special sense of belonging to Hong Kong. Education was provided for all, disparities in income lessened and a more mass consumer culture was created. Campaigns in the 1970s to clean up Hong Kong, both literally and in terms of corruption, also marked the transition, albeit more slowly than in Singapore, to a new civic culture.[9]

Thus as Hong Kong developed a sense of itself, it was still set between the looming shadow of China and the fading presence of Britain. The horizons looked wide open, and yet also vulnerable. Britain joined the European Community in the 1970s and, as London began to find a new post-war role, it became clear that role was to be played on the other side of Eurasia. Britain's military presence east of Suez was scaled back by 1971, although Britain had not really been able to defend Hong Kong for close to seventy-five years. A small garrison, including Gurkhas, was retained, although its role was in civil defence, as demonstrated in the case of the 1967 unrest.

Yet because of its pragmatic system of government and economy Hong Kong prospered in this uncertain world. The presence of Britain declined to an extent, but that of the United States and Japan, especially in the business world, more than compensated. Japanese firms set about using Hong Kong as a manufacturing base in the 1970s and the signs of Japanese consumer products began to dominate the skyline. With growth in neighbouring countries in Southeast Asia, Hong Kong prospered in a regional economy that was growing faster than the related international market economy. Hong Kong's success was not built on technical and engineering training, let alone by a disciplined labour force, but, rather, on its rapid response to world markets and the provision of trading and marketing expertise. Remarkably, until surpassed by Tokyo in the early 1980s, Hong Kong had the world's third largest financial market. By the mid-1960s the entrepreneurs of Hong Kong had overtaken the Greeks as shipping magnates. In the early 1980s Hong Kong overtook New York to become the world's second-largest container port (and passed Rotterdam, in 1987, to become first).

By the early 1980s it was no exaggeration to class Hong Kong as the most international city in the world. As a result, while Hong Kong was classed as an NIC, it was yet again unique, if only because of its volatility and precarious position.

Had the international economy been far more closed to trade, Hong Kong might well have withered. But it had the good fortune to be part of a booming region in an expanding system of market economies linking East Asia to North America and Europe. Hong Kong and the other NICs chose to avoid the sterile rhetoric of North–South confrontation and to focus instead on prospering within the system. Unlike even some of the NICs, Hong Kong never went through the stage of growth based on import substitution and was always far more committed to free trade and the international market economy. As trade grew, the Hong Kong authorities found wages rising and expectations of a better basic infrastructure increasing too. The prosperity provided the means to meet these demands and keep the growth going. The pace was relentless, but the opportunities continued to be presented.

Having hung on through the worst of the instabilities in China during the Cultural Revolution, Hong Kong was well placed to benefit from the opening of China that followed the normalisation of relations with the West in the early 1970s. Once the United States opened contacts with the communist authorities, the West as a whole, and Japan in particular, moved into the China market. Hong Kong, by virtue of its continuing, albeit reduced, entrepôt role, was well placed to take advantage of the shift.

The advantages to Hong Kong were manifold. First, it had the expertise in dealing with communist China and the contacts that could either be sold to others interested in the China trade or merely rented as the role of entrepôt returned. Second, Hong Kong could contemplate making use of the cheaper labour across the border in China and thereby improve its own productivity. Third, Hong Kong could offer itself to the mainland as a source of information, a place in which to learn about Western business practices as well as to make contacts.

By the late 1970s the position of Hong Kong in the international system could be best described as buoyant. True, it still lived under the shadow of China, but China was finding Hong Kong useful economically, especially as a way of earning foreign exchange. Nothing could be simpler than selling food and water for hard currency. True, too, Hong Kong did not get much protection from its nominal masters in London, but then little was needed. What is more, Hong Kong had demonstrated its ability to adapt to the international market economy and Britain was merely useful as an enabler. Certainly the fate of British foreign trade was nothing to be emulated.

In sum, Hong Kong had emerged as a unique city-state. Not only did it appear physically unique to those visitors who swooped down to the airport past high-rise living rooms, but also its prosperity was part of a system of government and economy not replicated anywhere else. The fate of Hong Kong depended on a number of factors, few of which were under the control of the people of the colony. The *laissez-faire* system could only be changed by a major shift in the international economy, which was not very likely. Much more real was the risk of policy-changing in China, for one thing was supremely evident: the fate of Hong Kong depended on the policies pursued in China. In the thirty-or-so years since communist power was established in Peking, the people of Hong Kong, while accepting the reality of Chinese power, somehow came to feel that they could do business with the communists. In fact, they had also come to believe that 1997 might not matter after all. It was evidence of the triumph of hope over experience.

3

Negotiating the End of Empire

During the age of Western imperialism, Hong Kong was not strictly speaking unique.[1] It was merely another colony, albeit particularly small, held by a European power but populated by non-whites. In the period after 1945, Britain, like most other colonial powers, gradually divested itself of its colonies. Given the diversity in the type of colonies, it is not surprising that there was no obvious pattern to the retreat from empire and Hong Kong was just another exceptional case.

Yet, as more European colonies were given their freedom, it became increasingly obvious that Hong Kong had to be classified in a category of its own. Hong Kong had been taken by force from an already existing, and still independent, power – China. Also, Britain had obtained only part of the colony in perpetuity, with crucial parts of it due to be returned in 1997. Finally, Hong Kong had prospered in the post-war world under a British 'flag of convenience', because its wealth and success depended on integration into the international market economy rather than on its relations with Britain.

Thus the choices about the fate of Hong Kong were always constrained by the looming reality of China and the vagaries of the international economy. In practice, although independence was given to nearly every other British colony in time, it was never a viable option for Hong Kong because China would not allow it. Nor did Britain have much control over the actions of the people of Hong Kong, for they had long ago come to recognise that their prosperity depended on the unstable mix of the interests of China and the wider world. The only other remotely comparable case was the city-state of Singapore, which might have ended up as part of Malaysia but eventually obtained its independence.[2]

31

British policy towards Hong Kong was always shaped by the actualities of China. While it may be fashionable to assert that Britain was 'mousetrapped', or it 'sold out' Hong Kong, the reality is far more complex. Hong Kong was always a special case in the eyes of everyone who watched its development. The British government, even in the Queen's speech of June 1983, noted the difference between the 'obligations' to the Falklands, the 'commitments' to Gibraltar and, merely, the 'aims' regarding Hong Kong.[3] The revision of Britain's nationality legislation in 1981 (which came into effect in 1983) also changed the status of British passport-holders in Hong Kong to ensure they did not have the right of abode in Britain.

China, too, had a special view of Hong Kong. In 1972, shortly after the People's Republic of China joined the United Nations, Peking wrote to the special committee on decolonisation, formally requesting that Hong Kong and Macao be taken off the list of 'colonies'. China claimed that the fate of the territories 'falls entirely within the sphere of Chinese sovereignty'. There seemed to have been a tacit Chinese assumption that Hong Kong would eventually become theirs, although there is little evidence that Peking thought seriously about how the transition might be managed.[4]

Thus any assessment of the way in which the fate of Hong Kong was decided in the 1984 Anglo-Chinese agreement depends on sorting out the extent to which Britain had an opportunity to change China's mind about eventually re-acquiring control of Hong Kong. If China could not be persuaded, as Malaysia had been in 1965, that holding on to a city-state was not worth the struggle, then there was little that Britain could have responsibly done to ensure independence was achieved. It seems the key decisions about the fate of Hong Kong were taken more often in Peking than in London.

Phase One Talks

The relationship between China and Hong Kong, for all its outward tranquillity, always contained the seeds of instability. As decolonisation around the globe worked its way down to the smallest of imperial territories, the anomalous position of Hong Kong became even more obvious. China made sure that everyone was aware that the incongruity of a rich Western colony claimed by Peking was not the norm in the process of decolonisation and that the territory was due to return to China. As China grew more confident in the late 1970s, Hong Kong was an increasing insult to Chinese pride in a revolution that had thrown out all other imperialist interests from China in 1949.[5] What is more, even in the first years of China's new reform programme in the late 1970s, between 1977 and 1980 Hong Kong still attracted some 400,000 people from the mainland. When given the choice, the people of China seemed to prefer Hong Kong to communist rule.

Even taking into account this background of a crisis waiting to happen, it is difficult to find a specific trigger for the negotiations that led to the 1984 Anglo-Chinese accord on Hong Kong. To this day it is not clear whether the initiative for the negotiations came from China or Britain, or whether it was simply the result of reactions by both parties to the reality beyond their control. Perhaps the most obvious but distant factor was the decision by China's communist rulers in December 1978 to adopt a programme of reform. As it evolved in fits and starts in subsequent years, the programme of reforms was designed to include a strategy of opening China up to greater involvement with the international community. The coastal regions, with the old treaty ports, were the obvious place to start as in those areas there was significant expertise and interest in establishing contacts with the international market economy.

As we have already seen, Hong Kong had been important to China precisely because the rest of the country was relatively closed to the international economy. So much of China's foreign exchange could be earned in the relatively easy fashion of selling food and water to Hong Kong. Thus the opening up to the outside world was both a potential threat and an advantage to Hong Kong.[6]

The threat to the colony was that, as China's doors opened wider, Hong Kong would become a less important source of foreign exchange and a far less vital window on the international trading system. Yet there were also advantages to be exploited as China clearly needed expertise in dealing with the outside world and Hong Kong was already well established as an international city used to dealing with Chinese communists. As the primary location for overseas Chinese business, Hong Kong was an obvious funnel for finance and expertise into the mainland.

As China looked seriously at the successes of those states in the region who took an active part in the international market economy, they saw the need to make basic changes in the way the mainland did business with the outside world. The strategy of creating special economic zones was a development of special processing zones recognised elsewhere in the developing world. South Korea, Taiwan and Singapore had shown the benefits of a determined effort to play an active role in the international market economy and China sensed the need to play the same game if it was not to fall further behind.

The first major, Special Economic Zone (SEZ) was established in Shenzhen, a sleepy fishing village just across the border from Hong Kong. As communists are fond of noting, the selection of Shenzhen 'was not by chance'. It was a deliberate attempt to exploit the benefits of easy contact with China's premier outlet to the international economy – Hong Kong. It was also assumed that Hong Kong Chinese capital would be more willingly slipped across the frontier in search of cheaper labour, while close contacts with the Hong Kong base (and lifestyle) were maintained. From China's point of view, the SEZ provided a controlled experiment in dealing with the international economy, while limiting the risks of 'spiritual pollution' that seemed to come with Western business. In the words of one observer, this was also designed as a 'dummy run' for Hong Kong, because if China showed it could cope with international capitalism, then it could cope with nearby Hong Kong.[7] Significantly, a border fence was built along the northern edge of Shenzhen county.

Despite the new location of the border fence, with the rapid development of the SEZs the linkage between Hong Kong and Guangdong province grew closer. The new rail, boat and air services linking Hong Kong and Canton made the practicalities of doing business easier. With the new atmosphere of reform in China after 1978 the enmities between Hong Kong and the communists eased and business became more pragmatic. Not that such economic integration made the people of Hong Kong want to join the mainland – if anything, the greater contact made them look down on their country cousins more than before – but it did show what could be done to make life more profitable and logical. The 'south wind' from Hong Kong into Guangdong brought all kinds of influences along with the wealth, including such things as television broadcasts which helped provide even more momentum for reforms. But the counter-current also made it clear to the people of Hong Kong that their fate was increasingly connected with that of the Guangdong area, and this despite the fact that by the late 1980s Hong Kong, with half of one per cent of China's population, had roughly the same amount of foreign trade as all of China.

The selection of the site of Shenzhen as the most important of the first four SEZs alone suggests that, even in 1980, China was aware that the fate of Hong Kong was something for which it needed to plan. It was never likely that China would simply allow Hong Kong to creep up to 1997 without attempting to regain at least the territory scheduled for return that year. It was also a reasonable assumption that any decision on the New Territories would be linked by China to the fate of Hong Kong island and the Kowloon peninsula. Peking never recognised what it called the 'unequal treaties' governing its hand-over to Britain and was determined to undo the 'wrongs of history' when it had the opportunity to do so at a reasonable cost.

But in addition to the pressure coming from China, it was clear that Hong Kong and its surrounding international community would be unwilling merely to let 1997 loom without some reaction. For international traders and the world of international finance, the main question was the length of leases for land in that part of Hong Kong scheduled for return to China in 1997. No legal provision could be made for such a lease when the government of Hong Kong was bound to return the land to China. Similarly, a Hong Kong government anxious to take long-term decisions such as that concerning a new airport required some sense of the post-1997 environment. It was therefore necessary to have some clarification about the fate of Hong Kong, if only because of the preciousness of land in the colony and the notorious sensitivity of land prices in this crowded territory. Most observers seemed to agree that, without the New Territories, Hong Kong was far less viable and could be made unviable if China was determined to force the return of all the territory. Unlike Malaysia, which was happy enough to make money from selling basic commodities to an independent Singapore, China made it clear it would not continue 'business as usual' with a Hong Kong rump after 1997.

When the Hong Kong Governor, Sir Murray MacLehose, went to Peking in 1979, he was told by Deng Xiaoping that investors should 'set their hearts at ease'.[8] Such Delphic utterances were accompanied by more specific statements declaring that China would indeed take control of Hong Kong, although it had not yet decided whether it would be before 1997, on the day, or even after.[9] So much for easy hearts.

China's silence on the fate of Hong Kong was either ominous or reassuring, depending on one's disposition. The prevailing optimistic line was based on what nearly became a mantra of Hong Kong – China would not kill the goose that laid the golden egg.[10] In the meantime, the people of Hong Kong were neither asked their views, nor spoke up in their own defence.[11] In April 1982, China's new draft constitution contained provisions for a Special Administrative Region (SAR), which, although couched in terms of easing the reunification of Taiwan, was also applicable to Hong Kong. The notion of an SAR had first been mentioned in September 1981, but it seems China's eye was always on the much bigger prize of Taiwan; Hong Kong was peripheral until the negotiations began in earnest. In any case, the idea that an SAR would have a high degree of autonomy and the existing economic and judicial system would remain intact was equally applicable to both Taiwan and Hong Kong.

Thus there is evidence that China was thinking about the future of Hong Kong, at least in general terms, before Britain formally raised the matter. But there is far less evidence that China had given any serious thought to the mechanism of taking control and how confidence could be maintained in the interim. As the audiences granted to prominent Hong Kong business leaders by Chinese leaders suggested, the future of Hong Kong was not really a matter to be negotiated as much as revealed. Unless Britain raised the subject of managing the transition and maintaining confidence, China would assume all was well.

In May 1982, in preparation for a visit to China by the British prime minister, Mrs Thatcher, Humphrey Atkins (a minister of state at the Foreign Office) observed that the initiative in talks about Hong Kong came from Britain. He claimed that China had as unclear a position as that stated by Deng in 1979.[12] But business decision makers could not do business with such uncertainty and so on 1 July 1982, with the New Territories lease set to expire in precisely fifteen years, a number of Hong Kong banks announced a decision to extend loan repayment terms on mortgages in the New Territories beyond 1 July 1997.

China did not respond formally to the needs of the

international business community, but on 16 July 1982 Peng Zhen, a vice-chairman of the Chinese Community party, told the standing committee of the National People's Congress (NPC) that Hong Kong and Macao could become Special Administrative Regions of China as set out in the draft legislation for the new constitution, and could retain their capitalist system so long as China obtained sovereignty. This was not a final decision on Hong Kong's future, but it was a more specific elaboration of ideas at a time of increasing concern about the future. From China's point of view, whether nationalist or communist, once the issue of sovereignty over Hong Kong was raised, no self-respecting Chinese leader could have done anything but claim Chinese control of the territory. What is more, the fate of Hong Kong was seen as part of the struggle to regain Taiwan, and if concessions on sovereignty were made regarding the lesser prize (Hong Kong), the bigger prize (Taiwan) would be surely lost.

With economic problems in Hong Kong at the time, albeit more due to the general recession in the international economy, sensitivities were sharpened. Yet it was not until September 1982 that the issues were clearly focused. A visit by Mrs Thatcher to Peking resulted in a secret, but unequivocal, statement by Deng Xiaoping of the obvious: that China would regain control of Hong Kong and there was no question of extending the lease. Some reports noted Deng's allusion to China's nineteenth-century experience with foreign imperialism and his belief that the future of Hong Kong was a matter of fundamental national pride.[13]

Thus the initiative to discuss the future of Hong Kong came from a combination of sources. The marketplace – which was so vital to the success of the territory – wanted reassurance about leases. Britain responded with an attempt to obtain clarification from China about the future. China in turn responded with a reassertion of a position of which it felt the rest of the world was already fully apprised.[14] If Britain, Hong Kong or the international market was unsure whether China would contemplate a revision of the lease or a compromise on sovereignty, the substance of the subsequent negotiations was all about making China's principled position very clear.

The two sides agreed to begin diplomatic consultation in order to reach a formal agreement on Hong Kong. But right from the start the atmosphere was turning dark. China's official news agency, Xinhua, appended an official statement to the copy of the joint declaration making clear the Chinese position on the complete recovery of the colony. On 27 September, on the first-ever visit by a British prime minister to Hong Kong, Mrs Thatcher responded with a bald reassertion of the validity of the old treaties and a sentiment that those countries who fail to keep to one treaty cannot be expected to honour another. The stock market and currency plummeted in what was to become well known as a regular process of barometer reading in the following years of talks on Hong Kong. On 30 September China issued its own rebuttal, thereby raising the temperature of the debate even before formal talks could begin.[15]

Mrs Thatcher's pugnacious style, coming as it did just after Britain's victory in the Falklands war with Argentina, was as much a matter of personal character as national interest. Despite a good deal of muttering to the contrary, there was never much economic, let alone military, rationale for Britain holding on to Hong Kong. Although some people in Britain thought a deal on Hong Kong might allow an increase in Sino-British trade, this argument was never taken very seriously by the British negotiators. Indeed, it was an enduring puzzle to China why Britain bothered to battle over seemingly tiny matters and constant queries were raised about some hidden and hitherto unstated British interest. The reality was that the easiest policy for narrow British interests would have been to 'cut and run'.

On reflection, there seemed to be no calm way in which the issue of 1997 could be raised. With China refusing to extend the lease and Peking feeling increasingly confident about its role in the international market economy, there was little chance that China would meekly make life easy for Britain. The choice in London was therefore stark. Either it could try to bluff its way into negotiations and challenge China to take the New Territories by force in 1997 – with all the dire consequences for the stability of Hong Kong – or it could try to negotiate about the terms of transition to Chinese rule. The reason why there was no middle ground was far more to do with Chinese than British policy.

The first round of preliminary talks were held in Peking in October, when matters of procedure were discussed. Hong Kong fretted and its economy staggered through the twin problems of political uncertainty and the recession in the international market economy. To make matters worse, Britain declined to brief its closest allies, including the United States, about the negotiations with China.

It is unclear the extent to which other interested parties might have played a constructive role at this time. The United States was closely involved with China as part of an anti-Soviet strategy and would have been unlikely to offer support to Britain in a determined effort to avoid returning Hong Kong in 1997. American business seemed convinced that China was serious about an Open Door strategy and would become a sensible trade partner. Under such circumstances, so it was reasoned, if China promised to handle Hong Kong gently, then it would do so. It is true that the United States had just been particularly helpful to Britain over the Falklands war, but the enemy was Argentina and therefore far less valuable to the United States. Argentina was certainly not a state bordering on the Soviet Union and part of the great power triangle.

Britain's position was difficult to sustain, especially because it had no means of taking on the Chinese. The only card that Britain had was a possibility of easing the transition in Hong Kong so that China might eventually obtain a prize worth having. If Britain conceded sovereignty at the start, then it would become clear that the talks were merely about technical subjects. Yet if sovereignty was not conceded, China felt Britain would seek an extension of the lease. The decision of China not to contemplate serious talks unless the principle of sovereignty was conceded was a gamble. Britain might have called China's bluff, but then the main losers would have been the people of Hong Kong. Britain had little to gain by holding out.

China's strategy was to stress that special terms for Hong Kong could be negotiated, terms which would ensure that little really changed in the life of the residents. At the same time, China refused to consider Hong Kong itself as a negotiating partner for fear of legitimising the notion that Hong Kong could have some *de facto* independent status. China wanted Britain to accept at the outset that the talks were about how to hand over sovereignty.

The details of the Chinese position seemed to have been worked out in the months after September 1982. It was then that Chinese leaders defined the range of freedoms that would be granted to Hong Kong to carry on their existing system. In December 1982 the new constitution promulgated by the National People's Congress included Article 31, which established Special

Administrative Regions. In June 1983 Deng, clearly in charge of the over-arching strategy towards Hong Kong, also noted that policy was being made at the highest level, including President Li Xiannian and Premier Zhao Ziyang.[16]

It was only the personal intervention of Mrs Thatcher that broke the Ango-Chinese deadlock. Britain accepted that sovereignty could be handed over, on the assumption that mutually acceptable terms were agreed. Thus Britain could retain the illusion that it had something to trade, while Peking could have confidence that it would obtain sovereignty in the end. On 1 July 1983 it was agreed that formal talks could begin on 12 July. It would take fourteen months and twenty-two rounds of talks until the final agreement was initialled.

Phase Two Talks

Agreeing to surrender sovereignty was one major concession, but it was not the end of the negotiations. Britain assumed that it knew better than China how to run Hong Kong and so set about establishing terms for the future of Hong Kong which might even allow for a continuation of some form of British administration after 1997. Much like in the case of Macao (which, after the 1974 revolution in Portugal, was offered to China but Peking refused to take control) so Britain hoped that China might accept a large degree of British administration of Hong Kong for some time to come. Of course, China's position regarding Macao in 1974, before the fate of Hong Kong had been agreed, was always likely to be vague until the much more important objective of Hong Kong was discussed. Thus a 'Macao solution' was never available for Hong Kong.

Britain pursued the idea of retaining administration through a discussion of the role of the people of Hong Kong in any negotiation about their future. Mrs Thatcher had used the phrase a 'three-legged stool' to describe the relationship between Britain, Hong Kong and China, and if the Hong Kong leg was not used the structure would become unstable. The problem for Britain in such a strategy was that putting too much stress on the Hong Kong leg required the establishment of a democratic process in the colony, something that had never been taken seriously before. By 1983, it was far too late to contemplate a credible introduction of democracy that did not appear simply to be a way of stymying the wishes of Peking.

As a result, China was able to subvert the British strategy with a classic campaign in the style of the formation of other 'united fronts'.[17] As far as Peking was concerned, Hong Kong was a matter for discussion between only China and the colonial master in London. Britain did not agree. In preparation for the next round of talks, Britain added the Governor of Hong Kong, Sir Edward Youde, to the British team. When asked at a press conference on 7 July 1983 who he would be representing at the talks, the Governor said, 'I am the governor of Hong Kong . . . I represent the people of Hong Kong.' On 8 July the Chinese foreign ministry immediately replied that Sir Edward was merely a part of the British delegation and represented no one but Britain.[18] The Chinese also denied a visa to the director of the Hong Kong government information service, who was intending to accompany the governor. Public opinion poll data from the time suggest very clearly that the vast majority of the people of Hong Kong did not want a change of the *status quo* and were satisfied with British administration.[19]

The first round of serious talks, on 12/13 July, ended with a communiqué declaring the discussions to have been 'useful and constructive' – a well-known euphemism for a sticky time. But the subsequent round of talks, later in July, was merely said to be 'useful' and the next round in August was just described as being 'held'. Things were going from bad to worse. Throughout the period, confidence ebbed rapidly from Hong Kong. China kept up a barrage of statements suggesting that Peking would take control, come what may, and it was best if Britain settled down to talking about how to hand over power. This was a worrying war of words, especially since Britain had nothing to fire back.

It seems that the British strategy at the talks, not to put too fine a point on it, was to educate China about the realities of Hong Kong. Early meetings included lectures about the international market economy, the secret of capitalist economics and Western legal systems, and the role of such international institutions as the GATT (General Agreement on Tariffs and Trade) and international agreements such as the MFA (Multi-Fibre Arrangement for textile imports).[20] Britain suggested, at least implicitly, that these lectures were necessary for the future of Hong Kong and that China did not yet inspire confidence in the people of Hong Kong.

Even if the residents of Hong Kong were not present at the talks, Britain was still determined to use the argument about the Hong Kong leg of the stool in order to force concessions out of Peking.

China was playing for high stakes in holding out for a collapse in the British position. China wanted to take over control of Hong Kong without a British role continuing beyond 1997. To do so, it would have to accept that the ebbing confidence in the colony would hurt the local economy and the value of the Hong Kong dollar. A falling dollar meant a cut in China's foreign-exchange earnings from trade with the colony and some 30–40 per cent of China's foreign-exchange earnings in 1983 came from Hong Kong.[21]

But, aside from the reputation of its diplomats, Britain had nothing to play for except the prosperity of Hong Kong. Certainly Britain, even by its own admission, had few cards to play.[22] If the colony was to be handed over in a shambles because London's negotiators held out too long for terms that ensured Hong Kong was not a shambles, then it was a pointless exercise.

China suspected Britain of deliberately manipulating the financial markets, but this suggested more about China's poor sense of how international capitalism functions than anything else. It was true that Britain did little to rescue the Hong Kong dollar on the international money markets and China's subsequent behaviour suggested that at least some of its arms of government, notably the Bank of China, recognised the rules of the international capitalist market place and sought profits in the markets before building confidence in Hong Kong.

The next round of talks, on 22/23 September 1983, was the low point, and the last British effort to test Chinese resolve. The continuing deadlock led to panic in Hong Kong on 24 September. The dollar and stock market hit new lows, supermarket shelves were cleared and trade partners insisted on dealing in United States dollars only. The Bank of China was among the major purchasers of US dollars, while Peking was denouncing the British for manipulating the currency markets.[23] It is estimated that China lost $1.1 billion in foreign-exchange earnings in 1982/3 owing to the fall of the Hong Kong dollar.[24]

Finally, the Hong Kong government stepped in to rescue the local dollar and the currency was pegged to the US dollar in mid-October. As a result, interest rates looked set to take the strain of confidence (and, indeed, in 1984 reached 17 per cent).

On the last day of September, Ji Pengfei, the head of the Hong Kong and Macao office, declared that China would make a statement regarding the future of Hong Kong by the end of 1984, whether or not there was an agreement with Britain. A deadline was set and Britain was under no illusion about China standing its ground. It is doubtful that China ever really saw its role as a genuine negotiator. While there is some evidence of differences of opinion on the Chinese side, Deng Xiaoping soon took clear control.[25] Even at the height of the crisis of confidence in Hong Kong, China continued to denounce what it saw as Britain's continuing colonial attitude to Hong Kong. For those used to an arrogant Chinese negotiating style, at least when China held the cards, Peking's policies between 1982 and 1984 were not surprising.[26]

The pegging of the Hong Kong dollar in mid-October seemed to be part of a package of concessions by Britain. London also then informed the Chinese that it was prepared to give up the administration of Hong Kong after July 1997, thereby caving in to the Chinese demand. Sir Edward Youde had led a delegation to London in the first week of October. This was apparently part of the decision-making process about the change of policy rather than an attempt, as Peking claimed at the time, to revive the idea of the three-legged stool. It was also announced in mid-October that Sir Percy Cradock, upon retirement from his post as ambassador in Peking, would return to London as a special adviser to Mrs Thatcher. Clearly there would be changes in Britain's policy towards Hong Kong.

Could it have been any different? In theory, Britain might have bluffed for longer and challenged China to ruin Hong Kong in 1983. Britain, along with other Western states, would have lost some commercial assets, as would China. Peking would certainly have lost more if one considers foreign-currency earnings and potential profits from a post-1997 Hong Kong. But would London have been allowed to carry on bluffing? Certainly there would have been pressure from other Western allies because Britain was harming more than its own interests. The United States had already shown in the Falklands conflict that it was prepared to exert some pressure on Britain – and that was at a time when Britain had some hope of using force of its own to regain its position. The United States, like Britain, recognised that China held the key to Hong Kong.

By holding out for some form of continued British administration, London had chosen to fight on relatively boggy ground. Had the notion of 'a three-legged stool' been more tenable, it might have been harder for China to refuse the demands of the people of Hong Kong for more control over their own fate. But because Britain had consistently refused to grant Hong Kong real democracy and the people of Hong Kong, unlike those of other British colonies, had so patently failed to agitate for any such thing, China was easily able to claim this was a red herring. By promising some measure of regional self-government, China further softened the impact of the autonomy argument.

Phase Three Talks

The next round of talks, in October, took place in the new atmosphere of British submission to the basic Chinese demands. Sir Percy Cradock had apparently returned from London with a personal letter, from Mrs Thatcher to the prime minister, Zhao Ziyang, which recognised that Britain could not play an administrative role beyond 1997.[27] Although it was not until 20 April 1984 that the foreign secretary, Sir Geoffrey Howe, would make it public that Britain had made such a concession to China, the reality was that London was ready to get down to the nitty-gritty of sorting out handover arrangements.

The October round ended with the return to the phrase 'useful and constructive' to describe the talks, which in the light of past ill feeling was a distinct improvement. Mrs Thatcher, speaking to the BBC World Service, said the talks were 'very constructive and went much better'. China was now paying increasing attention to British descriptions of what made Hong Kong tick, and Britain was paying attention when China spelled out what it meant by autonomy for the colony.

In place of the previous panoply of Chinese attacks on British policy was a new and much more positive line. Chinese officials described Sino-British relations as normal and Ji Pengfei elaborated some of Peking's ideas for Hong Kong's future. The proposal that the present social system could be retained for fifty years beyond 1997 was expounded. By the time of the 7/8 December Sino-British meeting, Britain was taking the initiative in setting questions to Peking about its plans for the future and the structure of the Basic Law that would govern Hong Kong after 1997. The December round was the first to end with a declaration that progress was being made.

By January 1984, Sir Richard Evans took over from Sir Percy Cradock as head of the British delegation (and as ambassador in Peking) and Zhou Nan took over from Yao Guang on the Chinese side. But Hong Kong itself, despite the earlier rhetoric about a three-legged stool, was kept in the dark regarding the details of the talks and the extent of the British concession. In February, Roger Lobo, a member of the colony's Legislative Council (Legco), suggested that plans for Hong Kong should be debated in the Council. The proposition revived Chinese fears of a Hong Kong leg to the talks and the pro-communist press in Hong Kong swiftly denounced the suggestion. With the decision in March of Jardine Matheson, Hong Kong's oldest trading company, to move its holding company to Bermuda, confidence was further undermined and the stock market reacted accordingly. It was against this background that Sir Geoffrey Howe's remarks about the decision to surrender administration of Hong Kong in 1997 made clear to Hong Kong the extent to which it would have to face China on its own.

A delegation from Hong Kong's Executive Council (Exco) appealed to Mrs Thatcher in London, but was poorly treated by MPs then briefly (for all of *thirty minutes!*) debating the future of Hong Kong. The reality of being set adrift by Britain was reinforced by Deng Xiaoping's declaration of the obvious: that PLA troops would be stationed in Hong Kong after 1997. In June another delegation of Exco and Legco members, this time to Peking, was met by Deng but pointedly the members were treated as individuals and told they were not Chinese patriots. Deng told them 'no three legs, only two legs', as if anyone had any doubts about China's attitude to the views of the people of Hong Kong.[28]

Hong Kong did get some support from one or two parties outside the Ango-Chinese bilateral relationship. Gaston Thorn, the president of the EC Commission, declared that it was in no one's interest to see the prosperity of Hong Kong put at risk. Nakasone, the prime minister of Japan, during a trip to China reported Hu Yaobang's assurances about the safety of all foreign investment. Yet these remarks also came in an atmosphere of Western courtship of China and at a time when outsiders saw the

China market as now open to Western business. Few would choose the prospects of Hong Kong in favour of the perceived opportunities in China. The message to Hong Kong was really one of the primacy of China.

Although the formal Anglo-Chinese negotiations were going well, there was a growing perception of the need to step up the pace in order to meet China's end-of-the-year deadline. Also, Deng Xiaoping had noted on 22 June that he wanted to see an agreement intialled by September and he clearly seemed to be taking the leading role in formulating Chinese strategy. It was he who was credited with the crucial notion that Hong Kong could have a fifty-year period with its own political and economic system.[29]

With a renewal of apprehension in the colony, it was all the more necessary to make progress and restore what confidence could be salvaged. China and Britain went into what was in effect permanent session by creating a full-time working group to work on the specific language of the agreement. David Wilson, assistant under-secretary of state at the foreign office, and later to succeed Youde as Governor of Hong Kong, led the British team.

Following some signs that serious blockages were developing in the faster-paced talks, Sir Geoffrey Howe arrived to break the deadlock. In a visit to Hong Kong on 1 August, after a few days of high-level talks in Peking, he announced 'substantial progress' (echoed by the Chinese) and a ten-point plan which summed up the details already provided so far by British and Chinese sources. Sir Geoffrey was most reassuring on the matter of the Joint Liaison Group (JLG) of British and Chinese officials, which, when first suggested by Deng, seemed to imply that China would take a role in governing Hong Kong even before 1997. Sir Geoffrey managed to persuade the Chinese to accept that it would merely provide for better liaison and would continue until the year 2000. This secured for Britain a role beyond 1997. Most importantly, Sir Geoffrey announced that substantial progress, the issues of aviation, land and nationality, had been made and the stock market rose as a result. These closing stages of the negotiations clearly involved small-scale compromises by both sides as well as high-level intervention in order to achieve them.

The remaining three formal rounds of negotiations focused on the three outstanding issues, the most important of which concerned nationality. Of the 5.8 million people living in Hong

Kong in 1989, some 160,000 were full citizens of Western or Asian countries. About 60,000 were white expatriates and most of the others came from neighbouring Asian countries. The majority of Hong Kong's population were Chinese eligible for British passports and were technically British Dependent Territories (BDT) citizens.[30] In 1984, at the time of the negotiations, there were 2.8 million people in this category (3.2 million in 1989).[31] They had the right to travel with British documents, but had no right of abode in Britain. If, after 1997, the people of Hong Kong could no longer use these documents, then they would have the far less useful Chinese passport. But in agreeing to BDT documents China would have to accept some residual sovereignty for Britain as well as risk Britain extending consular protection to the people of Hong Kong. In the end, China refused to accept the validity of BDT documents in Hong Kong or China, but essentially agreed dual nationality by allowing holders to travel elsewhere in the world with their BDT papers. China did insist that these documents could only be held by those born in Hong Kong before 1 July 1997 and that they could not be passed on to future generations. Peking also won agreement that this deal would not be part of the Joint Declaration; it would instead be consigned to an Exchange of Memoranda by the two governments.

On the aviation issue, China granted Hong Kong the right to negotiate bilateral agreements (except for those flights that terminate on the mainland) with other countries on behalf of Cathay Pacific, the local airline owned by the Swire Group. The question of land leases was more difficult because it touched on the sensitive matter of Chinese suspicion that Britain was likely to leave Hong Kong as an empty shell after 1997. The problem was who should take the profit from the sale of land leases running beyond 1997. Under the previous policy, the Hong Kong government took the profit and, indeed, this formed a major part of government revenue. China feared Britain would siphon off the funds before 1997 and so it was eventually agreed that 50 per cent of the proceeds would go into a fund for the future Special Administrative Region.

After frantic last-minute work, the final agreement was ready for initialling in Peking on 26 September 1984 – with Sir Richard Evans acting for Britain and vice-foreign minister Zhou Nan acting for China. Britain then issued a white paper called 'The

Draft Agreement between the Government of the United Kingdom . . . and the Government of China on the future of Hong Kong', while Xinhua's official English version merely called it the Sino-British 'Joint Declaration'.

Mrs Thatcher flew in from London for a fifteen-minute signing ceremony on 19 December. The Chinese prime minister, Zhao Ziyang, was the other signatory. The three-month interval had been taken up with a charade of consultation with the people of Hong Kong, although the agreement required formal approval by only the British parliament and China's National People's Congress. As the introduction to the British white paper made clear, 'the alternative to acceptance of the present agreement is to have no agreement. In this case the Chinese government has made it plain that negotiations could not be reopened and that it would publish its own plans for Hong Kong.'[32] The white paper also acknowledged that the need for 'confidentiality' in the talks was not good for confidence in Hong Kong but the failure to reach an agreement would have been even more damaging.

An assessment office set up in Hong Kong reported on 29 November that 'all but a few submissions' acknowledged the inevitability of Chinese rule. All but two Legco members supported the agreement. Only one member of both Legco and Exco resigned in criticism. Only one member of the urban council abstained and all eighteen district boards endorsed the deal.

It is true that the Hong Kong Bar Association refused to endorse the agreement, but this was because of unhappiness with the British Nationality Act, which failed to provide for the right of abode in Britain for those with British passports. While it is also true that the people of Hong Kong clearly had little choice in the matter, it has to be said their response to the deal was largely one of resignation. There was neither mass civil disobedience nor wild enthusiasm. The pragmatism was sensible, but it masked the extent to which the agreement could still be subject to major shocks to confidence. For the time being, it was a case of making the best of a bad situation.

As far as the world outside was concerned, there was a small, but still palpable, sigh of relief that nothing had been done to upset the economic prospects of the region. No one wanted a breakdown in the negotiations. United States Secretary of State George Shultz said that 'the agreement will provide a solid foundation for Hong Kong's enduring future'. United Nations'

Secretary-General Javier Perez de Cuellar praised the negotiations as a 'tribute to the wisdom, perseverance and imaginative thinking of the two governments'. Other officials in countries of the regions expressed similar platitudes.[33]

On 5 December, the British House of Commons held what passed for a debate on the Hong Kong agreement. Some 8 per cent of MPs attended. Foreign Office Minister Richard Luce tackled the subject of the refusal to grant the right of abode to the holder of BDT passports by noting that it would be an expression of bad faith to argue at this stage that there was a real need for an escape route for the people of Hong Kong. At this stage, at least, official confidence was being built on the agreement, although the Labour party (as embodied in the speech by the shadow foreign secretary, Denis Healey) suggested EC and Commonwealth countries should be asked to assist in re-settling those who may wish to do so. Only Paddy Ashdown, for the Liberal party, expressed an unequivocal concern that Britain had failed in its moral obligation to offer the people of Hong Kong a full escape route if the agreement failed. In any case, there was never any risk that the House would change the agreement or allow large-scale immigration from Hong Kong.

The Agreement

As has already been suggested, there were always limits to the kind of agreement that could have been reached. Reversion of sovereignty of Hong Kong to China was always the most likely scenario. Some form of continued British administration was a British hope at one stage, but never sustained for long. Thus the agreement was largely about the form of Chinese rule after 1997. The outcome might have been worse. China might have imposed its will, offering the kind of 'autonomy' held by Tibet or Xinjiang. In the end, the agreement was about building confidence in the future to encourage the people of Hong Kong to remain. China knew it would get the territory, but getting the people and the prosperity were (and still are) harder to ensure. Thus the central question was how much China would have to change its usual practices in order to obtain the people and prosperity. If China had it sway entirely, the takeover of Hong Kong would merely have been accompanied by a statement of platitudes and a request for blind trust. A minimalist argument would hold that whatever Britain obtained was better than nothing, even if it was not enough to secure the future. As British officials were quick to remind their critics, no one can do that.

The specific agreement begins with the obvious: China will regain sovereignty over Hong Kong. But the heart of the agreement, the twelve points of section three, immediately goes on to list China's basic policies towards Hong Kong, including the promise to establish a Special Administrative Region with a 'high degree of autonomy' except in foreign and defence affairs. The SAR will have executive, legislative and independent judicial powers and the laws 'currently in force in Hong Kong will remain basically unchanged'. The government of the SAR will be composed of local inhabitants, with a chief executive appointed by Peking by means of elections or consultations.

Section three also promises that the current social and economic system will remain. This includes rights, freedoms and private property presently in place. The SAR will remain a free port and open as an international financial centre. Using the name 'Hong Kong, China', the SAR may maintain its own economic and cultural relations and conclude relevant agreements with states, regions and international organisations. Public order will be maintained by the SAR.

Section four notes that Britain will continue to be responsible for the administration of Hong Kong until 30 June 1997, 'with the object of maintaining and preserving its economic prosperity and social stability'. The government of China promises 'its cooperation in this connection', as if either Britain or China could control anything so delicate as the confidence underlying stability and prosperity. In addition to other sections dealing with land leases and the JLG, the two parties also agree to implement the three annexes. The crucial exchange of memoranda governing nationality issues is also attached, but there is no agreement to implement its particulars.

Apart from the nationality question, other uncertainties include the promise to retain the existing legal system, except where it contradicts the Basic Law (passed by Peking's NPC in February 1990). But at least the power of final adjudication in the courts, which used to be held by the Privy Council in London, was now to be vested in Hong Kong and not Peking.

It was also agreed that entry into Hong Kong from the mainland will still be restricted after 1997. Those wishing to leave Hong Kong could do so, as before 1997, thereby leaving open the door to those wishing to find a better future – the so-called brain drain.

The remarkable detail of the agreement and its annexes was a clear attempt to boost confidence in Hong Kong and was mostly the result of a determined British effort to get China tied down as much as possible. Yet it was also clear that words were no guarantee of the unguaranteeable. Confidence is a state of mind and political freedom the result of a civil society that takes centuries to develop. Thus whether or not PLA troops were stationed in Hong Kong was irrelevant (they were nearby anyway) and they could be taken neither as a symbol of stability nor as evidence of evil intent. The stage was set for the testing of the agreement.

Some argued that only through convergence could there be assurance of stability, while the more independent-minded argued that only a fierce defence of basic rights and the accentuation of differences from the communist regime would guarantee success. Convergence, or what the social scientists called 'anticipatory socialisation', argued that success could only be ensured if both sides acquired characteristics of the other before the date of union.[34] But given the size of the gulf between the two sides, and the differences in their strengths, such a process was difficult to envisage. If China as a whole was not really becoming more capitalist and willing to be pressured by the international economy, then Hong Kong was the only one doing the converging. Perhaps the best hope for Hong Kong was that, with its help, Guangdong and southern China would evolve differently from Peking and thereby make for a better fit with Hong Kong. The future was as much about Peking's relations with all its regions as it was about Peking's specific relations with Hong Kong. The next stage was to await the Basic Law from the NPC – but in between came the unforeseen events of May and June 1989 in Peking.

On the Road to 1997

The first five years after the 1984 agreement provided strong evidence that both those urging convergence and those insisting on vigilance were correct. Confidence in the future was volatile. Unlike on previous paths to decolonisation, there was virtually no precedent for the task set out in the 1984 agreement. There was certainly no precedent for returning close to 6 million people to the rule of those from whom most of them had fled. It was not as if Hong Kong was a drain on the British people. Although Britain was not making any more from Hong Kong than from other developed capitalist states, the people of Hong Kong were themselves the third richest in East Asia behind Japan and Singapore. Thus the 'rich experience of decolonisation' was of little guide to the fate of Hong Kong.

Equally, China's usual practice of sending in the troops at an early opportunity was not a viable solution.[1] China's strategy was to demonstrate that the notion of 'one country, two systems' would work. This strategy, first evolved as a way to lure Taiwan back into one China, required a gentle demonstration that, even if China was the sovereign state controlling all of China, it could tolerate diversity in its various parts. The great unanswered question was whether Peking could indeed be so tolerant. The evidence of the first five years of practice suggested that China was not yet able to play the game successfully. After the Peking massacre of 1989 there was little question that confidence in the colony had taken a bad knock. The risk, then, was that if China continued to be unable to build confidence it would inherit a Hong Kong that was shrivelling away. The people of Hong Kong could of course simply roll over and accept whatever China said – Peking's sense of the convergence concept. But if it was vigilance that was required, then the people of Hong Kong could loudly state their opposition in their still protected environment. In between these extremes was the hope that Hong Kong could help the neighbouring territory of southern China to stake out its own greater independence from Peking and thus this larger region might stand a better chance in any dispute with Peking. Of course, if all else fails, Hong-Kongers can simply leave. Britain agreed to return the land but not the people in 1997.

Such pessimism was certainly not the main theme of the first few years after the 1984 agreement. The Joint Liaison Group, in managing the transition to 1997, was the embodiment of the notion of co-operation. This 'organ of liaison', rather than an 'organ of power', met three times a year and since 1 July 1988 has been based in Hong Kong itself. With up to five representatives from both China and Britain, it reached agreement on a number of technical but still important issues. Topics included seamen's identity documents, revised terms of service for the judiciary, improved pensions for civil servants and the localisation of British laws before 1997.

The first standing sub-group, on International Rights and Obligations, was set up in 1986. It agreed on Hong Kong's direct or indirect participation in such international organisations as the Economic and Social Commission for Asia and the Pacific, the International Atomic Energy Agency, the International Bank for Reconstruction and Development, the International Labour Organisation, the International Monetary Fund, the Universal Postal Union and the World Health Organisation. Other derivatives of the 1984 agreement, such as the Sino-British Land Commission set up under Annex 3, dealt with the disposal of land in the run-up to 1997.

One of the largest political uncertainties concerned the drafting of the Basic Law – the so-called Mini-Constitution for Hong Kong. The Basic Law Drafting Committee (BLDC) was appointed by Peking, but included people from both the mainland and Hong Kong. The first draft was published in 1988 and a second draft in February 1989. All the basic features of the Joint Declaration were faithfully included. But the supporters of a vigilant attitude to Peking's plans were quick to point out that Article 14 of the Basic Law allows for the use of the PLA 'in the maintenance of public order and disaster relief'. A China anxious to maintain confidence in Hong Kong would be foolish to exercise such a provision, but equally it would be foolish to rule out the use of troops in case the police could genuinely not cope with a major disaster. The draft Basic Law also granted the right of abode in Hong Kong to permanent residents (born in Hong Kong or resident for a minimum of seven years), but explicit racial discrimination was evident in the according of the right of abode to children of Hong Kong residents born abroad only if they were Chinese.

Ultimately, the power of interpretation and amendment of the Basic Law was to rest with Peking (Articles 157 and 158). Those seeking perfect guarantees might have hoped for something that set out Chinese control in a less stark fashion, but the Basic Law at least represented the reality: China was to be in charge after 1997. Most people seemed to accept this reality, as they did the Joint Agreement itself, but there was a more lively debate over the role of democratic government in Hong Kong as a means of checking Peking's policies.

The NPC had drafted regulations, appended to the second draft of the Basic Law, outlining a very limited role for representative democracy in Hong Kong. In February 1988, and much to the fury of local activists, the Hong Kong government published a white paper on political change that postponed direct elections to Legco until 1991. Even then there were to have been only ten (out of sixty) directly elected members, leaving the rest of the seats to government appointees and indirectly elected members. The demand for democracy was based on a belief that it might help check Chinese actions. Although no pluralist democracy relies on the power of popularly elected representatives to 'defend' its people against the tanks of a dictator, it was felt that it was better to have *some* moral suasion than none at all. Critics suggested that real democratic government depended on the establishment of a civil society that took decades or centuries to develop and the hastily erected Hong Kong structure would be useless in the face of determined Chinese action. Parts of the business community also feared that an elected government would mean higher taxes, left-wing government, or at least serious uncertainty resulting from political factionalism.

The decision to converge with Peking on the type of representative government was clearly not popular in Hong Kong, but then neither was it, at least before 1989, an especially important issue in a territory that had its mind on other things. Polls showed a general distrust of government, although the distrust of the Chinese was clearly uppermost. So long as the international economy was thriving and Peking seemed committed to reforms, there was little perceived need to create a major crisis over political representation. This was far more the 'decision' of the Hong Kong people than one imposed by Britain or China. To be sure, both Britain and China were arguing for such an apolitical strategy, but then there was no obvious revolt from the people most concerned – the residents of Hong Kong.

It was also clear that a number of the business leaders in Hong Kong had been doing their best to come to terms with the communist rulers of China. Whether they believed it or not, they certainly spoke the language of convergence. Deals were struck, such as that between Lord Kadoorie and the Chinese regarding the Daya Bay nuclear power station. Sir Y.K. Pao, an archetypal Hong Kong billionaire whose family had fled from communism on the mainland, was a frequent visitor to Peking.[2] Business instincts sensed deals to be done, with Guangdong especially, and the vast potential for creating a new Newly Industrialised Country out of this part of China. With Hong Kong as the key, an old NIC would have a worthy, and far more powerful, successor.[3] The frontier with Shenzhen was more blurred than ever before and it even seemed that the two ideologies blurred at the border as well. If anything, as the optimists argued, it felt as if Hong Kong were taking over the mainland rather than the other way round.[4] A new Governor, Sir David Wilson, arrived in April 1987; he was perhaps the best-qualified China-watcher to hold the post and a symbol of the convergence model.

Economic and Trade Issues

Indeed, there was much that had gone well in the economic sphere in the five years since the 1984 agreement to encourage the optimists, despite a major financial scandal in 1985 and another in 1987/8. The cause of these was to be found among the seedier aspects of Hong Kong's free-wheeling economic and social system. The Chinese stayed out of the mess and watched how Hong Kong operated. The basics of the Hong Kong economy remained sound and they responded to the United States-led recovery from the international economic recession. Even during some of the darkest times of the Sino-British negotiating crisis in 1983, the Hong Kong economy demonstrated just how much this was an economic, rather than political, place, where business was booming in response to international signals from the marketplace.

Even while confidence was being knocked by the difficulties of Anglo-Chinese negotiations, Hong Kong thrived as an entrepôt for the expanding China market. Peking could be excused for cynicism about Hong Kong, for economics did seem to come before politics. In this period the basis of Hong Kong's success remained the manufacturing sector, especially that concerned with fabrics and toys. But by the late 1980s well over half the work-force in the manufacturing industry owned by Hong Kong investors was located in Guangdong province. What remained in Hong Kong was increasingly a service-based economy. The re-export trade making use of the cheap labour across the frontier in China was booming. In 1984 re-exports from Hong Kong were 60.5 per cent of domestic exports and in 1988 the re-exports were 126.5 per cent of domestic exports.[5]

In addition, Hong Kong's role as a major trans-shipment point in the region increased. By the nature of this type of trade, statistics are hard to come by, but some analysis suggested that such business accounted for nearly a quarter of the total income from the export of services.[6] In this period there were several countries, including South Korea, South Africa, Taiwan, Israel and the Gulf states, who had no official diplomatic relations with China but were willing to trade. Hong Kong, as the main entrepôt, was well placed to play middleman in this process. This was not the only way in which such business could be done, but it certainly was the easiest and most efficient.

One of the most dynamic sectors of the Hong Kong economy was the property market. Rent indices showed a more than doubling in shop and office rates between 1979 and 1987. Foreign involvement in the property market is difficult to estimate but it is highly probable that Japan was the leading investor in this period. In 1987 it was estimated to have invested a total of HK$5 billion in the property market while Australian purchases were estimated at HK$2 billion. China and Taiwan were estimated to have invested HK$1 billion each.[7]

By contrast, foreign investment in manufacturing was far less impressive, although it is much easier to measure. In 1988 the United States accounted for 34 per cent, Japan 27 per cent, China 11 per cent and Britain 9 per cent. The electronics and textiles industries were by far the largest recipient of investment, much of it in joint ventures manufacturing components for overseas companies. Hong Kong was clearly a vital player in the complex game of company-to-company trade. States were considerably less important in this new world of global trading patterns, and market forces played the key role in determining where the investment went. Hong Kong would prosper only as long as its niche in the marketplace remained useful and effective.

Boom times in Hong Kong did raise property prices, thereby increasing costs. In some senses a political crisis would help profitability by cutting property costs, but certainly the larger *hongs* in Hong Kong could not easily relinquish their property holdings without doing serious damage to the local economy. Moving company headquarters to Bermuda, as Jardine Matheson did in 1984, did not deal with the major problem of investment tied up in the physical structures of Hong Kong.[8] The much more important trend that developed in the late 1980s was the so-called diversification of major firms – exemplified by Hutchison Whampoa buying a 43 per cent stake in Husky Oil of Canada – which was intended to begin shifting profits out of Hong Kong without wrecking confidence in the colony. Hutchison was openly attempting to increase its proportion of overseas assets from 20 per cent to 25 per cent in the early 1990s, while Jardine Matheson wanted to reduce its total of 75 per cent assets in Hong Kong to just 50 per cent. One of the more telling tactics was to sell assets in Hong Kong to mainland Chinese firms. Constituting a major player in the global market economy, firms in Hong Kong could easily undertake such deals and with little direct and immediate damage to the local economy. But the problem was that such changes, in the long term, might make it possible for a more rapid and indeed catastrophic loss of confidence and re-orientation of business.

There was also evidence that smaller firms in Hong Kong were seeking to diversify elsewhere in the booming East Asian economy. As regional economic interdependence began to focus on some of the less developed states of Southeast Asia, direct investment from Hong Kong and other NICs was evident.[9] Certainly from the point of view of people in Hong Kong, there was also a political reason for such diversification. Given the complex network of overseas Chinese in the region it made sense to stay closer to home, but to avoid at least some of the risks of relying on China.

But, overall, in 1984–88 GDP rose by 8.1 per cent a year. The immediate reaction to the Joint Declaration was a boost to confidence, on the basis of a booming international economy, especially in the East Asian region. During these years the average annual increase for private consumption was 7.9 per cent, for government consumption 4.6 per cent, for domestic exports 10.2 per cent, for re-exports 31.9 per cent and for imports 19.1 per cent. Although Hong Kong ran a deficit on merchandise trade at that time, this was more than covered by a large surplus on invisibles. Transport, travel, banking and insurance were all vital parts of the Hong Kong success story. All were also highly vulnerable to knocks to confidence.

The pattern of trade saw important shifts in this period. The United States' role as an export market declined, taking 44.5 per cent of Hong Kong exports in 1984 but only 33.5 per cent in 1988. China took 8.2 per cent of Hong Kong's domestic exports in 1984, but 17.5 per cent in 1988. West Germany and Britain kept roughly at 7 per cent each, while by 1988 that of Japan had risen to 5.3 per cent from 3.7 per cent in 1984. When data for re-exports was assessed, they showed that China continued to be the major player, taking about a third, while the United States had slightly increased its proportion, from 14 per cent to 18 per cent, by 1988. Hong Kong import figures showed China as the source of 31.2 per cent in 1988, up from 25 per cent in 1984. Japan declined, from 23.6 per cent to 18.6 per cent, in this period, as did the United States, from 10.9 per cent to 8.3 per cent.

The trade relationship between Hong Kong and China is complex, but crucial.[10] While it is true that Hong Kong ran a deficit of $2.9 billion in 1988, the same as in 1986, total trade had doubled in that period to $37 billion. China was earning easy money from water and food exports, but such exports were now a far smaller percentage of China's foreign trade. Because of the complex pattern of re-exports, Hong Kong's profits were also hard to identify. But the factories on the Chinese side of the frontier often had major investment from Hong Kong, thereby ensuring a significant portion of the profits came back to Hong Kong. China was also a major investor in Hong Kong, although figures are notoriously hard to come by. One estimate suggested that the total of $7 billion was akin to that of Hong Kong investors in the mainland.[11] Major Chinese companies such as the China International Trust and Investment Corporation bought a stake in such Hong Kong firms as Cathay Pacific (in 1988). The Guangdong Provincial Post and Telegraph Bureau bought a smaller, but politically significant, share of Hong Kong Telecom. At the end of 1986, mainland-owned banks held 18 per cent of all customer deposits in Hong Kong and 7.2 per cent of all bank assets and loans.

Certainly the boom in Western tourism to China also benefited Hong Kong. Some of the most striking growth figures were to be seen in the tourist sector. The total number of visitors to Hong Kong in 1984 was 3.1 million, which rose to 5.6 million in 1988. In this period there was an increase, from 18,031 to 22,882, in the total number of hotel rooms, with an occupancy rate of a staggering 92 per cent in 1988. Tourism, like many of the other service sectors, is potentially soft. It relies on confidence and security, both of which seemed to be present in Hong Kong at that time, but, as the events of 1989 were to show, they were easily punctured.

Thus the mainland found that interdependence with Hong Kong, which was intended to speed and ease the process of convergence, also gave China a stake in the prosperity of Hong Kong. Few of the Chinese assets would benefit from a major economic crisis. Although the nature of the Chinese stake had changed in the years since the 1984 agreement, the essential political point remained the same: China would lose economically if the Hong Kong transition did not go well. And as the process of integration between Hong Kong and the Chinese hinterland continued, it also became increasingly clear that it was harder to define Peking's and Canton's interests as being the same. As Guangdong province grew richer and more committed to reform than was Peking, it tended to share many interests with Hong Kong, even when Peking might have wanted to drive a harder bargain with Hong Kong and Britain.

One Country, One Instability

In April 1989, Hong Kong, like China before it, began to slide into crisis. It was always an essential part of the Hong Kong gamble that as long as China seemed to be serious about reform and openness Hong Kong could have confidence in the notion of convergence. Converging with chaos was quite another matter. By the night of 3 June 1989, when Chinese troops opened fire on the people of Peking, it certainly seemed that China was backtracking on reform and its leadership was in disarray.

The Peking massacre and the subsequent days when at least several hundred were killed were in fact part of the bloody process of sorting out Chinese leadership politics and restoring 'order' in the capital. To that extent, those who felt that confidence in China required stability could be cynically satisfied that events were 'moving in the right direction'. But far more damage was done to confidence for a number of reasons. First, the Chinese regime was obviously deeply divided about its strategy for reform.[12] The fate of Hong Kong seemed to depend on a reforming leadership in China and a willingness to tolerate different roads to modernisation. All these preconditions for confidence appeared to be under threat.

Second, for a time during April and May, there was a sense that faster reform of China's political system was possible and so Hong Kong people became closely involved in the demonstrations in Peking and other cities. The Hong Kong press, even some of its pro-communist outlets, criticised the hardline regime in Peking and supported the Party leader Zhao Ziyang. From the point of view of the hardline victors in Peking, Hong Kong was violating the idea of 'one country, two systems' by trying to change the communist system on the mainland. For Chinese communists, at least those who won the struggle, Hong Kong was subversive and, indeed, a vital part of the anti-communist conspiracy. In the aftermath of the crisis, Chinese leaders made it plain that they regarded the actions of Hong Kong people as unacceptable and the still-to-be-agreed Basic Law would have to take such subversion into account.

The vigilance school of thinking about the future of Hong Kong was convinced that such a reaction from Peking merely supported its claim to doubt China's good intentions. Every time the critics repeated their claims, Peking reacted in even more hostile manner and the cycle of recriminations grew ever harsher. Not surprisingly, confidence in the future of Hong Kong suffered a serious setback, and, as usual, it could be seen in economic indicators.

The stock market plunged 21.7 per cent on 4 June, but, unlike on Black Monday in 1987 when world markets plummeted, the Hong Kong market stayed open. Nor did the market close on 7 June when a one-day general strike was held to protest at the Peking massacre. After some initial technical adjustments, the market then climbed a staggering 35 per cent (from the post-massacre low) by the end of 1989. The major currency markets continued to function as normal – with Hong Kong playing its key role as a part of the 24-hour trading system. The local gold market, the world's fourth largest in trading volume, also continued to exploit its time-zone location. After the economy achieved 7 per cent growth in 1988, it slid to a still-respectable rate of 5 per cent in 1989. Inflation continued to be a persistent worry, and rising wage settlements were exacerbating the problem.[13] Hong Kong was clearly no longer a low-wage economy.

Despite the heated political rhetoric in the relationship between Hong Kong and China, many of the basic essentials of a successful economy remained in place. As in 1967, China did not turn off the water taps (China supplied 63 per cent of Hong Kong's water needs in 1988). Trade was affected by the larger problem of setbacks to economic reforms in China which pre-dated the 1989 events. But East Asians continued to be interested in doing business with China and, for those such as Taiwan and South Korea, Hong Kong still played an important role in the trade pattern. While Westerners were obviously distraught at the effect of the China crisis, East Asians were not. A more immediate effect was seen in the decline of tourism to the mainland and, therefore, the reduction in the number of those who passed through Hong Kong on their way to or from China. But overseas investment in Hong Kong manufacturing rose 24 per cent in 1989. Japan held top spot with 37 per cent of the 1989 total, although the United States still had the largest cumulative investment with 34 per cent, Japan second with 27 per cent, China with 11 per cent and Britain with 8 per cent.[14]

Uncertainty was bound to have an impact on the Hong Kong economy. It was not just that firms were agreeing to bonus payments for employees who stayed on or the obvious increases in pay necessary to hold vital personnel. Some companies were setting up overseas offices simply to satisfy staff demands for an opportunity to obtain a foreign passport.[15] By 1990 it was clear that the Hong Kong economy had moved into the slow lane in East Asia and the decline in the rate of overseas investment as confidence cooled was certainly a major factor.[16] The Hongkong and Shanghai Banking Corporation estimated the net capital outflow in 1989 was $3 billion, more than twice that in the previous five years.[17] Jardine Matheson not only moved its domicile to Bermuda in 1984; in 1991 it switched its main public listing to the London stock exchange. Jardine and its five blue-chip subsidiaries make up more than 10 per cent of Hong Kong's local market capitalisation.[18] Coming after the move to London by the Hongkong and Shanghai Banking Corporation, there could be little doubt of the crisis in confidence in the economic future of the colony. Of course, not everyone was, or is, willing or able to move out of Hong Kong, and Japanese and American firms have certainly been more prepared to invest in Hong Kong in recent years.[19] It is not that Hong Kong is about to collapse, but there certainly are sufficient worrying trends to undermine support for optimism or clarity about the future.

In October 1989 the Hong Kong government announced major new investment projects woth £10 billion. The flagship project, a new airport, was to be accompanied by a five-fold increase in the capacity of the container-port.[20] But the finance for these projects had to come in part from the private sector and therefore the availability of funds reflected at least part of the state of confidence. And yet failure to construct the projects would do serious damage to confidence. As will be described in greater length in the next chapter, China saw the project as a way to influence decisions in Hong Kong before 1997 and as a result the issue turned into a major test of confidence in Hong Kong in the run-up to 1997.

After much debate and negotiation, on 4 July 1991 Britain and China agreed on a Memorandum of Understanding which was in some senses a second Sino-British Joint Declaration (1984). The 1991 memorandum agreed that a new airport should be built and that the future Hong Kong Special Administrative Region would carry little of the financial responsibility – thereby easing China's fears that Britain was merely trying to bleed Hong Kong of its wealth. The most apparently important British concession was inherent in the very process of negotiations. By allowing China to force talks on the matter, Britain once again recognised that Chinese influence began well before 1997. This Chinese influence was always inherent in the 1984 accord, but the 1991 deal made it especially vivid to those who felt that Hong Kong could have genuine self-government.[21] In March 1992, when the Hong Kong government agreed to leave a larger-than-expected financial reserve when China took over in 1997, and raised corporation tax in order to do so, the same trends were again underlined.[22] China's presence was felt on major economic decisions in the colony well before 1997. Even in the run-up to the arrival of the new Governor, Chris Patten, in July 1992, China continued to withhold agreement to details of the airport deal, thereby demonstrating that the new Governor should not have any illusion about who was really in charge.

Although such intervention in Hong Kong's affairs by China was seen by some as detrimental to the success of the territory, it was nothing more than the rawest of political realities – China was in charge. But if there was any hope that China could be held at bay, it seemed to depend less on a strategy of denying China a role in pre-1997 decisions and far more on encouraging the southern parts of China to seek common cause with Hong Kong against Peking and other regions of China. As we have seen from Hong Kong's earlier history, this was a dangerous game to play and one that was rarely played in the open. But the expectation remained that if southern China could be sufficiently tied into the Hong Kong economy, then Peking would be more wary of intervening.

As we shall see in the next chapter, centre–province relations in China are very complex. But in the years after the unrest of 1989, Guangdong did manage to maintain a sufficiently prosperous economy so that it could effectively deflect many of Peking's economic demands.[23] When economic reform was given a new official lease of life in China in the spring of 1992 (following a trip by Deng Xiaoping to Guangdong), there was new hope that Peking would be more economically pragmatic about Hong Kong and leave it more to its own devices, much as it was leaving Guangdong more to its own devices. thus even many of those in Hong Kong who welcomed convergence with the mainland, and hoped that the Hong Kong tail could wag the Chinese dog, began to feel that their real hope lay in trying to wag a smaller Guangdong dog. In this sense at least, the fate of Hong Kong became tied up far more in the fate of Peking's relations with such successful economic regions as Guangdong in particular and centre–province relations in general.

Emigration

The ever closer connections between Hong Kong and Guangdong did not always contribute to building confidence in Hong Kong, if only because so many Hong Kongers either came from, or were descendants of those who fled from, Guangdong. Thus a major problem for Hong Kong, migration from the colony, continued to cast a pall over the prospects for economic prosperity. According to official figures, in 1980 some 22,000 people emigrated from Hong Kong, with numbers fluctuating by some 5,000 in the subsequent six years. But by 1987 the total was up to 30,000 per year and rising. In 1988 the natural increase in the population was 45,033, with a further 61,951 people arriving. Total emigration was 45,800. Some 42,000 left in 1989, 62,000 left in 1990, with a similar number leaving in the following years.[24]

To be sure, there has always been a steady stream of emigrants from Hong Kong. Even as late as 1987, Sir David Wilson was keeping up the happy line that Hong Kong's prosperity has never depended on stemming such a flow.[25] The Chinese government certainly shared this view. Indeed, some analysts in Hong Kong suggested that, because of the traditional flow of people, Hong Kong might in fact benefit from emigration in that it helps build regional Chinese business networks and therefore would be crucial to a Hong Kong playing a leading role in the future regional economy.[26] But a Hong Kong government task force set up in May 1988 reportedly found evidence that emigration was higher than earlier supposed, and especially among the better-educated part of the population. It was also becoming increasingly clear that, contrary to the assertions of the optimists, less than 20 per cent of those who left were likely to return after having secured a bolt-hole. Furthermore, one analyst estimated that 10 per cent of Hong Kong's 1.6 million families had documents enabling them to emigrate.[27]

Of course, the problem with the figures on emigration, even if they are reliable, is they do not highlight the fact that those leaving tend to be the far more skilled and wealthy.[28] It is the brain drain rather than simply the drain of bodies that is the problem. International business practice requires lawyers, accountants, doctors, computer specialists, not to mention nurses and engineers. One estimate cited by a senior British official suggested that Hong Kong was really run by only about 200,000 people and the key was to keep those in place.[29] A report by Price Waterhouse in late 1989 suggested that 700,000–800,000 passports with full right of abode would be required to keep the key people in Hong Kong. It also indicated that perhaps as many as 315,000 people already had such rights.[30]

But surveys in 1989 and 1990 indicated that at least half of Hong Kong's doctors were planning to emigrate and as a result they were charging more for their services in order to save money for emigration. Pharmacists, too, were in shorter supply.[31] An internal poll by the Hong Kong Society of Accountants said 80 per cent of the respondents were preparing to leave. Some 85 per cent of chartered surveyors were intending to leave before 1997 and the vital construction industry looked likely to be hit as a consequence. Property accounts for 60 per cent of all Hong Kong's capital investment, provides jobs for nearly 10 per cent of Hong Kong residents and accounts for 40 per cent of government revenue and expenditure.[32] A survey by the Hong Kong Institute of Personnel Management in 1989 revealed that less than a third of professional staff intended to stay beyond 1997. Less than 10 per cent of those who had left had returned to work in Hong Kong and a mere 3 per cent of the returnees said they definitely would stay.[33]

After the Peking massacre there was a reported trend to increased wage demands as many people sought extra money to put away in case they needed to leave. The government faced steeper wage demands from civil servants as a result of higher wage settlements in the private sector. These pay increases, coupled with a slowing economy and, therefore, declining government revenue, caused some worry that Hong Kong's traditionally low tax rate – long seen as a key to economic success – might have to be reassessed. Such extra pressures on the economy came at a time when the Hong Kong government announced major plans for enhancement of the colony's infrastructure, most notably with the construction of a new airport. Yet in the deteriorating economic climate there was concern that the private sector might not come up with the funds for the projects, thereby adding to the burden on the government.

The underlying cause for the shaky confidence was present before 1989. Jardine Matheson Holdings moved its legal domicile to the Atlantic island of Bermuda in 1984, but in 1989 alone some fifty, mostly public, companies also departed.[34] Of course, there has also been corporate immigration to Hong Kong. The Bank of America moved its Asian headquarters from San Francisco to Hong Kong in 1990. The key seemed to be the state of the China trade, for those doing business with the mainland often found it advantageous to deal through Hong Kong. Some estimates suggested that 40 per cent of the cargo carried into and out of Victoria harbour was merely passing through on its way to factories in Guangdong. Trans-shipments could be made in other ways but, for the time being, via Hong Kong was still the easiest way to do it.[35]

Without the trained support staff, the success of Hong Kong as a business centre will fade. Costs will rise as staff need to be paid more in order to be retained and this in turn will boost property prices. The international market economy may well take elsewhere that part of the business that is not directly related to the China trade. The problem was long recognised by Britain but, for a number of reasons, there was no strong reason to take any action. Not only was it felt that the introduction of public provision for halting emigration would make the self-same emigration more likely, it was also recognised that China would not like the issue to be raised. Needless to say, it was always unlikely that Britain, with its highly restrictive immigration policy, would actively seek immigrants from Hong Kong.

Yet the genuine horror at the scenes from Peking in June 1989, and the equally genuine surprise at the strength of shock in Hong Kong, led to a reassessment of British policy. Some people in Hong Kong (and an even smaller number in Britain) wanted London to grant the full right of abode to those holding BDT documents or, since 1 July 1987, those holding British National Overseas passports. The supporters claimed that most of those eligible would not take up the right to live in Britain because they wanted to stay in Hong Kong. It was said that the people merely wanted an 'insurance policy' in case they had to get out.

An important problem with this plea, apart from the obvious political one in Britain, was that such an instant grant of right of abode would not necessarily keep people in Hong Kong. Especially with the opposition Labour party in Britain claiming it would not necessarily keep the door so wide open, there was fear that the insurance policy might be revoked. There was also fear that the policy might not be available if China decided to close the door from Hong Kong. Would the rich of Hong Kong take to the boats or jumbo jets? Therefore, with another crisis in China – say, at the time of the succession to Deng Xiaoping – confidence in Hong Kong might be hit and people might indeed take up their right of abode. Even a short burst of extra applicants might trigger a larger, perhaps irrational, flood of emigrants.

The problem facing Britain was serious. If it were possible to issue the right of abode only to be taken up in time of crisis, then there might be some hope of keeping people in place. But then many might not trust the British government and most would rather go somewhere else. As a result, London chose to rely on what they were told – that most people in Hong Kong would rather stay in place, providing they had the right to leave if they felt they had to do so. In December 1989 the British government, with a rapidly sinking standing in the public opinion polls at home, took on public opinion by agreeing to a scheme granting 50,000 heads of household – some 225,000 people including families – the right of abode (a fuller discussion of this scheme follows in later chapters).

By March 1991 it was clear that a far smaller number of people than expected had taken the opportunity to apply for the British right-of-abode package. While this might have been interpreted, at least in more confident times, as a sign of faith in the coming communist Chinese control after 1997, in reality it was more an expression of dissatisfaction with Britain and a preference for living in North America or Australia. Certainly the level of immigration from the colony did not decline. With other countries also offering various schemes (again, more details in later chapters), there was an increasing range of options for people to take up. In 1984 Canada issued 6,350 visas in Hong Kong but by 1988 the figure was 21,843.[36]

However, the key, as always, was the extent to which there was confidence in the regime in Peking. The British government suspended the meeting of the JLG after the massacre in Peking and the next one in September was distinctly frosty (or 'frank', in diplomatese). The seventeenth JLG meeting, in December 1990, was more civil, despite the tricky discussions of the convergence of views on civil rights laws. More progress was made on such matters as the civil air services agreements and the localisation of merchant shipping safety regulations.[37] The eighteenth meeting, in March 1991, left most major issues unresolved although the atmosphere was described as 'good'.[38] There was agreement that Hong Kong had suffered a crisis of confidence, although Britain blamed China for the state of affairs and of course Peking returned the compliment.

To make matters even worse, in 1989 the emigration issue

became tangled in the thicket of international issues surrounding the emigration of people from Vietnam, many of whom ended up in Hong Kong in search of a better life in the West. While many of these people arrived in Hong Kong by boat, most apparently were making their trips via an overland trek through China. In late 1989 Hong Kong was housing 56,000 refugees, of whom 34,000 had arrived that year.[39] Thus the problem of a continuing flow of refugees into vastly overcrowded camps in Hong Kong was in part a matter that China could control. As 'compassion fatigue' set in in the West, fewer refugees were being taken out of these camps. Other places of first asylum, such as Malaysia, were towing boats out to sea, leaving the unfortunate people subject to pirates and the weather. To complicate matters even further, many of the new refugees were fleeing Vietnam in search of better economic opportunities; they were not political refugees. At a time when there were many more people in China who wanted to emigrate to Hong Kong in order to be reunited with their families, but were stopped by China and Britain, the people in Hong Kong were opposed to taking large numbers of refugees from Vietnam.[40] In sum, the people of Hong Kong felt neglected by the international community and impelled to contemplate the forcible repatriation of refugees to Vietnam.

Of course, the ironies in the issue abounded.[41] Just as the people of Hong Kong were growing increasingly concerned about their own future as immigrants and wanted greater compassion from the outside world, they were denying such compassion to others fleeing a communist regime. As the Hong Kong authorities took a firmer line and actually began forcible repatriation of Vietnamese refugees in December 1989, the exercise at least earned points from its local population, even if Britain took a beating in the world's press. Since Britain was trying to organise a co-ordinated Western response to the crisis of confidence in Hong Kong, the Vietnamese refugee problem made their task even more difficult. China might have done something to limit the flow of refugees, but in late 1989 it was not in the mood to help Britain, even in the cause of building confidence in Hong Kong. In October 1989, as part of China's war of nerves with Britain about revision of arrangements regarding Hong Kong, China had suspended the normal practice of accepting back an average of sixty nationals a day who dodged PLA patrols to get into the colony. A Chinese Olympic swimmer who fled the mainland into Hong Kong had very recently been allowed by Britain to leave for the United States.[42]

But unhelpful as China might have been, it was the United States, with its residual problems in coming to terms with its obligation to the people of Vietnam, that bore most of the responsibility for blocking an international accord to repatriate the Vietnamese. The United States would neither take the refugees across the Pacific nor allow them to be returned home. In 1991, when Britain and Vietnam finally reached an accord on the forcible repatriation of Vietnamese, the United States avoided formal opposition. In due course – by early 1992 – the flow of refugees from Vietnam declined and the problem looked as if it was coming under control. Nevertheless, for all the rationality of its case, the people of Hong Kong left the outside world with an excuse, should they ever need one, for treating them as mere 'economic migrants' and therefore not worthy of refuge. For Hong Kong, this was yet another factor that undermined confidence.

Democracy, and other Political Issues

The elaboration of the details of the British right of abode scheme came almost precisely at the time when China's NPC passed its final version of the Basic Law. China accepted that the number of directly elected representatives in Legco could rise to twenty in 1997, twenty-four in 1999 and thirty in 2003. But these minor concessions were accompanied by stiffer provisions about 'subversion' in Hong Kong and the prohibition of political groups forging overseas links of a political nature. This was at a time when the people of Hong Kong were playing a more active role in helping Chinese dissidents escape from the mainland and then forming political groups to campaign for a change of government in Peking.

The rulers on the mainland also decided that senior positions in the government of Hong Kong could not be held by those with right of abode elsewhere. This was a specific attempt to deal with a perceived problem that those with dual nationality who chose to remain in Hong Kong would be free of Chinese pressure and therefore able to take a tougher line against Peking. It was also decided that the final interpretation of the Basic Law would rest with the standing committee of the NPC, thus threatening the promised independence of the judiciary in Hong Kong.

The more conservative regime in China that followed the events of June 1989 seemed especially worried about Hong Kong serving as a base for subversion of the mainland. With the collapse of communism in Eastern Europe in the second half of 1989, China saw serious risks in uncontrolled dissident movements. While there was little that China could do to stop the United States or France from harbouring dissidents, let alone stopping Taiwan from supporting such dissident activity as a radio ship broadcasting into the mainland, Peking did feel it could scare Hong Kong into submission.

The particular problem for Hong Kong was that it was caught between promises of retaining its own existing system and China's restrictive definition of 'subversion'. Western notions of freedom included the right to criticise one's own and other countries, but from Peking's point of view China was not just another country, it was the sovereign owner of Hong Kong. Any such criticism would constitute subversion of communist rule, which, as the experience of Eastern Europe suggested, had to be caught at an early stage before it became too dangerous. While Hong Kong officials had always been especially careful about criticising the mainland Chinese government, they were less worried about the press in Hong Kong or statements by individuals. With a developing democratic political system, tolerance of diversity of views in the press and political circles would have been the logical standpoint.

But Peking regularly made it clear that such criticism would have to be controlled. When a dissident radio ship wished to stop in Hong Kong in May 1989, Chinese displeasure was made clear and the Hong Kong government refused it permission to enter.[43] When China deemed a film to be irritating to Peking's new sensibilities, the Hong Kong authorities agreed to censor it.[44] But nowhere was this narrow definition of democracy more evident than in the debates surrounding the final revisions to the system of election as set out in the Basic Law. Although there was a school of thought that maintained that the democratisation of Eastern Europe might have helped push Britain into holding out for more democracy in Hong Kong, China learned precisely the opposite lesson from the 1989 events and was always unlikely to accept a much greater level of democracy. That China was cajoled into a cosmetic modification was seen in both Peking and London as a significant symbol of pragmatism, although for obvious reasons Hong Kong activists were far from satisfied.[45]

The emotive imagery of 'surrender' and replacing 'one colonialism with another' was of course a replay of the earlier criticism of the 1984 Anglo-Chinese deal. All the old arguments about convergence and vigilance were still being raised. Yet it also remained true that, in the aftermath of the events of 1989 in China and Eastern Europe, it was somewhat peculiar for people to see democracy as something that could prevent a ruthless government from getting its way. The Peking massacre certainly showed that constitutional provisions were no protection when communist governments were determined to fight for their right to absolute rule. Eastern European events demonstrated that only when the supervising power – the Soviet Union – changed its mind about tolerating pluralism would real change take place. In Hong Kong there was no benign Soviet Union, only a bullying China.

Nevertheless, even the limited democracy granted to Hong Kong was swiftly taken up and political groups were organised in 1990. A liberal party led by Martin Lee promised to tone down its attacks on the mainland and concentrate on increasing democratic control over Hong Kong issues. The pro-Peking Federation of Trade Unions raised the prospect of strong communist support for other politicians. In the middle of this spectrum of trust for China were the larger business interests.

In the first direct elections for Legco on 15 September 1991, all but two of the eighteen contested seats were won by liberals, including eleven members of the United Democrats of Hong Kong (UDHK) which was sharply critical of China. Although the Governor replaced some of the most conservative figures on the list of twenty-one councillors that he appointed (twenty-one others were elected by professional associations), it was clear that there was a major difference between the liberal, democratically elected members and the professional, but still relatively conservative, majority. The liberals had hoped that their sweeping victory would 'force' the Governor to create a more representative Legco, but he decided that the elections were not as decisive as they appeared. The Governor's appointments to the Executive Council in October followed the same conservative lines. With a mere 39 per cent turnout of registered voters (only half those eligible bothered to register) for the Legco election, the argument could be made that the liberal victory (with two-thirds of the vote) did not represent broader Hong Kong opinion.[46]

Voting for the Macao Assembly in October had an even smaller turnout, of 15%.[47] The low turnout in Hong Kong certainly seemed to represent political apathy and an unwillingness to confront China with yet another contentious issue. The people of Hong Kong had been given a chance to demonstrate that they really wanted an independent political voice, but they chose to stay at home. It would now be far harder to make the case that the people of Hong Kong were desperately struggling to avoid Chinese rule.

There was some hope that the drafting of a Bill of Rights for Hong Kong might help entrench some of the basic rights that the democracy activists seemed most anxious to protect. Of course, as is the weakness in any constitution, no bill could prevent a ruthless communist government on the mainland from doing what it wanted. Nor could the bill override anything in the Basic Law – or even include such basic rights as that to self-determination or the right to elect political representatives – that had been agreed in the Anglo-Chinese agreement in 1984.[48] In fact, both the low take-up of the British right-of-abode scheme and the various public opinion polls suggested what many observers had long noted: the Hong Kong people remained apathetic about politics and suspicious of all government. Voter registration and turnout for elections remained remarkably low by the standards of most democracies. Compare the percentage of voters in Hong Kong with any of the first elections in the newly democratic East European states in 1990 and the apathy in Hong Kong is obvious.[49] The reaction of some people in Hong Kong was to blame 'weak government', but this in a colony that thrived precisely because it had 'invisible' government.[50] For some six million people who depended so heavily on other people's politics – most notably Peking's – the cynicism about government was both understandable and foolish. Peking's response to the elections was to appoint its own panel of forty-four prominent Hong Kong people as a form of shadow Legco. In the end, democracy was not on offer to the Hong Kong people, and it seemed that most Hong Kong people understood that reality.

Neither was there much opposition when a number of important legal issues were clarified in the run-up to 1997. A watered-down Bill of Rights was approved by Legco in June 1991 and in September Britain and China reached agreement on Hong Kong's Court of Final Appeal after the Chinese takeover. A dispute over the number of foreigners eligible to sit on the Court provoked little general public concern.[51] But in a rare act of defiance, Legco, with its new liberal cohort, passed a motion by forty-three to eleven (with thirteen abstentions) asking Britain and China to reconsider their agreement on the High Court. Yet Legco, even in its relatively tame form, does not always represent local sentiment. This was clearly seen in the debate over the building of a new airport in 1991, when public opinion polls showed far more willingness to see a compromise with China.[52] It seemed that politics in Hong Kong, even in its very limited form, often did not represent the more important grass-roots apathy about politics.

Towards 1997

Whether it was for economic reasons, concern over migration, or uncertainty about Hong Kong politics, the reality of Hong Kong in the early 1990s was of a shaky society. Hong Kong managed virtually to ignore its 150th birthday in 1991 as if it did not want yet another reminder of how it got into its present mess. The announcement of the retirement of David Wilson as Governor in January 1992 was another trigger for self-doubt and a new round of blaming everyone else for Hong Kong's troubles.[53]

What was effectively the sacking of the Governor by Prime Minister John Major was only the most visible part of what was emerging as an important shift in British policy towards China and Hong Kong. Mr Major had barely been in office six months in 1991 when he had to take a prominent part as host of the G-7 effort to deal with the death of communism in Russia. This stressful, but otherwise uplifting task involved the first trip by a G-7 leader to Moscow after the abortive coup of August 1991. But Mr Major felt humiliated by having to travel on from Moscow to Peking, the capital of what remained of communism, to sign what was seen in many quarters as a less than satisfying deal on building a new airport in Hong Kong. Mr Major swore to change Britain's China policy so he would never again be put in such a humiliating position by the diplomacy of the Foreign Office's China hands.

The most important step in the process of reform, the appointment of his friend Chris Patten as Governor of Hong Kong, could only be taken after Mr Major won a national election in April 1992 and Mr Patten lost his seat in Bath. The three close comrades, Patten, Major and Douglas Hurd, then set about formulating democratic reforms for Hong Kong that, while in keeping with the letter of the previous agreements with China and the Basic Law, was clearly an attempt to introduce greater democracy without China's prior approval. Patten fully expected criticism from China and the need to alter his proposals.

Patten's proposals of 7 October 1992 were essentially designed to widen the constituency for local and Legco elections. China viewed the manner of their proposal, as well as their content, as a challenge to their ability to assume gradual control over Hong Kong affairs before 1997. Despite Chinese threats, nerves remained steady in London, and only mildly wobbly in Hong Kong. Public opinion polls showed bedrock support for Patten and although the stock market fell sharply, it also recovered at regular intervals, in part because of regular buying by Chinese in Guangdong.

Peking was flustered and confused. Finally, in April 1993, they agreed to open talks with Britain on the Patten proposals, after swearing blind that they would never do so. Peking's supporters in the colony, including important sectors of the business community, also choked back their bile and settled down to a far more sensible twin-track policy. On the one hand they would behave more rationally on economic matters; for example, Peking allowed contracts to be signed for major projects extending past 1997. On the other hand they would continue to fillibuster during the political talks on democracy. The expectation was that Patten would have to break off the talks at some point in order to introduce legislation in Legco in time for district board elections in 1994. As this book went to press in mid-1993, the basic features of the clash between Britain and China about Hong Kong remained in place. The governor was therefore testing the limits of Chinese pragmatism, as well as the extent of the desire of Hong Kong's people to stand up for their own rights. If Hong Kong failed to achieve these marginal reforms, the primary fault would lie, as in the past, with the people of Hong Kong and their future rulers in Peking. A victory for Patten would at least leave some hope that a civil society might be created in Hong Kong that would provide at least some substance to the notion of Hong Kong's autonomy. If the people of Hong Kong were to abandon their support for Patten's reforms, then it would become even more clear that Chinese rule begins before 1997.

PART II
The Fate of Hong Kong

5

China: Taking Charge

No country is as important to the fate of Hong Kong as China. Indeed, Hong Kong is unlikely to be left merely to wait out the time before 1997 without being made more like China. This may be good for Hong Kong if the 'tail wags the dog of China', or it might be a problem if China slowly strangles the colony.[1] In between those extremes is the possibility that Hong Kong will wag a smaller animal called Guangdong province. But this possibility may actually pose a larger threat to Peking, and in the longer run mean that Hong Kong's convergence with China will become caught up in far more complex political currents. In any case, the evolution of Chinese policy towards Hong Kong must be the starting point for any assessment of where Hong Kong is going. What are the objectives and interests of China and all its various parts, and how will China manage its relationship with Britain in the years before 1997?

Chinese Sovereignty

It is in the first words of the preamble to the Basic Law of Hong Kong, and indeed in any major Chinese statement on the colony, that 'Hong Kong has been part of the territory of China since ancient times ... the Government of the People's Republic of China will resume the exercise of sovereignty over Hong Kong with effect from 1 July 1997, thus fulfilling the long-cherished common aspiration of the Chinese people for the recovery of Hong Kong'.[2] China's basic objective is the recovery of sovereignty over territory taken during the heyday of Western imperialism.

As is the case for most states, protecting and enhancing sovereignty is a key objective of the leadership. But in the Chinese case the sensitivity to issues concerning sovereignty was heightened by the fact that China was so badly mistreated by the outside world for so long. The communist revolution establishing the People's Republic of China in 1949 was also a triumph of nationalism. Among the first words of Mao Zedong's declaration of the Republic in October 1949 was the assertion that the Chinese people had 'stood up'.

China has repeatedly used military force since 1949 not only in defence of the territory it already held but also in pursuit of territory it claimed to belong to China. In 1950 Tibet was invaded (or liberated, in Chinese parlance). In 1955 some of the offshore islands disputed with Taiwan were retaken and further offshore islands crises followed in 1958 and 1962. Also in 1962 India was defeated in a border war that led to China obtaining the territory it claimed India held illegally. In 1974 China seized the Paracel Islands in the South China Sea from South Vietnam and in 1988 it took some of the Spratly Islands from a united Vietnam. Throughout all of this time China sought the return of Taiwan to the control of the mainland.[3]

No other great power had as many unsettled territorial claims and none was so clearly in the position of *demandeur* to the international system as was China. The communist government was not only revolutionary in its approach to development at home, it also wanted to see the international environment around it transformed. But though a dissatisfied great power, China was also often a weak great power, unable to take what it wanted. When China's adversaries had the support of stronger powers, then Peking had to back down. Thus there is nothing unusual or unclear about China's basic approach to Hong Kong. The colony was part of an unfinished agenda of an unsatisfied great power. Britain was too weak to deter China from satisfying its desires. All other Chinese interests in Hong Kong, including economic ones, are secondary to the interest of resuming sovereignty.

Yet China has rarely been rash in pursuit of its sovereignty. It has appreciated that there has always been a waxing and waning of the Chinese empire and it has learned when time was on its side. Britain was clearly a fading empire and China perceives its own power as waxing. As a result, China has often been remarkably pragmatic about precisely how it resumed sovereignty and the short-term compromises that might be made. The notion of a fifty-year transition phase and the very concept of 'one country, two systems' represent the pragmatic approach to sovereignty.[4] As long as the end is understood to be Chinese sovereignty (one country), the means (tolerating two systems) can be negotiable. The course of Anglo-Chinese negotiations in 1982–84 concerned the way in which the principle of 'one country' was related to the pragmatism of 'two systems'.

The achievement of one sovereignty involved two types of pragmatism on China's part. First, Hong Kong was allowed to retain many elements of the capitalist system for fifty years. Second, China began blurring the lines on its own side of the frontier to make the incorporation of Hong Kong less traumatic. It has always been a feature of Chinese security policy that its huge size and massive population allowed for something less than an immediate defence of rigid frontiers. Enemies could be allowed to penetrate to some extent in order for China to swallow them up in a 'sea of people's war'. Defence of the frontier has been layered defence and the approach to Hong Kong has also made use of the layered approach.

By embarking on major domestic reforms, creating Special Economic Zones, and even opening vast swathes of the country to special enticements to attract investment from the international market economy, China suggested that it was prepared to take a layered approach to sovereignty and socialism. The SEZs in particular were areas of political and economic experimentation. By placing the first of the SEZs, Shenzhen, next door to Hong Kong, China signalled its intention to treat Hong Kong as yet another layer. Hong Kong could be the outermost layer where the greatest experimentation could take place, but it had to be part of China and gradually it would grow closer to the rest of the Chinese people. When Chinese officials speak of 'co-ordination' of Hong Kong with the mainland in the transition to 1997 they are merely representing their sense that, from the time of the 1984 agreement, Hong Kong has been pulled in closer to China and that the ties that bind the two will grow.[5] If co-ordination is successful, 1997 would barely be a date of much importance, but merely another stage in a gradual process of transformation. China speaks of 'harmonising' policies before 1997, while denying that 'the mainland should strengthen interference in and control over Hong Kong's economic affairs'. Zhou Nan, China's leading representative in Hong Kong in 1990, spoke of 'common prosperity through mutual assistance and co-operation' as key features of the 'one country, two systems' concept. As another official noted, without such co-operation 'the stability and prosperity of Hong Kong' cannot be guaranteed.[6]

Lu Ping, the director of the Hong Kong and Macao affairs office under China's State Council, spoke in March 1991 of 'the river's surging waters' which 'originate from many sources', thereby implying that convergence was essential for the development of Hong Kong before 1997.[7] This, one of the more positive remarks from a Chinese official in 1991, suggested a more moderate view of what was in the interests of Hong Kong. Deng Xiaoping reportedly saw such convergence as part of the attempt to ensure a 'hand-over' rather than a 'sending-down' of cadres from Peking to rule Hong Kong in July 1997. Yet Deng also said China should not be 'afraid of intervention' in Hong Kong because 'participation is imperative in the later transitional period'. While accepting that keeping Hong Kong stable was 'no simple matter', he thought it essential that gradual participation would ease the pain of transition.[8]

This distinctive mix of sovereign pride and pragmatism in China's approach also has its rougher side. Take, for example, the matter of stationing Chinese troops in the colony after 1997. The People's Liberation Army (PLA) was the armed force that put the communist party in power and at various times (such as during the Cultural Revolution) has been instrumental in keeping the party in power. In June 1989 the PLA was the only force that the party could rely on to establish order. For any country, the armed forces are also a key part of the sovereign authority, usually present when celebrating great state occasions.

Although many people in Hong Kong do not like facing the fact of Chinese sovereignty, apart from the flag of the People's Republic of China the PLA is the primary representation of that sovereignty. Deng Xiaoping himself was apparently insistent that the PLA be present in post-1997 Hong Kong. Zhou Nan has reaffirmed the belief that the PLA 'is a symbol of sovereignty' and thus must take its place in the new Hong Kong.[9] When some people in Hong Kong made the bizarre suggestion that the name of the PLA be changed in Hong Kong, Zhou's response was equally bizarre in quoting Shakespeare: 'A rose by any other name would smell just as sweet' (*sic*).

In the aftermath of the Peking massacre carried out by PLA troops in June 1989, during a meeting of the Joint Liaison Group in September the British once again raised the issue of stationing

Chinese troops in Hong Kong. But Peking's response was the same: the PLA was a symbol of sovereignty and had to be present.[10] In 1992 it was suggested that a PLA representative might even sit on the Exco after 1997.[11] Indeed it was remarkable that anyone might think, especially after the PLA had been called in to Peking to carry out precisely the kind of tasks expected of it at a time of perceived threat to the regime, that the Chinese government would be sympathetic to a claim that the PLA would be damaging to stability. Although Peking insists that the PLA would not be used for maintaining internal order in Hong Kong and is there purely for defence, its role in Hong Kong would be the same as on the streets of the capital – any threat to the security of the regime would be met with whatever force was necessary, even if that included the PLA. Deng Xiaoping was reported in February 1991 to have said that if the opposition in Hong Kong 'create turbulence' and if 'there is major rebellion, the central government has to send troops'. Deng added that 'some people . . . have too many unrealistic illusions' about Chinese policy and that Britain in particular was often 'giving bad ideas and playing political tricks' – in other words, encouraging forces in Hong Kong opposed to Chinese rule.[12]

Nor did it make much sense to argue that PLA troops should not be placed in Hong Kong because, even if they were just outside, there is little doubt that they could be moved in rapidly to deal with any eventuality. Modernisation of the PLA in the 1980s and 1990s has created a more mobile force and the events of June 1989 demonstrate that it is one capable of restoring order, albeit in a brutal fashion.[13] It is likely that China will not station large numbers of troops in Hong Kong after 1997 and, in any case, reinforcements would have to be brought in case of major insurrection or public disorder, as indeed they were in Peking in 1989.

But just as Britain finds it impossible to restrain Chinese behaviour on military matters after 1997, so the Chinese sometimes find it a struggle to affect British actions before that date. When Britain decided unilaterally to move its naval base in Hong Kong and redevelop the land in such a way that meant China would not have the fine naval facilities it expected, China protested. Ke Zaishuo, China's senior representative on the Joint Liaison Group, complained that this matter should have been handled in the JLG and that China should have a say in the military redeployments.[14]

Of course, in the Chinese perception of blurring the lines between Hong Kong and China even before 1997, the British action was unacceptable. But in the British view they were still in charge until that date and, while China could express its feelings, it could not dictate British policy. As we shall see, on other issues the British have been sensitive to Chinese demands, but just as the PLA was a symbol of Chinese sovereignty, so the disposition of the naval base HMS Tamar was a symbol of British sovereignty. This was not a major dispute, but it was symbolic of the differing approaches to the transition period and the inevitable problems that will arise.

A more important issue concerns the use of Hong Kong for what the Peking authorities regard as 'subversion'. Needless to say, if convergence is what Chinese policy is all about, then Hong Kong cannot be allowed to be used as a base for subverting the mainland. In the aftermath of the events of May–June 1989 when people from Hong Kong were involved in the Peking protests, the sensitivity on this matter grew in both China and Hong Kong. Zhou Nan noted that convergence would be damaged if 'the socialist system were subverted' and that the mainland had to have 'unity and tranquillity' in order to help maintain prosperity and stability in Hong Kong. His analogy was that 'with the skin gone, to what can the hair adhere?'[15] When the Basic Law was promulgated, the wording strengthened the section dealing with subversion. China had clearly grown more concerned that, once Hong Kong was integrated more closely into China, it would be a threat as well as an asset.[16]

The obvious difficulty is deciding what constitutes subversion. The two sides might agree that physical support for dissidents in China was subversion. But did this include finance for the underground network that allowed dissidents to flee the mainland? Probably. Did this include financial support in Hong Kong for dissidents in France and the United States who called for the overthrow of the present regime? More difficult. And did this include support reported in newspapers and on radio and television for a change of government in Peking? Clearly not, at least from Hong Kong's point of view. China and the people of Hong Kong would have problems in defining what constituted support for dissidents.

The traditional Chinese approach to dissidents in exile is either to ignore them or woo them. As the post-1989 wave of exiles washed up in a number of countries, the Chinese could afford to ignore them, and even add to their number by allowing the dissident astrophysicist Fang Lizhi to join them in exile. But it was quite another matter for Hong Kong to allow leading dissidents to come to the colony and, indeed, heavy pressure was exerted by China in November 1989 to prevent such visits.[17] Nor would Hong Kong allow a dissident ship intending to broadcast subversive messages to the mainland to dock in the colony.

Was this limitation on free speech in the name of limiting subversion of the mainland? There seemed to be an inevitable clash between the two concepts of free speech and subversion. There also seemed to be clear evidence that Hong Kong basically accepted the Chinese message that convergence should take place before 1997. There were, however, limits on this acceptance of the Chinese line, although these remained unclear. It seems inevitable that a more conservative regime in Peking would define subversion more broadly and insist that support of most kinds, perhaps even including verbal support for what China considered subversion, was unacceptable. There would be a tendency in Hong Kong towards self-censorship for fear of creating an incident, and on the part of some others a tendency to speak more boldly in order to demonstrate that China is not yet in control. This radicalisation of politics seemed a likely outcome of the Chinese concern with subversion and the differing definitions in the Western and communist systems. At such times, the notion of 'one country, two systems' seemed far less like a pragmatic policy and much more like a recipe for future uncertainty and conflict. A more moderate regime in Peking might ease tensions, but not remove them entirely.

Economic Interests

As has already been outlined in earlier chapters, there is a vital economic link between Hong Kong and the mainland. In keeping with the convergence theory, Peking clearly would like to see that link strengthened. But the convergence notion carries risks for both Hong Kong and the mainland, for if the socialist economy falters it risks pulling that of Hong Kong down with it. Hong Kong can contribute to growth in China, but it cannot make up for poor policies in Peking. And yet, Guangdong province and much of southern coastal China has come to share such a concern with Peking's policies. In large part because of the growing integration between Hong Kong and its Chinese hinterland, it is increasingly necessary to distinguish between policies in Peking and those in southern China.

Of course it is sometimes difficult to distinguish between the role that Hong Kong plays for China and the more narrow linkage to south China. It is clear that Hong Kong serves as an entrepôt for important parts of China's trade, but a large section of what is called Chinese trade is in fact Guangdong and south China's trade. In 1989, Hong Kong took 48 per cent of total Chinese exports, more than twice the level in 1979. Yet only 9 per cent of Chinese exports were retained in Hong Kong, while 39 per cent were for re-exports. In 1979, 15 per cent of Chinese exports were retained in Hong Kong, while only 7 per cent of its exports were for re-exports. In 1979 Hong Kong accounted for a mere 2.5 per cent of Chinese imports, rising to 11.8 per cent in 1983. In 1983, 4 per cent of the 11.8 per cent were imports from Hong Kong that stayed in China and the remainder were processed and re-exported. By 1989, Hong Kong accounted for 31.8 per cent of China's imports and 22.4 per cent of that total were for re-export from China. Because south China was developing as a single export processing zone, it could be argued that Hong Kong was integrating with southern China more than with China as a whole.[18] In 1989, 62.1 per cent of Chinese exports to the United States went through Hong Kong, up from 17.4 per cent in 1979. Exports to other OECD states saw similar rises, but Hong Kong declined as a re-export platform for countries in East Asia, such as Singapore, who established more direct trade links with the mainland.[18]

A GATT report in 1990 recorded that Hong Kong grew even more dependent on the Guangdong economy than in the previous five years. Domestic exports of labour-intensive products were being replaced with re-exports, in part because Hong Kong manufacturers moved their production into the nearby hinterland. The jobs of almost three million workers in Guangdong were estimated to depend on investment from, or trade with, Hong Kong. Thus when austerity measures were introduced by China in 1988, the Hong Kong economy stagnated in line with that of southern China.[20] The connections between south China and Hong Kong begin with cultural factors and a shared dialect. It extends to trade and investment to the point where the Hong Kong dollar is now a common currency in south China. More than 100,000 people cross the Hong Kong–Guangdong frontier every day, along with 14,000 vehicles.[21] Some 75 per cent of Guangdong's investment in 1990 came from Hong Kong. In 1991 there were 16,000 Hong Kong-owned factories in Guangdong. Hong Kong took 81 per cent of Guangdong's exports in 1990, up from 48 per cent in 1980.

Peking's representatives understand this close relationship and use it to encourage Hong Kong to help maintain stability in China as a whole.[22] Hong Kong is also seen as a key transfer point allowing trade between northeast and southeast Asia and even northeast and southeast China.[23] When Western countries imposed sanctions on China following the Peking massacre, Hong Kong was quick to join China in complaining about the impact on China and Hong Kong. The fall in Hong Kong–China trade in 1989 because of the economic downturn on the mainland was used by Peking as part of the argument for why Hong Kong should be active in supporting Chinese claims to have Western trade sanctions lifted.

As the gross national product of south China (including Taiwan, Fujian, Hong Kong and Guangdong) powers on to $550 billion (with a population of 140 million) in the year 2000, up from a GNP of $280 billion and a population of 121 million in 1990, it is obvious that the attitudes in Hong Kong and China will inevitably change. For one thing, Hong Kong will have to focus on the services sector of its economy. Peking will notice that growth in this region will spread into the hinterland, making it harder for policy objectives to be set from Peking. Indeed, market forces far more than governments will become major 'players' in the process determining Hong Kong's fate. In March 1992 Peking gave the go-ahead for the development of a special free port zone on Hainan island, once a part of Guangdong. This operation, led by a Hong Kong-based subsidiary of a Japanese firm, was evidence of the increasing complexity of the economic interdependence that was developing in the region.[24] Earlier in 1992, discussions were held in Hong Kong about even setting up a more formal mechanism for greater co-operation among the economies of south China.[25]

What might have been a more suspicious attitude in Peking towards the growing connections between south China and

Hong Kong is tempered by the sense that growth in south China, at least in the meantime, is good for overall growth in China and its international image. Of course, Peking claims to dislike what it sees as sharp business practices in Hong Kong, such as re-labelling of goods to beat quotas in the developed world, but these tricks of the trade are useful for China as a whole. Peking is certainly aware that Guangdong is China's major earner of foreign exchange and the province's growth helps pull along parts of the Chinese hinterland. GNP growth in Guangdong in 1990 was 50 per cent higher than the national average. Guangdong accounted for 25 per cent of all Chinese exports in 1990. The linkage with Hong Kong also allowed firms from all of China to use Hong Kong as a way to connect with the international economy. Some reports suggested that in 1990 Chinese investment in Hong Kong was so high that the colony was a net recipient of Chinese investment.[26] Chinese firms were often investing in their own country via Hong Kong as a way of protecting their assets in a time of political uncertainty in China. In 1991, China emerged as the biggest foreign holder of Hong Kong dollars, thereby reinforcing both China's influence and its stake in a prosperous Hong Kong. Chinese holdings were also part of the general internationalization of the Hong Kong dollar.[27]

For the leadership in Peking, the increased interdependence between Hong Kong and south China is likely to remain a difficult issue. If Guangdong is merely 'one step ahead' of the rest of China, but willing to play by the rules set in Peking, then the problem can be controlled.[28] But the risk must be that, with rapid growth, south China will become more distinct and therefore less likely to accept diktats from Peking. To some extent this process was already evident after 1989 when Guangdong rebelled against Peking's efforts to claw back more of their profits. But in early 1992, and in part in reaction to the collapse of the Soviet Union, Deng Xiaoping led an effort to revive south China as a model for the whole country.[29] The transfer of Guangdong's Governor Ye Xuanping to Peking is a sign both of the importance of the province and the need for Peking to balance centre–province relations. Guangdong still needs good relations with Peking, if only because the region needs major investment in transport and energy. Moreover, Guangdong and Hong Kong knew that their success has also stimulated other parts of China, most notably Shanghai, to seek its own regional independence. Shanghai and

Hong Kong may well compete as financial hubs for larger regions. Thus, to an important extent, the fate of Hong Kong depends as much on Peking's relations with south China and other emerging regions as it does on Peking's relations with Hong Kong, London or any other part of the globe.

Management of Britain

Peking's argument that China and Hong Kong should converge in the run-up to 1997 is in flat contradiction to the notion that Britain rules Hong Kong until the date of transition. The tension created by this line of argument is meant to be resolved through the mechanism of the Joint Liaison Group. But in the difficult months after the Peking massacre, the JLG became the forum for airing disputes and, where they could not be resolved, the problems soon became public. Thus a number of issues elbowed for prominence and, in the end, the conclusion was the same nearly every time: China was taking a more active part in running Hong Kong even before 1997.

Ke Zaishuo, China's senior representative on the JLG, was among the most noisy complainers about Britain's role. In October 1989 he said that 'the British side has the unshirkable responsibility for the present problem of confidence in Hong Kong', precisely at the time when Chinese actions were doing their best to undermine confidence in the colony.[30] In a very public meeting of the then vice-foreign minister, Zhou Nan, with the Governor of Macao, the Chinese official bemoaned the fact that Britain was not as compliant as Portugal about the management of the period of transition.[31] Xu Jiatun, the head of the Xinhua News Agency and China's effective 'ambassador' in Hong Kong, added that Britain had 'tied the bell on the tiger' (meaning it raised the confidence issue) and thus had to build confidence in the period before 1997. He too contrasted Hong Kong and Macao and said if China was responsible for the lack of confidence, then why was it not affecting both colonies? He noted a series of disputes with Britain, from the Tamar naval base to political reform (see below), all of which were said to be problems created by Britain and made 'convergence with the Basic Law' more difficult.[32] Chinese officials suggested that they would not intervene in the daily affairs of the colony, but, as the parties moved into the second half of the transition period (1984–1997), China increasingly defined issues that were in the daily headlines as issues of concern to them.[33]

Deng Xiaoping was quoted in February 1991 as encouraging his officials not 'to be afraid of tension' in the relationship with Britain because the period of transition would require resolute behaviour. But he added that Britain was leaving a system which had many good features, including the role of the Governor, and therefore China should work with Britain to ensure a smooth convergence. He was clear that although other countries such as the United States were important, Britain was the key to a successful transfer of power.[34] By stressing the role of Britain, China thought it was better able to keep other states from becoming involved, leaving it more free to sort out Hong Kong on its own.

The fact that there were issues in dispute with Britain was not so surprising, but what was particularly worrying was the tone of the conflict. In fact, maintaining confidence was something over which Britain did have some influence, even though the major responsibility lay with China. But when Britain sought to do something about confidence, China judged the action on the basis of whether it contributed to convergence with the mainland. Two of Britain's major efforts, the granting of passports with the right of abode in Britain and the seeking of greater democracy, were seen as separating Hong Kong from China.

Both issues are covered in other chapters, but some attention should be given to China's reaction as evidence of how it is likely to handle future disputes before 1997. On the question of greater democracy in Hong Kong, it is clear that China does not want a local government that by 1997 has the confidence of the people and can try to stand up to Peking in any dispute over policies adopted by the new rulers. China's expectations are that, in the old ways of 'United Front' politics, it can make use of such bodies as the trade unions to build a strong base of public support. Ji Pengfei, as director of the Hong Kong and Macao office at the State Council, urged the trade unions to take an active part in the electoral process on precisely those calculations. Of course, China does not really want to see party politics emerge in Hong Kong and Lu Ping even said he would oppose a political party advocating socialism in Hong Kong.[35]

China officially accepted the notion of democracy, but defined it as the principles as 'specified by the Basic Law' and not the sort of fully representative democracy as understood in Europe.[36] The trade unions were asked to take 'as their primary task' the managing of the transition to rule by the Basic Law. Deng has spoken of the need to distinguish between 'patriots' and 'troublemakers', the latter being supported by 'outside forces'. Deng accepted both the need for greater 'participation' and 'changes' in Hong Kong, but he made it clear he would judge the process on the basis of whether it 'is changing in a healthy or sour direction'.[37]

But Britain and the people of Hong Kong, while not agreeing on the precise form of representative democracy, were sure they wanted more than China. The squabbles over the number of directly elected seats featured in the debates of 1989–90. Yet the basic acceptance of the Chinese position sent a clear message that China would get its way on the running of the democratic system.[38] Those members of the Basic Law Drafting Committee from Hong Kong such as Martin Lee who were most outspoken about how China was handling the democracy issue were told in no uncertain terms that they would be ignored because their views did not fit with those in Peking.[39] Martin Lee and Szeto Wah were later expelled from the BLDC because of 'their antagonistic stand against the Chinese Government'.[40] Zhou Nan noted that only those who 'love the motherland and Hong Kong and support the Basic Law and the motherland's reunification' should rule Hong Kong after 1997.[41] Other Chinese commentaries noted frankly that Britain had never granted democracy to the people of Hong Kong so why should the Chinese authorities now do so. The Basic Law was meant to make Hong Kong converge with China, not with Britain.[42]

When elections in 1991 elected anti-Chinese candidates to the Legco, China was quick to declare that it dismissed the process as out of touch with reality, and in any case was on an insufficiently high turnout to impress.[43] China's response was to choose a group of forty-four 'consultants' from the colony who would 'advise' on Hong Kong affairs. This tactic, well known from the revolutionary days of creating a 'United Front', would be used to show that Peking was trying to understand Hong Kong's real views.[44] In reality, the people of Hong Kong were too apathetic about policies to treat the whole matter very seriously. In June 1992 the Legco decided not to press for an increase in the number of directly elected members, thereby capitulating to Chinese demands.[45]

But with the arrival of Chris Patten in July 1992 and his proposals for widening the democratic process in October, Legco was given a new opportunity to stand up to China. Their backing for the Governor angered China because it was both a symbol of the limits of Chinese power and the putting in place of an opposition that might bother China after 1997. The infection of democracy might spread into Guangdong and beyond.

Relations are also likely to be kept sour by the continued operation of forces opposed to the Peking regime working out of Hong Kong. In 1989 the fact that Hong Kong allowed the dissident swimmer Yang Yang to go to the United States angered Peking and even led it to refuse to take back the illegal immigrants that regularly flee China for freedom in Hong Kong.[46] Assuming that dissidents continue to leave China, then such problems are far from over, even as the memories of the Peking massacre fade. Britain will have to defend its definition of what is subversion of China and continue to suffer verbal abuse from Peking. There is no obvious calm water after the storms of 1989–90.

Britain's second strategy for building confidence, the issuing of passports with the right of abode in Britain, has already stirred a storm of protest from Peking. As we shall see in the next chapter, it was no simple struggle for Britain to change its nationality legislation. It did so in order to accommodate at least some of the Hong Kong demands about passports and to offer some reassurance. Britain expected that China would accept the small number of passports on offer as evidence that Britain was not anxious to drain Hong Kong of its talent. But when China made plain it would not recognise the passports, the drive to leave Hong Kong was bound to accelerate, thereby making it more likely that those with passports and right of abode in Britain would take up their places. In March 1991, when it became clear that there was relatively little demand for the British right-of-abode scheme, China's attacks on the scheme moderated. China's attacks on the 'insurance package' devalued the deal as a way of insuring for the future.

The Chinese refusal to support the British scheme was based on the notion, as one official stated in 1989, that 'there must be relations between democracy and patriotism . . . A guest is in no position to exercise the authority over his host'. Because Hong Kong is an international city, Hong Kong residents of non-Chinese nationality can be given the right to vote, but not to be elected.[47] When Britain announced its passport scheme in December 1989 as a form of insurance policy, China denounced the arrangement as damaging to confidence in Hong Kong. 'There are safety devices and lifeboats on all ships. If the ship can carry 1,000 passengers, it usually has 1,000 life jackets or enough lifeboats for the passengers. When the ship is in danger, the passengers will leave before the crew and the captain and other administrative personnel will be the last to leave.'[48] China suggested that, by granting passports with the right of abode to only an élite, Britain was operating the precise opposite of the lifeboat principle. Great social problems are likely to emerge as a society divided between those with, and those without, passports take up different political views as they approach the iceberg of 1997. China foresees that some people will then be likely to follow British interests, and not those of China or what China claims to be in the 'long-term interests of Hong Kong'. Even the civil service will be riven by divisions along these lines. In any case, as the passport scheme takes years to implement, some will be too anxious to wait and may well seek their own exit routes, thereby strengthening the flow of emigrants.

China seems to think that without such divisive legislation, 'more than 95 per cent of Hong Kong people will stay'. But the legislation has now been passed and will be implemented. There is little reason to believe that any of the problems discussed by the Chinese will not come to pass. But, rather than hurrying to improve matters, China was slow to make its peace with the legislation and at least to try to ensure confidence. On the contrary, it expressed 'regret' over the legislation and said that the passports 'will not be recognised by the Chinese' because they will 'cause confusion in Hong Kong society'. Britain must bear the consequences for the action and, indeed, 'the Chinese government reserves the right to take further measures at an appropriate time'.[49] By the spring of 1991, when the right-of-abode package turned out to be less popular than first thought, the Chinese were restraining their criticisms.

Yet even with the less panicky atmosphere, it was clear that the brain drain was not stemmed. There was still a real fear in Hong Kong that people needed to seek some sort of arrangement that would prevent them being trapped after 1997. Thus even though the take-up of the British scheme was not great, it still remained likely that, despite China's doubt about the validity of foreign papers, many people would take the British option. Britain might well have to honour most of the documents, even though they were probably issued only in the expectation that many would not be used.

There are some more positive signs from other Chinese officials who note that those with foreign passports can come and work in Hong Kong, even as civil servants: their Chinese citizenship will automatically be relinquished.[50] Under such circumstances the passport scheme would operate as it was intended, keeping people in Hong Kong. It is possible that a more reformist regime in Peking will return to the original formula under which Britain could offer the right of abode without China taking any further action. If the worst was that these people could live in, but not govern, Hong Kong under Chinese rule, it was a small price to pay. The key is whether Peking will recognise the validity of these documents and therefore afford the protection to the people who wish to stay but do not trust the Chinese authorities.

Trusting Peking is the nub of the question of confidence, and, as we have seen, confidence took a bad knock after the events of 1989. But China does not consider that granting the people of Hong Kong another option apart from Chinese rule will be conducive to confidence-building. They are right to suggest that this is a way of trying to get the Chinese authorities to abide by their promise of recognising 'two systems' and not to impose the narrow Chinese definition of another system. The right-of-abode issue is what China claims it is: an attempt to 'internationalise' the Hong Kong problem.

Of course Britain also is ambiguous about whether it is a good idea to involve the international community closely in Hong Kong's future. The United Nations, for one, made clear before 1989 that it wanted no such role. However, by 1991 there were signs of change. When a UN panel of jurists urged the British government to safeguard human rights in Hong Kong, both Britain and China rejected the UN intervention.[51] Of course, the Chinese have already accepted that Hong Kong is an international city in the sense that it is part of the global market economy and a hub for many foreign business interests. Indeed, that is part of China's interest in taking over this thriving economy. But China is against any attempt to involve outsiders in the fate of Hong Kong. When Britain proposed discussing the Hong Kong problem at a Commonwealth summit, China was 'firmly opposed'.[52] China described such efforts as 'playing the international card' and in direct contradiction to the 1984 accord.[53] Prime Minister Li Peng said such cards as internationalization or 'popular will' were vain attempts to exert pressure on China.[54]

The purpose was to impose pressure on the Chinese to live up to their obligations under the 1984 accord as interpreted by Britain. A *People's Daily* report in November 1989 made much play of the fact that being an international city did not mean the city should be governed by international forces. China asserted that the 1984 accord was between itself and Britain and no other body was involved. At a time of acute sensitivity about Western attempts at 'peaceful evolution' in China, Peking was especially concerned that Hong Kong should not become a base for United States-led subversion.[55] By pointing to the 1984 agreement, China hoped to keep its strong hand when playing against a weak Britain.

As the concern over the Peking massacre in 1989 faded, Hong Kong settled back to dealing with Britain and China in a most pragmatic manner. Britain seemed resigned to finding ways to build confidence in Hong Kong. The most prominent project was the proposed construction of a £7 billion international airport. It was hoped that China's state-owned firms might become involved in projects such as this as a way of bolstering mutual confidence in the future of Hong Kong.[56]

However, predictably China did not see the projects in such a light, and its opposition soon began to damage the very confidence that the British scheme was intended to build. In essence, while China was not displeased to be consulted about the plans, it was worried that it was not more closely consulted as part of the steps towards convergence. More specifically, Chinese officials worried that the project was so grandiose and poorly costed that it would eat into the colony's financial reserves. Peking always had a tendency to fret that Britain was seeking ways to drain the colony before 1997, and the major building projects were seen by some as a way in which British firms might be paid Hong Kong money which might otherwise be left to the post-1997 Chinese rulers. It was not so much that China did not want a new airport to be built as a way of promoting confidence in the colony; it was a case of China demanding that Hong Kong's accumulated reserves should be kept at roughly stable levels until 1997. Lu Ping, speaking to business leaders in Hong Kong in March 1991, was explicit about the fact that the problem was one of the scale of development.[57] Other Chinese officials were openly incredulous of British projections for financial reserves in the coming years. The huge sums involved in the project led some Chinese to recall the massive drain of capital from Shanghai just before communist rule was established as well as the grandiose construction projects launched by various Chinese regions in the 1980s that helped lead to the over-heating of the economy.[58] When Hong Kong's unofficial central bank, the Hongkong and Shanghai Banking Corporation, moved its assets to a London-registered holding company, China saw a plot to withdraw funds that it might otherwise obtain after 1997.[59]

In the heat of public debate on the issue in early 1991, Chinese officials challenged Britain's right to rule in Hong Kong when the issues concerned post-1997 Hong Kong, thereby suggesting they considered the British to be lame-duck authorities.[60] But by remaining so openly hostile to the British plans, the Chinese ensured that investment from the private sector would not be forthcoming. Without major new infrastructure projects, Hong Kong would be at a disadvantage as a business environment.

At times during the airport wrangle, British officials, usually unofficially, suggested that they would press ahead without Chinese support. During a trip to China in the spring of 1991, the British foreign secretary, Douglas Hurd, suggested as much, only to find he could not conclude a deal with China anyway.[61] It was the old story. China held all the cards and when Britain threatened China the Chinese authorities demonstrated a remarkable determination to pursue their own agenda despite the damage done to confidence in Hong Kong. The message was clear: China was in charge of the fate of Hong Kong.

On 4 July 1991, Britain conceded that Peking had to be a major decision-maker in Hong Kong before 1997 and the airport deal was done. Britain's role was being whittled away in much the same way as Western imperialists grabbed bits of China in an incremental fashion in the nineteenth century.[62] Of course, this so-called second Sino–British Joint Declaration was little more than the recognition of a powerful reality accepted in the 1984 accord. In the same vein, when Hong Kong set its budget in March 1992, including higher than expected reserves, it was clear that this was part of an attempt to reassure China that they would not inherit an empty shell.[63] In the event, Chinese officials still criticised the budget because it raised taxes. The spectacle of a communist China urging lower corporate tax was evidence of how it was impossible for Britain and its colonial government to satisfy China. Ultimately, China was primarily concerned with reinforcing the message that it was well down the road of convergence with, and ruling over, Hong Kong.

These issues were commonplace in the early 1990s. For example, in October 1991 China blocked an agreement on Hong Kong's air services with other countries.[64] It was not so much that China had a specific vision for Hong Kong, but, rather, it was establishing and reinforcing political principles. When the Hongkong and Shanghai Banking Corporation moved its domicile to London in 1990, China's prime minister was consulted in advance. When the Corporation then took over Britain's Midland Bank in 1992, they also consulted with Peking.[65] Even though the Hongkong and Shanghai Bank was explicitly trying to reduce its presence in Hong Kong before 1997 and its directors would now be based in London, China was satisfied that the process of consultation met the minimum conditions.

During the 1992-93 struggle with Chris Patten over his proposals for greater democracy, China threatened to destroy economic prosperity for the sake of political principles. It eventually assumed a more pragmatic position and began to separate decisions on economics and politics—becoming more pragmatic on the former. But the separation was always difficult because it was increasingly unrealistic. As economic prosperity in southern China developed, with Hong Kong's help, Guangdong and other coastal provinces were increasingly able to stand up to Peking. The central government was discovering that a difficult Hong Kong was making Guangdong even more difficult to handle. Struggles over increasingly intertwined politics and economics in relations with Hong Kong were becoming more tied up with struggles about the fate of China as a whole.

6

Britain: Dignity in Retreat?

It must be counted among the oddities of the 1990s that Britain, an island off the west coast of Eurasia, remains the nominal ruler of some six million people clinging to the eastern fringes of Eurasia. It is all the more remarkable that Britain should retain this limpet of imperial times when the claimant of the territory, China, is the looming power of East Asia. What can Britain's interest in Hong Kong possibly be and how is Britain likely to react to Hong Kong's coming union with China?

British Interests

As Dean Acheson aptly noted, Britain's roles and interests are not always the same. Britain's primary role regarding Hong Kong is to hand the territory and people back to China. Not since the end of the Second World War was it ever credible that Britain should do anything else, although of course it took Britain and the world a while to realise this sad fact. The pattern of British foreign relations since 1945 has included massive decolonisation and it was only the fact that Hong Kong seemed to be so independent of Britain that led some people to think that it might not follow the route of all Britain's other holdings.[1] The real decision-makers in this process were either the Hong Kong people – who might have agitated for independence – or the Chinese, who had to decide when they wanted Hong Kong back. Britain's role was passive.

Yet it might be said that Britain had an interest in holding on. China was ruled by a communist regime and in the Korean war British and Chinese troops had killed each other. But Britain also took a less Manichaean view of the Cold War, especially in the developing world. It was not about to turn Hong Kong into an outpost of 'the free world' and defend it as it prepared to defend Europe in NATO. London settled for what was effectively a holding policy – holding Hong Kong so its people could prosper and until other people, such as the Chinese in Hong Kong or Peking, decided what was to be the fate of the territory. As we have already seen, the people of Hong Kong failed to make their feelings known at an early enough stage and China finally decided it wanted the territory back.

The negotiations in 1982–84 were about the terms under which Hong Kong would be returned, and only initially (and not credibly) about whether it should be handed back to China at all. In any case, in the 1980s China was seen as the most reformist of the communist regimes and whatever Cold War ethics prevailed in British calculations they were not focused on China so much as on Eastern Europe and the Soviet Union. Then came 1989, a most confusing year for attitudes towards communism. China's brutal suppression of opposition in June 1989 made it the hard man of the communist world. But the death of communism in Eastern Europe later in 1989, and in the Soviet Union in 1991, effectively ended the struggle with communism. The winning of the Cold War meant that communism in Asia could be treated as more Asian than communist and that Britain was relieved of some of the guilt that it was 'surrendering six million people to ruthless communists'. Now they were only ruthless Asians, and Asia was a long way from Britain. What is more, Hong Kong had always been associated in the British mind with sweatshops and sharp business practices and by the 1980s, as the people of Hong Kong often noted, the colony was in some senses richer than the master. Certainly in comparison with the Falkland Islands, Hong Kong evoked little natural sympathy in Britain.

Nor did Britain have any overpowering economic interests in either Hong Kong or China. To be sure, the total net assets of companies controlled from Britain was at least £6 billion in 1989 and in 1991 the gross stock-market value of British-owned or managed companies in Hong Kong was £25 billion, accounting for 40 per cent of the Hong Kong stock market. British companies' net assets in Hong Kong in 1989 was between £2.5 billion and £3 billion. Net British investment in Hong Kong in 1987 was £280 million, compared with £176 million in Singapore and £87 million in Malaysia. Hong Kong had ranked below both countries in the 1984 table of British investment in Asia. Net earnings from direct investment by British firms in the 'invisible' sector of the Hong Kong economy in 1987 was £486 million and total earnings by

British firms in this sector in that year were over £1 billion. Britain's average annual trade surplus in the late 1980s with Hong Kong was less than £500 million. Britain also ran an important intelligence listening post on the south coast of Hong Kong island.

But Britain's connections were clearly on the wane, as seen in the fact that by 1991 it held less than 5 per cent of Hong Kong dollars overseas.[2] It was said that once Britain and China resolved the Hong Kong problem, then British trade with China would rise.[3] Yet in the years from 1984, British trade remained in the middle ranks of EC trade with China. In 1989 China accounted for 6 per cent of all British trade with Asia and 0.4 per cent of total British trade. Hong Kong accounted for more than three times the Chinese share of British trade. Germany had long been the EC's largest trade partner with China. China's trade with Britain was roughly at the level of British trade with Greece, Thailand or New Zealand. Britain ranked eighth among exporters to Hong Kong and fourth as a destination for Hong Kong's domestic exports in 1989.[4] However, Hong Kong was Britain's second-largest export market in East Asia, after Japan, although nineteenth in Britain's total. In the preceding years Britain had gently declined in importance, especially as a source of imports into Hong Kong. In both imports and exports, Germany has been more important for at least a decade.

If there is a British interest in Hong Kong it is that the very hand-over of Hong Kong gives Britain a claim to special status. At the G-7 summit in Houston in July 1990, Britain, like the United States and Japan, had a reason for breaking ranks on opening a dialogue with the Peking regime and a junior foreign office minister was duly despatched to China.[5] When countries like France and Britain look around for arguments why they should hold seats on the United Nations Security Council while Germany and Japan must sit outside, they have to do more than simply point to wartime legacies and nuclear weaponry. Managing problems like Hong Kong is part of the rationale for why Britain is a great power and not merely a major partner in the EC. When Hong Kong is returned to China, Britain will lose prestige, not so much through the loss of a colony *per se* but because some of its world role will have been lost as well.

Of course, practitioners of international relations are not usually exercised by such high-flown ideas as they deal with day-to-day management of problems in their in-trays. As a difficulty on the desk of ministers, Hong Kong remains one of the most pressing problems for Britain outside of the Euro-Atlantic theatre. Thus Britain has a more short-term interest in making sure that it is not embarrassed by events surrounding the hand-over of Hong Kong. Britain has an interest in keeping the Hong Kong problem off the front pages.

Yet there is not much that Britain can do to manage the news that puts Hong Kong in the headlines. The unrest in China in 1989 had nothing to do with Britain and yet forced the foreign office into crisis-management mode. It is fair to say that the problems of elections in Hong Kong, let alone the passport and right-of-abode issues, would not have arisen in anything like their modern form if not for the crisis in China. Nor will Britain be able to decide when Deng Xiaoping and his comrades die. Therefore Britain can be sure that it will be forced to react to changes in the level of confidence in the colony as Hong Kong responds to the new politics of its future master.

There are, of course, mechanisms for managing such crises. The Joint Liason Group as well as continuing high-level Sino-British contacts are intended to smooth out the troubles as they arise. It does not require a well-polished crystal ball to perceive that in the years before 1997 confidence in Hong Kong will be upset by such issues as confidence in the Chinese economy, political succession and Western trade relations with China (such as the United States' dithering over whether to revoke China's Most Favoured Nation status). At all times the British policy will be to calm the concerns.

In 1990, it appeared that by dealing with democracy and passports the most troublesome decisions had already been taken, but this was to prove wishful thinking. In a matter of months it became clear that Britain would face a series of issues in a continuing process of convergence before 1997. Various economic issues in Hong Kong, not to mention the election of opponents of China in the 1991 elections, all demonstrate that there will be much to manage before 1997. Elections will be held and more radicals may well be elected. Problems will increase in number and intensity as the era of British rule comes to an end, just as they did in the last days of the Indian Raj.

By the time the day arrives, Britain's interest will have become even more focused on getting out with as much dignity as can be arranged. It is likely that British trading interests will have declined in Hong Kong and London will have grown more reconciled to its new role as a European power in a vibrant and united EC. Britain's trade with East Asia as a whole may rise, but it will be chiefly because of rising trade with Japan, South Korea and Singapore.[6] With the new Europe emerging from the end of the Cold War, Britain's interests and role are more clearly drawn back to home ground. With the United States increasingly dealing with the EC as a unit and United States–Japan problems still unresolved, the much cherished 'special relationship' with the United States is changing shape. Despite the close Anglo-American co-operation in the Persian Gulf conflict in 1990/91, the conditions for a precise repeat of such a scenario in Asia seem remote. By 1997 Britain will be a major partner in the EC, and with far fewer illusions about what its international role might have been.

Nationality

Hong Kong will rank, along with problems in the Middle East, as an important issue. A major reason why this will be so is the fact that in 1990 it committed itself to offering to the people of Hong Kong 225,000 passports with the right of abode in Britain. When this figure is added to 200,000, the number of residents of Hong Kong already said to have such status, it is axiomatic that Britain has a vested interest in keeping the transition smooth and avoiding having to resettle, possibly at short notice, close to 500,000 people on an island not known for its tolerance of sudden influxes of immigrants. Indeed, the domestic impact of the nationality question is among Britain's most important interests in managing Hong Kong.

Britain has a self-image as a crowded island which has been decent to refugees and immigrants. It is true that Britain is among the thirty most crowded states on earth, but Holland, Belgium and even Germany have more people per square kilometre than Britain. It is certainly true that many of the more densely populated places are wealthier than Britain. Nor is Britain's population particularly static. In 1986, 302,000 people left its shores, over 52 per cent of whom went to Australia, New Zealand and Canada, 9 per cent to the EC, and 9 per cent to the United

States. In 1988 only 237,000 people left, with 26 per cent going to Australia, New Zealand and Canada, 25 per cent going to the EC, and 13 per cent to the United States. Of the 206,000 leaving England, 109,000 were from the southeast. Some 21,000 left Scotland.[7] Clearly the population of Britain is far from unchanging and, with the EC developing into the Single European Market, these trends are set to increase.[8]

The British population has not been as settled as many would like to believe. Indeed, Britain is among the most ethnically mixed of European states, despite the self-image of an 'English race'.[9] The very word refugee was first used almost exclusively to denote Protestants driven from France at the end of the seventeenth century, many of whom settled in Britain. By the late eighteenth century the term was used to denote all those who flee their country in times of distress and Britain, an island of relative tranquillity next to turbulent continental Europe, remained a safe haven.[10] Britain watched and sought to manage the process of change, for, as Lord Curzon noted before the First World War, there was a 'winnowing of people' in such areas as the Balkans.

But Britain was never particularly liberal in taking refugees, preferring to manage international relations from a distant and relatively safe island. In the period between the two world wars Britain took in 250,000 aliens, while France took 3,000,000 in the same period. Britain declared itself not to be a country of immigration and, indeed, for the past century it has been a net exporter of people. Between 1933 and 1939, as the Third Reich was being constructed and Jews persecuted, Britain took only some 50,000 refugees from Germany and even implemented a very restricted policy toward Jewish immigration to Palestine.

In the post-war period there have been major movements of people in Europe, most of which passed Britain by. Of the 200,000 Hungarians who fled their country in 1956, 180,000 went initially to Austria: Britain in the end took just 14,000. An even greater percentage of the 3,500,000 Germans fleeing East Germany in the decade from 1951 settled in West Germany. Britain took only a handful of the 80,000 who fled Czechoslovakia after 1968 and virtually none of the 260,000 Russian Jews who fled, mostly after 1971. Holland took in 250,000 from Indonesia after the end of colonial rule in 1949, Belgium took in 90,000 from the Congo, France took 1,000,000 from Algeria, and even Portugal took 360,000 from its African colonies (the highest proportion of any

European state, adding 7 per cent to the Portuguese population). In this period, Britain took 28,000 Ugandan Asians, a small proportion of its population by the standards of other European colonial powers or the special case of Germany.[11]

By far the biggest problem in the future will be the potential immigrants – those who hold British nationality and the right of abode but who reside abroad. Some reports suggest there are up to 200,000 such people in Hong Kong and a staggering 1,000,000 whites in South Africa (350,000 British nationals and a further 750,000 with the right of abode).[12] But while most of South Africa's 'delayed immigrants' are white, the vast majority of the people to be granted the right of abode in Britain from Hong Kong under the 1990 nationality package are Chinese.

Chinese are already the third largest visible immigrant community in Britain.[13] But of the 25 million overseas Chinese (those who live outside China, Hong Kong and Taiwan), the vast majority remain in Southeast Asia. They used to see themselves as merely sojourners rather than immigrants, and Hong Kong was traditionally their trans-shipment point. Hong Kong may well be merely a longer-stay half-way house for a further several hundred thousand. Up to the Second World War there were fewer than 5,000 Chinese in Britain, but by the early 1990s there were up to 150,000 (compared with 6–7,000 in all of the rest of the EC, mostly in Holland, Germany and France). At the turn of the century this tiny population was the focus of numerous scare stories about drugs and sex as the Boxer rebellion of 1900 and the Russo-Japanese war of 1905 fed wild rumours about oriental practices. The early immigrants were seamen, many of whom fled persecution in the United States at the end of the nineteenth century. The China trade after the Opium War led to a rise in the need for Chinese seamen, but the restrictions on aliens in Britain kept the growth of the Chinese population in Britain to a minimum.

The main wave of immigrants arrived in the early 1950s from Hong Kong. Most came to work in the restaurant trade and they had the benefit of family and informal ties based on local communities, unlike most Chinese immigrants in the United States who came as contract labour. Wives and families followed, especially in the decade after 1963. Until 1962 there was no restriction on immigration from the Commonwealth and West Indians were actively recruited to work in post-war industries. A quarter of the men and half the women who came were trained, non-manual workers. Then the Commonwealth Immigration Act restricted numbers unless there was employment for the immigrants, and the restaurant trade ensured the jobs were made available.

By the 1960s Soho in London had become easily the largest Chinese community and business centre in Europe. But the relatively low profile of the Chinese community, due to its tightly knit groups, mostly kept immigrant Chinese out of the growing public debate over immigration. Their diligence, lack of major claim on the social security system and the fact that most were refugees from communism helped the Chinese cause. As racial tensions rose in the 1960s, both in Britain and the United States, the rules on immigration were tightened. Afro-Caribbean immigration tailed off and virtually ended in the mid-1960s. But immigration from the Indian subcontinent picked up sharply at this time (in 1959 there were only 850 immigrants from Pakistan and in 1961 there were 25,100). In August 1985 the Labour government tightened the 1962 Act by requiring more skills among the immigrants. The entry of Asians from Africa and Enoch Powell's 'Rivers of Blood' speech prompted the 1968 Commonwealth Immigration Act, which restricted automatic entry in future to United Kingdom and colony citizens who had patrial (and therefore, in most cases, white) ties to Britain. The perceived loophole to be closed concerned people from the former British colonies of Uganda and Kenya who had retained their British passports: the policy of Africanisation in these countries was leading Asians to leave for Britain. The Labour government pushed the legislation through in three days.

The Conservative government in 1971 passed further regu-lations (which came into force in January 1973) that focused on the patrial distinction. Other immigrants needed a work permit before they could enter and thus non-white immigration was often restricted to those on contract labour. Immigration from the 'black and brown Commonwealth' peaked at 68,000 arrivals in 1972 and since then most of the growth in the size of communities has come from births. In 1987 only 46,000 people were accepted for settlement in the United Kingdom, of which 21,000 were from the new Commonwealth. The Conservative government of Mrs Thatcher was particularly rigorous about immigration and the 1981 British Nationality Act introduced three new categories, with most Commonwealth citizens becoming British Overseas Citizens. In 1988 a new Act tightened some of the entry rules and changed the appeal process.

The popular debate about immigration remains peppered with myths. Many people believe that most immigrants have been non-white, that they comprise a large proportion of the population and that they have resulted in a large increase in the total population of an already crowded island.[14] But of the people living in Britain who were born overseas, more than half are white. Some 51 million people in Britain are white. Only 4.5 per cent of the population are non-white, with 1 million black or brown. The British population did grow steadily in the two decades from 1951, but between 1971 and 1983 more people left the country than entered. Since the mid-1980s the figures are more confused, but basically because of the large flows to and from the EC. In 1990, total immigration into Britain stood at 52,390, virtually the same as in the previous few years.[15]

In the 1981 census there were 154,363 Chinese in Britain, which did not include those with British-born parents. Some 50 per cent of Britain's Chinese live in London and 14,000 in the northwest of the country. In the 1980s an influx of Vietnamese, 70 per cent of whom were of Chinese origin, brought new numbers and new problems to what had become a very settled and relatively prosperous community. The very isolation and prosperity of the Chinese in Britain made it easier for the government to contemplate a nationality package allowing in hundreds of thousands of new immigrants. But the new immigrants would be of a very different kind from those who came to work in the restaurant trade and rivalries were bound to develop. Some 50 per cent of the present Chinese in Britain are of Cantonese origin, 30 per cent are Hakka, and the rest are from Southeast Asia, other parts of China and Taiwan. The new immigrants from Hong Kong would mostly be Cantonese, but wealthier and more skilled. This should make them less of a burden on the local economy than any other type of immigrant, and yet so much depends on where they settle and whether they come in large numbers or in a steady but smaller flow. The mainstays of the present community, a tightly knit group that keeps away from mainstream British life, might not appeal to all of the new Chinese immigrants. Needless to say, the new immigrants are less likely to include the gang members that play a part in the present community. They are also likely to be far more proficient in English than those already living in Britain, for the British-Chinese have shown a widespread lack of English proficiency. A Home Affairs committee report in Parliament in 1984 also highlighted the fact that the local Chinese had little notion of British law and the benefits available from the welfare state. A study by the Commission for Racial Equality also suggested that although young Chinese in Britain dreamed of becoming doctors, lawyers and accountants (like the prospective immigrants from Hong Kong), they usually ended up in the restaurant trade.[16] There are signs of change and there is an increasing Chinese middle class integrated with the rest of the population, but the numbers are still small. The influx from Hong Kong might well make the transformation more swift and, indeed, raise the profile of the community in Britain.

The 1990 Legislation

Even before the Peking massacre in June 1989, the British government was planning to make special provision for additional immigration from Hong Kong. But before 1989 the issue of confidence was not nearly so acute that Britain, and least of all a very conservative Conservative government, felt it had to allow large numbers of people to come. Even when the legislation was first outlined to the House of Commons in December 1989, the 'sales pitch' was that the changes to legislation were an insurance policy intended to encourage people to stay in Hong Kong. Although the new Act was to allow up to 50,000 households (or some 225,000 people) to live in Britain, the intention was not that they should do so. The reasons for such a ruse have to do with the past record of British governments on immigration and the needs of Hong Kong.

As we have already seen, Britain's record is not over-generous in welcoming refugees and immigrants. Ever since the Labour party was perceived as being 'softer' on immigration issues in the 1960s, there has been a rivalry between the two main parties in demonstrating a 'firm' approach to immigration. Mrs Thatcher's Tory government, which came to power in 1979, had a tough line on immigration as an explicit plank in their election platform. Thus it was no small change of political heart to agree to allow 225,000 people from Hong Kong.

Mrs Thatcher reportedly had an ambivalent attitude towards Hong Kong. While she respected the industry and self-reliance of its capitalists, she was never the kind of Tory who enjoyed the upper-class snobbery that seems so prevalent in some Hong Kong circles. She also had an ambivalent attitude towards China. Although Mrs Thatcher lived up to her 'iron lady' image as a staunch anti-communist, she had a serious respect for those communists such as Mikhail Gorbachev and Deng Xiaoping who seemed determined to reform their countries. But the negotiations on Hong Kong were not the high point of her diplomatic career. After the triumph of the Falklands war, it was somewhat of a disappointment to discover that the foreign office was right, that Hong Kong would have to be returned to China. Her distrust of the foreign office sometimes seemed nearly as strong as her distaste for the likes of Deng Xiaoping.

In the months before December 1989, the Thatcher government was aware of two conflicting sets of pressures. With Hong Kong calling for a generous nationality package, and back-bench Tory MPs warning of the consequences of a U-turn on immigration, the prime minister allowed the precise deal to be thrashed out in cabinet and the corridors of power. The foreign secretary, Douglas Hurd, who learned Chinese when training as a China specialist of sorts in the foreign office, and who once wrote a novel (*The Smile on the Face of the Tiger*) about a Chinese takeover of Hong Kong, was also a former home secretary. He seemed particularly concerned to be as generous as politically possible. He reportedly initially suggested that some 60,000 heads of household be granted the right of abode. With a working multiplier[17] figure of 3.7 to account for average family size, this would have meant close to the 300,000 that many of the business groups in Hong Kong were saying was the minimum number required to preserve confidence in the colony.[18] With the home secretary as well as the trade and industry secretary leading the opposition, a compromise of 50,000 heads of families was agreed.

By April 1990, the details were worked out for a complicated scheme that would identify groups of people whose applications would be graded by a point system which values age (30–40 years old as best), experience, education and training, special circumstances, knowledge of English, British links and community service. Of Hong Kong's nearly 6 million people, some 3.2 million held British Dependent Territory passports and were therefore eligible for the new nationality package. The government was targeting the business sector as the key to staunching the brain drain, but financial means were not weighted as heavily as many feared. Since the risk of a labour shortage seemed acute in such jobs as computer specialists, nurses and engineers, the scheme had to be more flexible than one merely based on ability to pay.

With a Labour party claiming it was a scheme for the rich, the weighting of categories was a particularly sensitive problem. A category for 500 'key entrepreneurs' provoked the most outrage.[19] The colony's 342,000 business managers, administrators and professionals were offered 19,703 passports; the 60,000 in the disciplined services were offered 7,000; the 12,500 accountants were offered 1,615 passports; the 57,300 engineers, architects and surveyors were offered 3,230 passports; the 10,300 computer personnel and journalists were offered 1,938. Doctors, nurses and paramedical staff, comprising some 44,700 people, were offered 2,584 places; the 3,700 lawyers and judges were offered 323 places; and the 82,700 teachers were offered 2,907 places. Those in the so-called 'sensitive services' (such as the police) were offered 6,300 places. The government expected some 750,000 people to apply for the 50,000 places, although the delay in implementing the scheme meant that many would-be emigrants had sought alternative exits in any case. Only 43,500 passports will be given in the first allocation, with the remaining ones handed out closer to 1997.

In announcing the package in December 1989, and by way of response to the former Tory minister Norman Tebbit who opposed the nationality package,[20] Douglas Hurd said, 'This is the last main chapter in the story of this country's empire. I am sure he is rather keen that the last chapter should not end in a shabby way.' Yet Hurd was also explicit that this was a compromise, for the up to 5.28 million people who might have a BDT passport could not all be allowed in.[21] This was a specific measure to do the minimum to give Hong Kong a chance and the government would not amend the 1981 Nationality Act.[22]

Reaction to the package was entirely predictable in Britain (although not in Hong Kong), except for the relative ease with which the legislation was passed by the two Houses of Parliament in 1990, and this despite a public hostile to the deal.[23] A public opinion poll in April 1990 revealed that 25 per cent favoured granting the right of abode to 50,000 Chinese families and 65 per cent were opposed. Among Conservative party voters the figures were 34 per cent in favour and 55 per cent opposed. Some 39 per cent said Britain had an obligation to take any Hong Kong refugees, with 50 per cent saying there was no obligation. The remarkably insular trends went on to record that 83 per cent opposed more Indian and Pakistani immigrants, 83 per cent opposed more West Indians, 77 per cent opposed more Chinese, 67 per cent more Jews, 54 per cent more white Commonwealth people, and 60 per cent even opposed more EC individuals, despite the run-up to the Single European Market of 1992. A whopping 84 per cent wanted tighter restrictions on immigration with only 13 per cent opposed.[24] Just after the Peking massacre, the polls showed Britain evenly divided on whether immigrants from Hong Kong should be treated as a special case.

Thus Norman Tebbit did represent the views of the country far more than the prime minister, and yet Mrs Thatcher pushed the legislation through the two Houses with far less opposition than expected. The Labour party officially joined the Tebbit conservatives in the 'No' lobby, but a serious rebellion on the Labour back benches, along with strong support from the Liberals and Social Democrats, ensured a safe passage. An all-party House of Commons select committee on foreign affairs report in 1989 had recommended even larger numbers. Most of the leader columns of the press were strongly supportive of the government and many commentators urged an even more generous settlement.[25]

The Labour party's position was especially worrying to the people of Hong Kong as Labour led the Tories in the public opinion polls throughout 1990. Labour did not pledge to abide by the scheme and, because it certainly would not be fully implemented before the next general election, there was a risk that those who did not get a passport before a Labour government came to power might not do so at all. This added to pressure on those seeking alternative arrangements and, unlike with the British scheme, the Canadians, Australians and Americans all required a residency period before a passport was issued, thereby draining Hong Kong before 1997. The Labour party in Britain, although probably not likely to sabotage the package once it had passed the House of Commons, was doing its best to undermine the purpose of the deal even before it went into operation. It was equally unlikely that, if a Labour government was in power when a flood of people began to come to Britain, they might revoke the legislation.

But the uncertainty in British party politics was yet another complex element in what now became a guessing game about future scenarios for immigration. Would Britain have to take all these immigrants? The answer, at least from the potential migrants, was 'yes, but probably not on quite that scale'. Various surveys showed that most Hong Kong people would prefer to live elsewhere if they had to move, with Canada, Australia and the United States scoring highest.[26] But if the only passport they had was British, and especially with the British passport opening up the rest of the booming EC as a place to live and work, a considerable number could be expected to take up their new rights.

As always, the question was not so much 'would they come to Britain?' but 'would they wish to leave Hong Kong?' Once the leaving question was decided, the *where?* question was relatively easy to answer. As we have seen in other chapters, any such discussion of the calculations on whether to leave is based on a calculation of confidence in Hong Kong and its future rulers in China. In the period before a succession to Deng Xiaoping and before clarification of the question of whether reform would be revived, the drain of people from Hong Kong would be likely to continue.

By March 1991, when the deadline for applications for places in the British right-of-abode scheme had passed, it was clear that the people of Hong Kong clearly did not want to come to Britain. By the last date of application, 28 February, some 66,000 applications had been received. The vast majority came in a bizarre last-month rush. For a scheme that was supposed to be a competition for scarce places, the take-up rate suggested there was an *under*whelming demand for places in Britain. The Hong Kong government originally announced that it was gearing up for 750,000 applications and had printed one million forms. The low take-up could be seen both as a victory both for the Chinese, who claim that far fewer people fear their rule than the doom-merchants suggested, and a victory for Britain, which claimed that it had judged its right-of-abode programme nearly perfectly and might have been embarrassed if there had been a vast over-subscription. One Hong Kong official noted that 'if people have confidence in Hong Kong and feel no need for such an insurance policy, it's fine by me'. Victory might also be claimed by North American governments and Australia, for there was good evidence that the flow of people desiring to leave the colony for those destinations had not diminished. The low take-up was seen as a vote of no confidence in Britain.[27]

Perhaps the clearest implication of the low number of applicants was that Britain would now be under far less pressure to do more in the way of an 'insurance policy' for the people of Hong Kong. As one observer noted before the final numbers were counted in January 1991, 'If this scheme is not oversubscribed then there's no chance for making further approaches to Britain if something disastrous happens in a few years' time.'[28] If the un-confident did not want to come to Britain, then why should Britain do much more to help them go elsewhere? It was also a sanction of sorts for Britain to resume normal business with China on a wide range of issues including the future of Hong Kong. It seemed as if many people in the colony were far less fearful of staying on after 1997 and therefore might actually approve of Britain negotiating with China before 1997 about measures to ensure that there was a 'through train' that went past 1997 with a form of *de facto* joint administration.

Although Douglas Hurd was careful to avoid any suggestion of a 'through train', he was clear that Britain had to be freer to deal with China in a businesslike manner than many of his critics allowed. As he noted before the numbers on the right-of-abode scheme were known, 'we do not treat Hong Kong as if its future could be separated from the future of China'. He added that 'on recent evidence you would get shorter odds on Hong Kong lasting fifty years than on socialism doing so'.[29] Indeed, this re-statement of the notion that the 1984 deal was the 'best available prospect' was often denounced as reflecting the views of the traditional foreign office cabal on China. But such a critical assessment of British policy was certainly harder to sustain after the figures became available on the numbers interested in the British right-of-abode scheme.[30] It seemed as if the foreign office and the Hong Kong people had reached similar conclusions.

As a result, Britain began experimenting with ways in which the through train might be started without officially admitting as much. Perhaps the most obvious place to start this through train, apart from the operation of the JLG itself, was on the question of such long-term construction projects as the new scheme for an airport for Hong Kong. As we have already seen, this contentious scheme was opposed by China for many reasons, but in April 1991, when Douglas Hurd became the first Western foreign secretary to break the ban on high-level contacts with China after the Peking massacre, it became the major stumbling-block in Anglo-Chinese negotiations. Although the agenda for the talks in Peking included a wide range of issues after the Gulf war and the ending of the Cold War, it was once again Hong Kong issues which caught the headlines.[31] Given China's key role in the state of confidence in the colony, it was always going to be China that held the stronger hand. The airport was designed to be a confidence-building scheme, but, because of China's desire to take more control of the colony before 1997, it was a confidence-sapping scheme until a deal was reached in July 1991.

The airport deal, like the battle over the Patten proposals of 1992–93, indicated that Peking and London were locked in an unavoidable struggle over how much influence Peking would have before 1997. The truth was there was no escape from such struggle and it seemed bound to get worse before 1997. Changes in personality in British politics might well bring about a change, for John Major and Douglas Hurd have been staunch supporters of Chris Patten and a break in that triumvirate would be significant. But far more important are possible changes in Peking.

Assuming that Deng Xiaoping does not quite make it until 1997 to see Hong Kong returned to the mainland, then the hope has to be that there is a quick resolution of his succession and reforms are speedily resumed. But if there is lingering uncertainty, as there was after the death of Mao in 1976, the lack of confidence in Hong Kong may well produce a drain of skilled people. By then, the vast majority of the British places will have been allocated and the numbers offered may well be seen as insufficient to meet the new demand. Under such circumstances those with places in Britain may well take them up, especially if Britain and the new Europe are seen to be economically successful. Thus in the mid-1990s the steady stream may turn into a flood. At that point, far more attention will be paid to the policies of other countries, and it is to a consideration of these states' policies that we now turn.

7

The United States:
The Inactive Superpower

When the United States was one of two competing superpowers, it was seen as the only power with the ability to support Hong Kong and possibly even deter China from undesired action. By the time the Soviet Union disintegrated and the United States became the only superpower, it was clear that the Americans would not take such an active part in the defence of Hong Kong. The United States had come to accept some time before that Hong Kong would be returned to China and the agenda of Sino-American relations was filled with far more important issues. And yet the emergence of Chris Patten with high profile proposals for greater democracy in Hong Kong caught the American imagination in 1992. At a time when the United States was increasingly anxious to press China on human rights, the new Clinton administration became far more supportive of British policy on Hong Kong.

In 1990 China accounted for only 1.2 per cent of American exports (down from 1.3 per cent in 1984), but imports from China in 1990 accounted for 3.1 per cent of the American total, up from 0.9 per cent in 1984. These are figures used in the International Monetary Fund's *Direction of Trade*. But according to China, if trade through Hong Kong is properly counted in the figures the massive Chinese trade surplus in 1989 and 1990 becomes a small American surplus. In 1989, according to the Americans, total trade through Hong Kong of $9.7 billion was distinct from the total of $18 billion for Sino-American trade. China asserted that direct trade was valued at $12 billion. In 1990, according to the Americans, the trade through Hong Kong was $12 billion, and $20 billion in direct trade.

The emergence of China as a major exporter to the United States and the trade imbalances that ensued clearly put economic

112

issues on the Sino-American agenda and broadened the nature of the relationship. In the two decades since the Nixon administration opened a high-level dialogue with China, China had been assessed primarily in terms of its role in the strategic balance between the United States and the Soviet Union. Although the United States was the main supporter of the Guomindang forces led by Chiang Kaishek, when they lost the civil war the United States was forced to settle for the defence of Taiwan and the uneven imposition of the Cold War framework in East Asia. The United States fought Chinese troops in Korea and again took on what it perceived as a Chinese-backed North Vietnam for a decade from 1965.[1]

Since the official Sino-Soviet split of the early 1960s, China was seen as a possible strategic counterweight to the Soviet Union. In the 1980s, after the start of a major Chinese reform programme, once again Americans came to believe that China was on the verge of going capitalist and the potential of China could be tapped. The events of 1989, which so shocked Hong Kong, had a major impact on the American psyche as well. The strategic dreams of military co-operation had been gradually lost in the 1980s as China pursued a more independent foreign policy line.[2] In 1989 a Sino-Soviet summit normalised relations between the communist giants, just as the Soviet Union was moving beyond notions of a communist-versus-capitalist world. The virtual death of communism and the Cold War in Europe later in the year turned the Soviet Union into a different sort of adversary and isolated China even more as a peculiar leftover of the communist system. This sense of being left behind was strengthened by the actions taken by the Chinese regime in 1989 when faced with a challenge to its authority. The Peking massacre in June 1989 was the antithesis to the liberating events later in the year in Europe. Sino-American relations worsened as a result. With the disintegration of the Soviet Union in 1991, the Cold War could be clearly declared as over and it became fashionable to argue that the United States no longer needed to work with China because the Soviet adversary was gone.

Yet, as time wore on, it became clear that it was not in the United States' interest to isolate China. Even with these major strategic changes, the United States knew there was much that a dialogue with China could achieve that was in the American national interest. The Bush administration made a special point, despite the sanctions imposed after June 1989, of maintaining contact with China and trying to cajole it into a return to its reformist path. During the Gulf war of 1990/91, China, as a member of the United Nations Security Council, also demonstrated that it was an important part of any international co-operation and could not be ignored. After the demise of the Soviet Union it was going to be impossible to get international agreement on nuclear proliferation or controlling the arms trade unless China was part of the deal. Western contacts with China gradually returned to normal. China was also too important in terms of the growing importance of the Pacific region, where the United States was trying to develop a more co-operative atmosphere for economic prosperity. Although United States power had waned in recent years as Japan and the EC picked up some of the slack, the United States still remained the leader of the world market economy, the *primus inter pares* of the G-7 and the leading guarantor of stability in the Pacific region.

Of course, a relative decline of American influence was felt in both Asia and Europe. In Asia there was no one to replace the American influence as the region's guarantor of stability and there were serious risks that, if the United States simply departed, a strategic vacuum would be left that might be filled by China or even Japan. In Asia/Pacific there were no multilateral institutions to help shape the post-Cold War international politics, while in Europe there was the EC to pick up the mantle of leadership. The reunification of Germany meant the United States would be an actor in Europe because it wanted to be, not because the Europeans needed them.

This more equal relationship with Europe also meant a major change in the Anglo-American special relationship. Ties between London and Washington in the post-war era had been based on a mix of historical factors and the fact that Britain was a convenient link between the EC and the United States. As the effective bridge in the North Atlantic part of NATO, Britain's importance to the United States gave it a claim to a special relationship with the United States. Britain also continued to be the heaviest direct investor in the United States and the particularly close ties between the prime minister, Margaret Thatcher, and the president, Ronald Reagan, reinforced the linkage. But 1989 changed all that. Not only did Germany emerge as the more vital partner, but there was simply far less need for a bridging state. Of course, Britain did not cease to be important. During the Gulf war of 1990/91, Britain, in sharp contrast to Germany, demonstrated the still-valuable military dimensions of the special relationship. Germany may well have been more important in the context of the emerging EC or international economic policy, but when it came to strategic issues Britain was still of special importance. The Hong Kong issue involved various dimensions of power and the United States was certainly aware that it played a special part in helping shape the future of the soon-to-be-ex-British colony.

During the Reagan administration there was little evidence that the more special relationship between Britain and the United States manifested itself in a special policy towards Hong Kong. The main American interest in the colony in the period before the beginning of Sino-American *détente* was as an intelligence-gathering outpost targeted against China.[3] The huge American consulate in the colony was welcomed by Britain as part of the worldwide co-operation against communism, even though Britain thought the American attitude towards China excessively harsh. It was no doubt useful to Britain during the Cultural Revolution and the excesses of the pro-Chinese forces in Hong Kong that the Americans had such a stake, even though the colony was insignificant as a trade partner. To an important extent the American military presence in the Pacific, and the frequent rest-and-recreation visits to Hong Kong by American troops engaged in the Vietnam war, was an informal military guarantee for the colony and part of a global anti-communist strategy.

At no time after the early post-Second World War years did the United States attempt to affect the British policy towards Hong Kong. The United States never tried to apply the principles of self-determination through the United Nations. Nor did Britain seek to involve the United States in the affairs of Hong Kong – an omission of no small consequence when the time came for Britain to seek support in its negotiations with the Chinese. It was only with the gradual opening of China in the 1970s that Hong Kong was transformed into a significant economic force in East Asia and became of special economic interest to the United States. As the entrepôt for the China trade, Hong Kong's trade with the United States began to boom and direct investment flooded in. In 1984 Hong Kong imported $3.1 billions' worth of goods from the United States and the United States was Hong Kong's largest market ($7.9 billion or 45 per cent of total exports). There were 14,000 American residents in Hong Kong, with some 500,000 Americans visiting annually. Many large American corporations established regional headquarters in Hong Kong and over 800 firms were in operation by the mid-1980s. United States investment was hard to measure with any confidence, but it was put at $4-5 billion in the mid-1980s, or second in Asia after Japan.[4] In 1990, Hong Kong accounted for 1.7 per cent of American exports (up from 1.3 per cent in 1984) and 1.9 per cent of American imports (down from 2.4 per cent in 1984). The colony was the United States' fourth-largest export market in Asia – a region where Washington was particularly pleased to see any partner appearing to be a fair trader.

As a result of this major investment in the stability of Hong Kong, especially as the United States grew more interested in its Pacific destiny, it was curious that the American attitude to the Hong Kong negotiations was one of an 'interested bystander'. Far from taking an active part in the fate of Hong Kong, the United States left it to Britain to hand back its colony. Just before the conclusion of the Anglo-Chinese negotiations on Hong Kong in 1984, Secretary of State George Shultz said the United States had a 'deep interest' in a meeting with the Governor of Hong Kong. Shultz was briefed on the talks and said that, 'while the United States does not perceive a role for itself in the ongoing negotiations over Hong Kong's future, we have a deep interest in preserving Hong Kong's stability and prosperity and strongly support efforts to reach a settlement.'[5] Other American officials noted that the negotiations were 'strictly an issue between the UK and the People's Republic of China'.[6]

The United States was clearly watching events, but basically seemed to leave it to its ally Britain to look after Western interests. The special American concern was with Taiwan, although it was of less concern to Britain, but otherwise the Americans could rest assured there was more or less a coincidence of interests. As a result, despite sporadic consultation on the progress of talks and subsequent liaisons, the United States left the fate of Hong Kong to Britain. Certainly the American response to the 1984 accord on Hong Kong, as expressed by State Department spokesman Alan Romberg, was pleasure at the deal and the basis for 'sustained confidence in the future of Hong Kong'.[7] The United States was also the first country to announce that it would accept the international validity of the new British National Overseas passports, thereby relieving some anxiety in the colony that they would be stranded by the international community. As the leader of the Western world, the American pronouncement was vital, and indicated the Americans' leading role in any issue affecting the international status of the colony.

Indeed, once the agreement between China and Britain was reached, it could be argued that the United States' role in determining the future of the colony rose in importance. Much play was made of the fact that in 1988 there were more United States residents in Hong Kong than there were residents from the United Kingdom. It was said that of the 15,870 Americans, some 7,500 were people from the colony who had obtained American passports and then returned to work. The decline in the British total was in part attributed to the determined effort to reduce the number of foreigners involved in the administration of Hong Kong.[8] Thus, as the transition took place, the United States looked like becoming a more important international actor.

It was certainly true that the United States was far more important to Hong Kong as a trading partner than was the United Kingdom. When the American economy declined or demand fell for Hong Kong products, the economy in the colony was hit especially hard.[9] When confidence in the colony was being badly undermined during the Sino-British negotiations leading up to the 1984 accord, the United States dollar was made the peg for the Hong Kong dollar. In 1988, when President Reagan announced he would withdraw Hong Kong (and the other NICs) from the list of developing states that enjoyed preferential trading privileges in the United States, the local economy worried about its export potential.[10] Although the NICs were merely being granted recognition of their new trading status as more developed states, there was still a great deal of worry that Hong Kong was more vulnerable than the other NICs because of the hand-over in 1997 and therefore deserved better treatment.[11] Hong Kong's concern with American legislation, especially in the textile sector, seemed to be even more acute as business nerves were more jittery in the late 1980s, even though such issues had been on the agenda for years.[12]

To some extent the American treatment of Hong Kong regarding trade issues was more lenient than it was with the other NICs, but this had more to do with the linkage of the Hong Kong dollar to the United States dollar and, therefore, the fact that currency rates remained in line. American trade officials also acknowledged that Hong Kong's economy was remarkably open to foreign trade and consequently should not be hurt by curbs placed on other NICs for 'unfair trading practices'.[13] Hong Kong was also worried that curbs on China imposed through COCOM, the Cold War regulating commission set up to limit high technology exports to communist countries, would eventually also hurt Hong Kong, especially after 1997.[14] These debates about American policy in East Asia were front-page news in Hong Kong in the late 1980s as the United States struggled with its new role as importer, rather than exporter, in the Pacific. Hong Kong sought special treatment and only sometimes received it. On 7 October 1991 Hong Kong was included among the exclusive list of those licensed to receive high technology under COCOM, and this despite the fact that the increasingly complex trade between the colony and China made it virtually impossible to halt the seepage of such technology to China. To this extent, at least, the United States had given Hong Kong an extraordinary concession which seriously undermined American China policy but was testament to its concern not to destroy the Hong Kong economy.[15]

Following the Peking massacre, there was no significant change in the American attitude that Hong Kong was a low-profile issue. Hong Kong was apparently not discussed at any of the high-level meetings held in defiance of the Western ban on any such contacts with China, that task being left to Britain, who also broke the ban because of its special concerns over Hong Kong. But neither was the United States oblivious to Hong Kong's problems. In a very unusual public comment, the United States Consul General in Hong Kong in May 1990 cautioned Peking about imposing restrictions on freedoms in Hong Kong after 1997. He added that 'it was vital that Hong Kong remain an open city, an international financial and commercial centre which fully participates in the world trading system'. The statement was interpreted as being part of an American attempt to help Britain staunch the flow of people out of the colony, which was harming American interests in the colony.[16]

The United States also seemed aware of the particular vulnerability of the Hong Kong economy after the events of 1989. As part of the American debate over whether to rescind the Most Favoured Nation (MFN) trading status China held in the United

States, the British and Hong Kong governments launched a major effort to make sure China kept its rights. With so much of Hong Kong's trade dependent on major investment in Guangdong, it would be Hong Kong more than China that would be hurt by the revocation of the MFN status.[17] Chinese officials were clearly aware that Hong Kong could be an important ally in the struggle over MFN and explicit appeals were made to Hong Kong and Britain to look after their common interest. From the point of view of Peking, this was a fine example of the convergence of interests.[18] From the American point of view, it was an equally fine example of the limits on its policy when it was increasingly tied in to the regional economy, which in turn was increasingly important for the United States. So far, the Americans have recognised the weight of these pressures and extended MFN status, thereby, at least tacitly, acknowledging some responsibility regarding the fate of Hong Kong. As in the case of the American COCOM decision, the closer integration of Hong Kong and China placed a major limit on American ability to pressure China and gave Peking a greater stake in speeding up the integration of the colony with the mainland. Thus, the United States, and the other developed market economies, were key participants in the speeding up of the convergence of Hong Kong and south China.

Yet the MFN issue also demonstrated the extent to which the direct link between the United States and Hong Kong was not developed. Most of the contact over the Hong Kong issue was either directed through United States–Britain relations or Sino-American relations. The people of Hong Kong had little direct access to the single power that might have been able to exercise some authority on their behalf. There were the annual visits by the Hong Kong Governor to the United States, but at least until 1989 these were usually merely occasions to repeat the usual line that the fate of Hong Kong was a matter for the United Kingdom and China and trust should be placed in the convergence of Hong Kong with the mainland.[19]

In the early 1990s the United States was somewhat more outspoken in its concern about how confidence was being maintained in the colony and especially on the question of enhancing democracy in the colony. In particular, the American Congress, which opposed President Bush's strategy of constructive engagement with China, tried to set out rules for

American policy on Hong Kong. Needless to say, China regarded the congressional efforts as meddling in internal affairs.[20] China was evidently concerned that the United States was seeking new ways of pressing China on human rights and was stepping in to internationalize a problem just as China felt it had 'house-trained' the British.[21]

The passage of the 'US–Hong Kong Policy Act of 1992' in May 1992 did little more than reconfirm those aspects of the 1984 Anglo-Chinese accord on the autonomy of the colony in signing international agreements. But, by passing the Act, Congress was at serious risk of contradicting itself, at least in the sense that its attempts to revoke MFN status for China would only hurt Hong Kong. Nevertheless, the essential reality of American policy remained the same. The United States was supportive of British policy and in its actions was strongly supportive of the notion of convergence of Hong Kong and South China.

When Chris Patten, under attack from China, turned up in Washington just before the first American debate on MFN in the Clinton administration, the new importance of the American factor for Hong Kong was demonstrated in unusual ways. China had agreed to talk to Britain about the Patten proposals in part because they wanted to avoid another dispute with the United States. Patten was ostensibly in Washington to argue against the removal of China's MFN status, but in reality his presence was signalling to Peking that he and Hong Kong were increasingly important in Washington. The limited form of conditionality imposed on China's MFN status in May 1993 strengthened Patten's hand and kept the pressure on China, but it was a hard act to sustain. For the United States the best way to reconcile its important interests in both China and Hong Kong was to accept convergence and, indeed, to speed it up. It was likely to remain difficult for the United States to maintain a simple policy towards Hong Kong and China at a time of growing integration in south China.[22]

Immigration Policy

The fate of Hong Kong, and also the American companies operating there, depended in part on the flow of skilled workers from the colony. As a major investor, and unlike Canada and Australia, the United States could be said to have more of a stake in people staying in the colony than leaving. There was also the United States' fear that the collapse of Hong Kong might lead to problems between China and Taiwan, thereby forcing the United States to take a more active military role in a region where it hoped economic prosperity could be maintained with less forceful means.[23] In essence, the United States saw clear advantages in creating the best environment for the convergence of Hong Kong with south China. The United States hoped that China would change as part of a more general trend to peaceful transformation from communism in the post-Cold War world. Thus Britain and the United States had a common interest in both building confidence in Hong Kong and in stopping the flow of people from the colony.

In fact, at least until the early 1990s, one of the least developed issues in American policy toward Hong Kong was that of immigration, and this at a time when the United States was in the midst of its own debate about immigration policy. As the country of greatest immigration, the United States has a particular reputation as a country of refuge. There is the apocryphal story of President Taft, who met an old Indian chief and asked whether the chief had any words of wisdom for the United States president. The chief said, 'Watch your immigration.' Indeed, virtually all of the United States' population are immigrants or the descendants of immigrants (some 0.6 per cent of the population is Amerindian). The United States took in most of the 55 million people who left Europe in the century after 1815 and it was not until the late nineteenth century that the United States implemented serious curbs on this inflow. Yet some 34 million immigrants arrived between 1901 and 1986, of which a mere 3 million arrived between 1925 and 1950.[24]

Nevertheless, the United States has kept its doors remarkably wide open to immigrants since then, although the nature of the flows of people has changed. In 1961–65 there were 290,000 immigrants per year, with 42 per cent from Europe, 7.5 per cent from Asia and 41 per cent from Mexico and Canada, whereas in the 1969–76 period the annual average was up to 383,000, with only 24 per cent from Europe, 30 per cent from Asia and 37 per cent from North America.[25] Only 5 per cent of the American population is now classified as immigrant, whereas in Australia 20 per cent of the population is immigrant and in Canada 16 per cent.[26] While the United States continues to take more immigrants than any other country when measured in absolute numbers, the proportion of the American population that is foreign-born is at its lowest since the 1850s and now the United States ranks ninth among Western nations in terms of its liberality in accepting immigrants.[27] The United States has the lowest population density of any industrialised state except Canada and Australia.[28]

In 1882 the United States banned the immigration of Chinese labourers and the ban was maintained until 1943. Various immigration acts restrained oriental immigration in particular but the 1900 census still counted 119,000 Chinese and 86,000 Japanese in the United States. By the time of the 1940 census the restrictive policies had taken their toll and, especially because of the shortage of Chinese women, the total Chinese population had dropped to 106,000. The Japanese community grew to 285,000 because there were no similar restrictions on women. During the Second World War, the Chinese Exclusion Act was repealed but the total number of people from China allowed in was a mere 105. With major inflows of refugees after the war, only a small number were admitted from China.[29] A new immigration act in 1965 abolished the national origin quota system and replaced it with a preferential admissions system that was intended to stress the skills of the immigrants. In the event, the question of family reunions took precedence in the operation of the system. In 1955 some 2,700 immigrants came from China and 160 from Hong Kong. In 1970 there were 14,093 from China and 3,863 from Hong Kong, and in 1985 there were 24,787 from China, 14,895 from Taiwan, and 5,171 from Hong Kong. Taiwan was recognised for immigration purposes as an independent entity in 1981 and was given a separate quota of 20,000. This had the effect of doubling the quota available to 'China'.

Once in the United States, the Chinese immigrants, like many others, have fewer problems adjusting there than in Canada or Australia,[30] but the Americans did of course invent the 'melting pot' and its genuinely multicultural society is far more mixed.[31] Yet racial problems are clearly worse in the United States and the social security net is far less secure than in Canada or Australia. Chinese-Americans are very clearly divided into several groups, depending on where they are from and whether they now live in Chinatowns or are mixed in with the general population. Immigrants from Hong Kong certainly fit in the more cosmopolitan category.

Nearly one million people from Vietnam, mostly of Chinese origin, have come to the United States since 1975, including 45,000 in 1989.[32] But between 1950 and 1974 some 210,000 people from China and Hong Kong came to the United States, compared with 300,000 from the Philippines, 175,000 from Japan and 130,000 from Korea.[33] In 1981–87, of the 4,067,600 immigrants to the United States, 1,902,200 came from Asia, with 257,000 from China and Taiwan, and a further 35,300 from Hong Kong. In 1988 some 8,500 came from the colony, compared with 9,700 from Taiwan and 28,700 from mainland China.[34]

The 1990 census recorded 7.27 million Asian and Pacific Americans, accounting for 2.9 per cent of the population (up from 3.5 million or 1.5 per cent in 1980). There were 1.6 million Chinese, 1.4 million Filipinos and roughly 800,000 each for the Vietnamese, Korean and Japanese communities. Half the increase in the American Asian population since 1965 was due to immigration. Some experts project the total Asian population to grow to some 10 million by the turn of the century and perhaps 18 million by 2050. In 1990, California was home to 39.1 per cent of the Asian and Pacific Americans, while New York and Hawaii each had 9 per cent. The Asian and Pacific Americans accounted for 61.8 per cent of the population of Hawaii, 9.6 per cent of that of California, 4.3 per cent of Washington State and 3.9 per cent of New York State.[35]

In 1985 Asians represented nearly half the total of immigrants to the United States but Asia may not produce the largest flows of immigrants in the 1990s. In January 1992 the United States announced that instead of the 20,000 citizens of the Soviet Union that were allowed in to the United States each year, the breakup of the Soviet Union meant now some 300,000 per year from the former Soviet Union could obtain immigration visas.[36] While the vast changes in Europe since 1989 made it considerably more likely that Asians would figure far less prominently on the immigration agenda of the United States, other migration issues also loomed large.

The main problem in the last half of the 1980s was seen to be the major flow of illegals who crossed the southern borders (there were nearly one million apprehended in 1989).[37] Some 10 per cent of the Cuban population has moved to the United States since the early 1960s. The 1986 Immigration Act was established to deal with the flood of illegal immigrants, but the problems continued unresolved.[38] While the Chinese from Hong Kong seemed more prepared than anyone else to pay $20,000 to $50,000 per person to enter the United States illegally, by far the larger numbers of immigrants come from the poorer southern neighbours of the United States. Of the reported 300,000 Chinese in New York City, some 30,000, mostly from Fujian province, are said to be documented.[39] As these legal and illegal flows increased the non-white proportion of the United States population, the debate deepened on the implications for policy. In 1991 more than three-quarters of all Americans were white; by the middle of the next century that proportion may have fallen to below half.[40]

After various false starts, in October 1990 the United States Congress finally passed a new immigration act, the first major change in legislation since 1965.[41] Under the provisions of the act the number of immigrant visas granted each year will rise from 500,000 to 700,000 between 1992 and 1994 and then fall to 675,000 thereafter. These figures do not include refugees. Pre-1991 immigration favoured applicants with close family members already in the United States and, since almost 90 per cent of all United States immigrants are from Asia and Latin America, the old legislation effectively shut out applicants from other parts of the world. The new legislation almost triples employment-based immigration by raising the number of visas set aside for that purpose from 54,000 to 140,000 a year. Some 40,000 visas are set aside for people from specific countries, including Italy, Ireland and Poland, that were traditional source of immigrants but have been vastly under-represented in the current immigration pool. In 1995 the figure will rise to 55,000 and the range of countries will be widened. But more than half the visas (465,000 in the first three years, rising to 480,000 thereafter) are still set aside for family reunions. The ceiling for any one country will rise from 20,000 to 27,000.

The act also stresses the need to revitalise the economy and thus 10,000 'investor' visas will be available to those who invest $1 million in urban areas or $500,000 in rural areas and create at least ten jobs for United States workers. As was apparent in the Canadian and Australian schemes, these arrangements are likely to increase the number of immigrants from Hong Kong. But the United States went even further by raising the limit for Hong Kong immigrants from 5,000 to 10,000 per year from 1991. From

1994 Hong Kong will be treated as a 'separate foreign state, and not as a colony or other component or dependent area of another foreign state', thereby earning a quote of 27,000 each year. Another 12,000 visas would be set aside for Hong Kong employees of United States companies in the fiscal years 1991–93 and, as with the British right-of-abode scheme, immediate family members would be able to join the applicant and not be counted against the ceiling of 12,000. The latter feature was a major boost to American firms operating in the colony and also satisfied Britain's desire to see more people encouraged to remain in the colony as long as possible.[42] What is more, in specific reaction to British wishes the new legislation created an extended-use visa for Hong Kong residents which will remain valid for five years after 1997, until 1 January 2002. In theory, between 1991 and 1997 some 190,000 Hong Kong people could be granted United States visas, a figure roughly similar to the expected flow to Canada.

No other country had been quite as helpful to Britain and Hong Kong as the United States and for a time it looked as if Britain might soon be able to turn up the pressure on Canada and Australia to make similar changes. But the low take-up of the British right-of-abode scheme demonstrated that in fact most people in Hong Kong would rather not come to Britain, especially when there were opportunities to go elsewhere. The fact that the United States, a highly sought-after destination, was also implementing a delayed-action visa scheme probably meant that the United States would become the preferred destination for Hong Kong people. Under the American regulations, those who wanted to stay behind in Hong Kong and make money, even beyond 1997, could now do so and still retain an American 'insurance policy'. Canada and Australia might then lose out in the competition for Hong Kong immigrants, not because they did not co-operate with Britain *per se* but because the United States did.[43]

Perhaps the most important reaction to the new American legislation came from China. In September 1990, Li Hou, deputy director of the State Council's Hong Kong and Macao Affairs Office, told an American Chamber of Commerce delegation that China was not opposed to the American plans. Mr Li seemed most concerned that the United States help reduce the exodus of Hong Kong people and promised that China would recognise the visas issued under the new legislation.[44] Pro-Chinese papers in

Hong Kong soon added that Mr Li's comments were not meant to endorse the 'internationalization' of Hong Kong, but they at least implicitly supported the suggestion that China would not sabotage such efforts to build confidence in Hong Kong.[45]

The United States as the Superpower

On the subject of immigration the Americans, for their own good reasons, remain closer to the British position on the future of Hong Kong than do the Canadians and Australians. Indeed, it can be argued that the American interest of preserving its investments in Hong Kong and good relations with Hong Kong might well be served by pressure on Canada and Australia to adopt the notion of deferred entry for citizens as a way of testing whether confidence in Hong Kong could be maintained. But the problem is that Canada and Australia do not share the primary concern with Hong Kong and China, let alone in maintaining good relations with the British. For them, the primary interest is the self-interest in getting the best immigrants possible. The low take-up for the British right-of-abode scheme was announced in March 1991, just after the United States had amended their immigration rules as Britain had desired. The implication of these two events was that the flow of people from Hong Kong was likely to continue and, indeed, North America would become the destination for a growing number of people. While the Canadian scheme was damaging confidence in Hong Kong, the change in American policy offered some hope that confidence could be retained.

And yet, the United States and the other developed market economies can be said to share a common interest in seeing Hong Kong grow more closely integrated with south China. For all these states, such a solution would ease the pressure from those who say one has to choose between supporting Hong Kong or China. From an American point of view, encouraging such regionalism in south China would also help evolve a more suitable strategy for a post-Cold War Asia/Pacific. If the United States could help give all the states of the region a powerful stake in economic integration, the risks of tension and military conflict might diminish. In the post-Cold War world the United States is reducing its military capability and would not want to get drawn into conflict in Asia. Failure of the integration process in south China might not only involve a call for American support for Hong Kong, it might even require action in support of Taiwan. The United States, like Britain, would be happy for Hong Kong to converge with south China.

Nevertheless, if there should develop a basic crisis of confidence in Hong Kong, the Americans are likely to be asked to act again to help Britain and the people of Hong Kong. At such a time, Canada, Australia, Britain and the United States will be the key actors and will have to co-ordinate policies, perhaps more in the realm of refugees than simple immigration rules. If such a crisis develops when there are other major demands on American compassion – for example, from Eastern Europe or the former Soviet Union – the people of Hong Kong may well not be at the head of the queue for American and Western sympathy. Under such circumstances, a failure of American leadership might also damage the future of the Pacific century. In that sense, getting a sensible American policy for Hong Kong is part of a more general scheme of rethinking strategy towards the Pacific in the post-Cold War world. The process is clearly far from complete. The United States must hope that by encouraging a *de facto* south China strategy it will not result in the breakup of China as in the Soviet case, for such a disintegration might well involve crises over Hong Kong and Taiwan. But if the decentralization of China is part of a more general loosening of definitions of sovereignty in East Asia and a pragmatic approach to economic integration, then the United States can rest more easily. The development of greater multilateralism in East Asia, on both security and economic issues, would certainly help the United States ease itself out of the Cold War world into a new era in the Pacific. The fate of Hong Kong is in many respects merely part of this much larger process.

8

Canada: Immigration Without Responsibility

Canada is one of the United Kingdom's closest friends, but it is also a country with a remarkably liberal record of 'importing people' through a modern immigration programme. With the people of Hong Kong constituting some of the most sought-after immigrants in the modern world, and Britain anxious to anchor as many of them as possible in Hong Kong, Canadian policies, and especially its immigration policy, pose some of the biggest problems for Britain and Hong Kong. As Britain has sought greater co-operation from its allies in managing the Hong Kong problem, Canada (like Australia and the United States) has often made a different calculation of its interests, stressing relations with China and an immigration policy that attracts the best and the brightest.

Canada, like the United States, has discovered, especially in the past decade, that it is both a Pacific as well as an Atlantic state. Hong Kong, as one of the thriving NICs, has drawn Canadian attention as its exports to Canada have risen sharply and as the NICs have generally played an increasing part in the international market economy. Of course Canada can hardly be seen as a major power in the Pacific. It does not rank in the top ten sources of Hong Kong's imports, although it is the sixth-largest destination for Hong Kong's domestic exports (tenth in Hong Kong's re-exports), ranking ahead of Singapore and Taiwan. Some 25 per cent of Canadian exports to Hong Kong in 1990 were re-exported; of those, 80 per cent went to China. Hong Kong is also important to Canadian firms as many have Asian headquarters in the colony.[1] In 1989 Hong Kong was Canada's twelfth-largest export market, with 56 per cent of Canadian exports composed of precious metals and Maple Leaf coins. Of the estimated $12 billion of total investment from in 1989, the Canadian share was reportedly 20 per cent.[2]

But Canada has also grown more interested in China as the communist regime undertook far-reaching reforms in the 1980s. Like the United States, Canada has seen Japan as the main Pacific power. But Canadians have always been more appreciative than the United States of China's positions, especially in the period before the Nixon visit to China in 1972.[3] Of course Canada ranks behind the United States in trade terms, accounting for less than one per cent of Chinese exports although some 3.3 per cent of Chinese imports come from Canada. Wheat dominates Canadian exports and is handled in both countries by national bodies rather than private firms. Canadian trade is dominated by the United States. Trade with the EC and Japan are also of major importance and trade with Britain is worth more than twice the trade with China (although Canadian exports to China are only some 25 per cent smaller than exports to Britain). Canadian troops have been deployed with NATO, although there has been only sporadic military co-operation in the Pacific theatre.[4] The image Canada projects is that of a firm member of the club of developed market economies, but one with special expertise as an aid donor to the developing world and as a believer in international peacekeeping through the United Nations. It is a country with a conscience, although with wealth rather than military power to support its ideals.[5]

Relations with Britain have traditionally been among the warmest in the world. The granting of control to Canada of its constitution in 1982 (the Canada Act) was a long-overdue step in the emergence of a fully independent Canada. By the time Britain committed itself more completely to the EC in the 1970s, Canada was already well established in the American sphere of trading influence. The 1988 United States–Canada free-trade agreement was yet further evidence of Canadian orientation. There have been disputes between Canada, which sees itself as the senior state in the Commonwealth after Britain, and Britain over various issues, most notably sanctions against South Africa. But these have not undermined the fundamentally solid basis of the relationship and none of the major issues in dispute affected the Pacific theatre. Canada's commercial relationship with Britain is, by almost every measure, the most extensive Canada has in Europe. Britain is Canada's third-largest trade partner (after the USA and Japan), although Britain enjoyed a $1.5 billion trade surplus in 1990. Britain remains the second-largest foreign investor in Canada, with holdings exceeding $16 billion, and Canada ranks fourth as a destination for British investment.[6]

Of course, in the past decades the Canada–United Kingdom relationship has become less intense and there has been less British inclination to consult particularly closely with its Canadian ally. Both countries are members of the Group of Seven leading Western nations and, if only for that reason, Canada has become part of the broader multilateral dimension in Britain's relations with its allies. When the Hong Kong agreement was signed in 1984 there was no special consultation with Canada and none was expected or sought. The fate of Hong Kong was viewed as a British problem. Canadian interest, apart from that of the wider international market economy, came to be focused on one issue – immigration. But that issue, and its connection to the internal debate in Canada about the kind of country it really was, soon had important implications for Canada–United Kingdom relations.[7]

Canadian Immigration Policy

The Canadian record on immigration has evolved into one of the most liberal in the developed world. But its earlier years were often less savoury. Some 2.5 million immigrants came to Canada between 1896 and 1914, with close to one million coming from Britain, three-quarters of a million from the United States, and more than 500,000 from continental Europe.[8] Yet World War I ushered in a period of restricted and prejudiced policies towards immigration and it was not until 1962 that a *de facto* White Canada immigration policy was abandoned. The Gold Rush in British Columbia in 1858 had brought a large number of Chinese but the Immigration Act of 1910 (amended by the Act of 1919) gave the power to exclude would-be immigrants of certain categories. In 1881 the Chinese population of Canada was 4,383 and by 1911 it was 27,831.[9] The basic motive was to preserve a society that was seen to be another version of the United Kingdom's, and it was sustained by a widespread ignorance and prejudice about the people of Asia as a whole. The 1923 Chinese Immigration Act totally excluded the Chinese from entering Canada and by 1941 the Chinese population had shrunk back to 34,627 from 46,519 in

1931. The inter-war years mixed economic depression into these policies and the doors remained closed to Asian immigrants. By the late 1950s most of the discriminatory clauses against the Chinese had been removed from federal and provincial statutes and the 1923 Chinese Immigration Act was repealed in 1947. The population of Canada doubled between the end of the Second World War and the 1970s. Although the White Canada policy was sustained for some fifteen years after the war, there was a desire to take displaced Europeans from a war-ravaged continent. The Chinese population of Canada rose to 58,197 by 1961. But new immigration regulations in 1962 removed racial discrimination as the major feature of Canadian immigration policy, while retaining one privilege for Europeans – sponsorship of a wider range of relatives. Between 1966 and 1967 a completely new immigration selection system – the point system – was introduced and the last remaining biases in the system removed. Consequently the Chinese population increased to 118,815 in 1971 and doubled again to reach 289,245 in 1981 – nearly twice the total of Chinese in Britain, with a Canadian population almost a third the size of Britain's.

A new Immigration Act, which was passed in 1976 (entered into force in 1978), was important in improving the management of migration. The 1967 regulations had permitted visitors to apply for landed immigrant status from within Canada and this soon led to a flood of applications and a chaotic system. The subsequent Adjustment of Status programme in 1973 meant full citizenship was obtained by some 25,000 people, of which 28 per cent were from the United States and 22 per cent were from Hong Kong.

A full-scale review of immigration policy then followed, culminating in the 1976 legislation. Canadians were concerned both with their own needs as a vast country with a shortage of manpower, and such international issues as the development of world population.[10] The 1976 Act explicitly outlined the Canadian goals in encouraging immigration and set out new systems of planning and management. The point system was revised in new immigration regulations in 1978. In 1979 Canada took in some 112,000 new immigrants, but the numbers fell to 84,000 in 1985 and rose again to 160,000 in 1988.[11] The changes in policy had something to do with a response to labour needs created as a result of industrial expansion. Canada had been losing many professional and technical workers to the United States (there was a net outflow of some 41,000 in the decade from 1953) and with immigration managed a net gain of some 125,000 professional and skilled workers between 1953 and 1963. Thus the changes in legislation and the point system had a great deal to do with attracting the right kind of people for a developing economy next door to the United States.

In 1979/80 a sizeable group of Chinese came to Canada as refugees. Canada accepted 60,049 Indo-Chinese refugees, about 30 per cent of whom were ethnic Chinese. Of the total Chinese community in Canada in 1981, some 40 per cent lived in Ontario, 34 per cent in British Colombia, 12.8 per cent in Alberta and 6.3 per cent in Quebec. The wave of post-war migration gradually altered the size and structure of the Chinese community in Canada. Many of the new migrants were urban dwellers (from Hong Kong and Taiwan) and the migration from mainland China virtually ceased. Most of the post-war Chinese immigrants came in their prime working years and with a more diversified occupational background.[12] They settled mostly in cities, with Toronto and Vancouver each having about 85,000 Chinese in 1981, or a total of 60 per cent of all Chinese in Canada. Although they lived mostly in the suburbs, their sheer numbers meant the local Chinatowns also expanded as there was a greater demand for their services.

Not surprisingly for such a new community, for the most part they remained out of local politics and retained a strong identification with their ethnic origin.[13] They showed the highest level of original language retention of any ethnic group, but still managed to demonstrate remarkable levels of upward mobility. They did well educationally and occupationally and data on home ownership show them doing extremely well. Nevertheless, Chinese-Canadians did less well than Canadians of Jewish or British origin and their incomes were less than what might be expected from their higher educational level as compared with other groups. Needless to say, the Chinese have not been immune from racial prejudice and public opinion polls in the 1970s gave them an unfavourable rating of fifteenth among nineteen ethnic groups. As numbers increased, the Chinese-Canadians were often seen as foreigners who kept to themselves, were relatively rich and were adversely affecting the lifestyle of Canadians. But, in general, the level of racial tension was remarkably low, even as the China tide grew larger in the 1980s.[14]

The 1980s saw a particular focus of Canadian immigration policy on the steady flow of people from Hong Kong. In fact, by the late 1980s some 20,000 Hong Kong Chinese were settling in Canada every year. The vast majority of the immigrants came under the point system in an immigration programme that was taking 160,000 to 180,000 people per year. The global ceiling for immigration which was 180,000 in 1990 rose to over 200,000 in 1991 and to 250,000 for the few years after that. But with a stagnating economy in the early 1990s, there were signs that Canada was unlikely to liberalise its entry procedures and might even begin to reduce its quota.[15]

In 1988, of the 160,768 immigrants, 43 per cent came from Asia and the Pacific (down from 48 per cent of 143,287 in 1980). Hong Kong provided 14.2 per cent of the 1988 total, easily taking top spot with their share sharply up on the 4.4 per cent from the colony in 1980. In 1989 some 24,132 immigration visas were issued to Hong Kong people and 25,262 in 1990. There were some 35,000 landed immigrants from Hong Kong in 1992, with 47% going to Ontario and 25% to British Columbia.[16] While there was no official quota for the number of immigrants from Hong Kong, the number of immigration officers was a *de facto* limit, as was the overall ceiling on immigration into Canada. The quality of the Hong Kong applicants was rising as the situation in the colony drove more people to seek a safe haven in countries like Canada that took people on the basis of their qualifications as likely contributors to Canadian growth.[17] Some of Hong Kong's population were so anxious to get to Canada that they were applying in Buenos Aires, Singapore and Tokyo where the queues were shorter.[18]

The more controversial category of immigrants from Hong Kong came under the Entrepreneur Program which sought those with a net worth of C$500,000 or more with a proven track record in business who would invest at least US$100,000 into a new business in Canada and in exchange be granted a passport. First introduced in 1978, the scheme was criticised for 'selling citizenship', a tactic that certainly did appeal to thousands from Hong Kong who wanted the insurance policy of a passport and did not want to have to live in Canada to qualify.

Canadian officials claimed that in 1984 some 2,094 immigrant entrepreneurs were admitted, promising to invest $817 million and creating 8,271 jobs. Since the programme began, some 11,000 business immigrants had been granted landed-immigrant status, and they had promised to invest $3.4 billion, creating almost 25,000 jobs. Some 51 per cent of the 2,136 visas issued to business migrants in 1985 were given to people from Hong Kong.[19] This programme was notoriously hard to evaluate because the figures for funds invested and jobs created were a statement of intention rather than reality. Nor was there much control over the types of people who could effectively buy passports.

In January 1986 the Conservative government introduced a new scheme, the Investor Program, which was aimed at even wealthier foreigners. Investors are those with a minimum net worth of $500,000, a proven business record, and who are willing to invest at least $250,000 for a minimum of three years to a programme that will develop business and create jobs. Unlike the Entrepreneur scheme, which required hands-on management, the new programme allowed immigrants to leave the work of managing their money in the hands of investment syndicates. The syndicates were approved by the provinces but not closely monitored.[20] The obvious opportunity was created for some to cash in on anxiety in Hong Kong about the need for a passport. The provinces less wealthy than Ontario, Quebec, Alberta and British Columbia asked for an even smaller investment (C$150,000). In 1988 only 245 investor-immigrants entered Canada, 107 of whom were from Hong Kong. New rules in April 1988 allowed investment by a third party, but the applicant's net worth had to be C$700,000 and the investment had to be a minimum of C$500,000 locked in for a minimum of five years – and this in a country that has perhaps the fairest point system and most generous approach to immigration. The numbers in this business-class passport group are not large, but the principle highlights the purpose of the system – to attract the best immigrants, and all at the expense of Hong Kong's prospects. Of the 3,954 business immigrants in 1989, 1,006 were from Hong Kong. The colony took top spot for the fifth year running, providing 43 per cent of all investment under the business immigration scheme. In 1988, official estimates said $3.4 billion in investment was earmarked that year alone.[21]

As an immigration counsellor at the Canadian High Commission in Hong Kong said in 1987, 'Canada is in the immigration business. These are the kind of people we want. They bring family values, a devotion to law and order, and especially a drive towards competitiveness and achievement which we seem to breed out of our own young people.'[22] Thus Canadian provinces compete through their offices in Hong Kong to attract precisely the kind of people that Britain is trying to anchor in the colony and that China needs in order to inherit a vibrant economy. Canadian lawyers and business ventures open shop in Hong Kong in search of clients and investment funds.[23] Canada, especially after the bad economic times in the early 1980s, was convinced that Hong Kong offered a pool of precisely the best kind of qualified and monied people that would help diversify the Canadian economy and avoid the typical demographic problems of developed countries where low birth-rates lead to a 'greying' of the population.

In their defence, Canadian officials argue that the flow of Hong Kong people to Canada has helped give Canada a stake in the future of the colony. As Barbara McDougall, the then Canadian minister of employment and immigration, said in Hong Kong in September 1990, the largest foreign branch of Canada's largest business organisation – the Canadian Chamber of Commerce – is in Hong Kong. Over 30,000 Canadians live and work in Hong Kong, more than twice the UK figure, and about 150,000 Canadians visit Hong Kong each year. Some 15,000 Hong Kong students study in Canada and they comprise more than a quarter of Canada's total foreign-student population. More than 70,000 university graduates in Hong Kong graduated from Canadian universities. Mrs McDougall also noted Canada's strong support for the 'rapid development of democratic institutions' in Hong Kong and support for Hong Kong's membership in regional and global international organisations. Canada has been instrumental in helping Hong Kong draw up its Bill of Rights as well as other less headline-grabbing legislation as that on conflict of interest in business. Canada spent millions of dollars on a Canada Festival in Hong Kong in the summer of 1991 and Hong Kong did the same in Canada in the summer of 1992.[24]

Mr Mulroney, the prime minister, said in the autumn of 1989 at a Commonwealth heads of government meeting in Singapore, 'Hong Kong involves us all, and we have to accept part of the responsibility and provide some leadership.'[25] And yet Canadian 'leadership' was lacking in most respects except that which furthered Canada's own narrow interests. When Mulroney visited Hong Kong in May 1991 to launch Festival Canada he even stirred up trouble by suggesting, apparently in jest, that his own dire election prospects would be improved by taking more immigrants from Hong Kong. More seriously, it was certainly important that Mulroney's visit to Hong Kong did not involve a trip to China – thereby demonstrating a basic commitment to real autonomy for Hong Kong.

And yet the main aspect of Canadian policy remains its immigration policies. The transformation that all this immigration is making in Vancouver and Toronto is nothing short of remarkable. There is even a mini-industry in books about the phenomenon.[26] The Chinese population in the greater Vancouver area (called Hongcouver by some) is said to be 250,000, or 20 per cent of the total. Some predictions suggest this will rise to 40 per cent although Toronto also now claims to have a slightly larger Chinese population (300,000 in 1991). Some 6,500 arrived in Vancouver in 1989 alone, an increase over the 5,000 in 1988 and the 3,514 in 1987.[27] Some $750 million was reportedly invested in the Vancouver property market in 1988 by Hong Kong money. Major office blocks are being purchased and Li Ka-shing, a prominent Hong Kong businessman, bought the Expo '86 site. Residential house prices in this city with a far better climate than Toronto are rising and locals sometimes express concern that 'Chinese Yuppies' (Chuppies) are changing the face of Vancouver. By the late 1980s reportedly C$1.5 million was being invested per year in Vancouver by Hong Kong Chinese. The city was being transformed in the image of other Pacific-rim metropolises.

Needless to say, there is some ill feeling in what has so far been a remarkably smooth process of change.[28] There is still no racial violence, not surprising in a country well known for its peaceful ethnic relations and reasonable management of social problems. The Chinese influx has certainly helped feed an economic boom which, although it makes people complain about house prices, has brought a rise in the net worth of many residents. The fondness of the rich migrants for building garish new homes also rankles, and this in a country that until 1947 did not allow the Chinese to vote.[29] The local press runs regular reports on the fears regarding the influx of Triad gangs and the Canadian Association of Chiefs of Police prepared an official report on the subject in 1990.[30] In a province where the Lieutenant-Governor is of Chinese origin, the message is that integration is possible, but there always will be problems when it is undertaken at such a pace.[31]

Similar problems and complaints abound in Toronto, but also against the background of a booming local economy (at least until 1991). Toronto claims to have the fastest-growing Chinese community outside of Asia because of the influx of its 'yacht people'. Toronto is already the most ethnically diverse city in the world, and one of the most prosperous and pleasant. According to some conservative estimates, by 1986 there were already 126,000 people of Chinese ethnic origin among Toronto's 3.5 million inhabitants. One report said 80 per cent of all Chinese immigrants to Canada come to the province of Ontario.[32] An estimated C$2 billion has been spent annually over the five years to 1990, mainly by Hong Kong immigrants on real estate. Vast new complexes of shops, sparkling clubs and new suburbs are changing the face of Toronto.[33] There are nine daily Chinese-language newspapers in a city boasting only three English-language ones. As the Chinese move out to the suburbs (the Agincourt district is known as Asian Court), shopping malls are sinofied to suit the new locals. In the Scarborough district of Toronto, 170,000 people of Chinese descent live on tree-lined streets with names like Silver Spring's Boulevard and Blairwood Terrace.[34]

It is fair to say that no country has given a warmer welcome than Canada to those who wished to leave Hong Kong. In the seven years to 1991 some 110,000 people had arrived and, according to one Canadian bank, these people were bringing on average $1.7–3.5 billion a year in capital. Most of the funds have gone into property but money has also gone into the various investment schemes set up under government supervision. 'Asian banking centres' have opened in many Canadian cities and Cantonese- and Mandarin-speaking staff are also available. The Hong Kong Bank of Canada, which is wholly owned by the Hongkong and Shanghai Banking Corporation, became the biggest foreign bank in Canada and Asian émigrés account for approximately a quarter of its business.[35]

The Canadian success at multiculturalism has made such an integration remarkably problem-free, and this despite the fact that many of the Hong Kong immigrants had a better life back in the colony (with a tax rate of 15 per cent). But the business climate in Canada is still one of the more honest in North America and the route to acceptance into a multi-racial society has been remarkably easy. As David Lam, the Lieutenant-Governor of British Colombia, notes, 'you must burn your bridges and become Canadian', and he can deliver that message without sounding racist.

Relations with China and Britain

The Canadian success in enticing people from Hong Kong has had an impact on relations between Canada and China. In 1988 the Chinese government reportedly approached the Canadians to persuade them to slow their intake of people from Hong Kong.[36] Canadian officials admit to regular exchanges of views with Chinese counterparts on the Hong Kong question, but no attempt is made by the Chinese to punish Canada for taking people from Hong Kong who are necessary for the prosperity of China's future territory. China will obviously take Hong Kong in 1997, even if no one is left, but it would also obviously prefer a thriving economy, which requires the very entrepreneurs that Canada is taking. The Canadians, for their part, have no interest in raising the question of emigration from Hong Kong with China although Canadian officials admit to having to play a role in the general process of building confidence in Hong Kong and encouraging sensible policies in Peking.

In fact, the Canadian government has recognised its increasing role in building confidence and has said so to the Chinese in 1990.[37] The former external affairs secretary, Joe Clark, took a particularly high profile in East Asian international relations, most notably on the question of North Pacific security and confidence-building. In a statement in June 1989 following the Peking massacre, he outlined a clear view of Canadian interests in continuing reform in China and a careful attitude towards Hong Kong.[38] But in keeping with other leading Western countries, Canada imposed sanctions on China following the massacre, only to lift them in 1990/91 as business slowly returned to normal. The major role of wheat in Canadian exports meant there was little real effect on the overall pattern of trade. In the end, so long as the Chinese do not protest too strenuously at Canadian immigration policy, Canada is able to continue with its policy of taking the best migrants from the colony.

And yet in recent years, and especially since the Peking massacre, there are signs that the Canadians have grown somewhat more concerned that they have earned the image of narrow-minded poachers of people from Hong Kong. As has already been noted, Canada has been stressing the extent to which its role in Hong Kong has increased and its contribution to stability is being stepped up. As part of its attempt to treat Hong Kong as a special kind of 'not colony, not sovereign state', the Governor of Hong Kong, Sir David Wilson, was received as a head of state in May 1990. This, the first official visit to Canada by a Governor of Hong Kong, elicited strong Canadian statements about the warmth of the relationship between Hong Kong and Canada, although there were few concrete commitments. Joe Clark noted in his speech of 22 May that 550 Canadian soldiers died in the defence of Hong Kong in 1939. On more up-to-date matters, he also noted that the first bilateral air agreement between Canada and Hong Kong was signed in 1988 and in April 1990 a bilateral mutual legal assistance treaty was initialled.[39]

From Britain's point of view, Canada's self-interested policy might have been expected to provoke a row with its old friend. It certainly seems clear to all parties that the outflow to Canada is likely to be the largest for some time to come. The British nationality package was intended to staunch such an outflow, without naming the Canadians (or the Americans and Australians) explicitly. The British idea of granting to applicants the right of abode without their having to leave Hong Kong to meet residency requirements is supposed to be easier for them than meeting the Canadian terms, even though most immigrants would rather go to Canada than Britain (neither of which has an enticing climate).

After the Peking massacre and the crisis of confidence in Hong Kong, Britain asked its Canadian, American and Australian friends to staunch the flow of people. Britain was particularly keen on a change in Canadian immigration policy that would allow a deferral of the taking up of an entry visa, in order to build confidence in the colony. But in September 1990 the Canadian employment and immigration minister said explicitly in Hong Kong what officials had been saying privately for some time: that Canada would not consider any such arrangement. The standard response was that to do so would be interfering in the free flow of people, a right that was fought for in relation to the Soviet Union

for so many years. Barbara McDougall noted that a basic
requirement for all immigrants is that they 'share a commitment
to Canada and to Canada's future. That is why we cannot and will
not allow our immigration program to be used simply as a kind of
"insurance policy".'[40] Some cynical Canadian officials suggested,
albeit unofficially, that Britain merely wanted the best people for
itself and thus the Canadian Entrepreneur or Investor Programs
were merely intended to do much more what Britain did already,
without forcing residency terms on the prospective immigrant.
Who would not compete for the best-educated and richest
immigrants to be seen since the Second World War?

The level of acrimony on this issue remained remarkably well
contained. Interviews with British and Canadian officials reveal
that although Canada expected and received what it called a
'full-court press' (a basketball term for intense pressure, not
always understood by Foreign and Commonwealth officials) on
the question of Canada's immigration policy after the Peking
massacre, neither party really expected the initiative to succeed.
For at least eighteen months after the Peking massacre and until
the failure of the British right-of-abode scheme in early 1991, the
subject of Hong Kong appeared regularly on the agendas of
Canada–United Kingdom meetings, even at the highest level.

But Canada remained firm in its policy for a number of reasons.
First, Britain's 'press' was not really very hard and Canada
assumed the issue would soon fade. Second, Canadian policy
towards Hong Kong was made mostly in the China desk of the
External Affairs Department and thus was no longer as closely
connected to the pressures from the West European section.
Third, Canadian immigration policy was already such a sensitive
domestic matter that it would have been extremely difficult to
engineer a change of policy if it were seen to come under British
pressure. Fourth, with the growth of interest in immigration from
Eastern Europe from 1990, Canadian immigration lobbies would
have strongly opposed special treatment being given to the
people of Hong Kong, who were already viewed as a pampered
class. Finally, the main agenda of Canada–United Kingdom
relations was so clearly focused on the challenges of the new
issues in Europe – the Single European Market in 1992 and the
new military security after the collapse of the Warsaw Pact – that
the Hong Kong issue simply could never be given much space. As
members of the G-7, both countries saw a need to focus on the

main issues in shaping a New World Order. It might also be added that immigration was an issue where Canada felt it was particularly successful. In contrast to Britain, which struggled less effectively with the creation of a multicultural society, Canada felt it had little reason to listen to British officials on the matter.[41] Of course, throughout, the discussions remained remarkably civil.

With the failure of the full-court press, Britain seemed resigned to waiting for a change in China, Hong Kong, or even Canada. When the United States amended its immigration policy in the last half of 1990 to allow deferred entry of people from Hong Kong and also offered special places for employees of United States firms in the colony, it seemed for a brief moment as if Britain might try again to press Canada for a change of policy. But by the end of February 1991, when it became clear that the people of Hong Kong had not applied for places in the British right-of-abode scheme in anything like the expected numbers, Britain too began to reassess its policy towards China, Hong Kong and even Canada. It seemed clear that although the people of Hong Kong did not want British passports they were still interested in leaving for Canada, Australia and the United States. By failing to apply in large numbers for the British 'insurance policy', the people of Hong Kong had effectively taken Canada off the diplomatic, and even moral, hook. Britain now no longer felt it had to plead for special treatment for the people of Hong Kong if they did not want to come to live in Britain (or even Europe, for that matter). The continuing strong preference for places in North America and Australia seemed to vindicate the judgement of Canada that its policies were in the best interest of the people of Hong Kong.

As the numbers coming to Canada, Australia and the USA looked like reaching their limit, the people of Hong Kong would soon be forced to opt for places of second choice. Having missed the British and European boats in 1991, they would have to choose between even less pleasant options. It did not seem far-fetched to suggest that, as the young professionals of Hong Kong made their 'life choices' in the early 1990s, by 1995 at the latest there might well develop a crisis for those who were increasingly desperate to leave Hong Kong and yet no longer had the option to go to the places they wished. The fear of 'jumbo-jet people' was already being discussed among Canadian immigration officials as a scenario for the near future. Under such conditions, an Orderly Departure Program, as was arranged for the Vietnamese refugees, could become a serious proposition. Canada and Britain might well find themselves working more closely together in managing the problems of Hong Kong. By that time Canada will have taken in so many people from Hong Kong that, if only for reasons of worried relatives, Canada will have one of the greatest stakes in the fate of the remaining people of Hong Kong.

9

Australia: Pragmatism in the Pacific

In many senses Australia's reactions to the Hong Kong problem and its relations with Britain bear many resemblances to the Canadian case. Like Canada, it is essentially a white-settler state created by Britain in the heyday of European imperial power. Australia was, if anything because of its island home, more dependent on Britain in the early years. It lacked the looming American presence that Canada felt and it was not until the Second World War that it was clear to Australians that the United States was the dominant military power. In the ensuing three decades, the British influence faded as Australia built up its own self-esteem and mixed it with American-led global culture.[1]

In contrast to Canada, Australia recognised the importance of 'thinking Pacific' at an early stage in post-war politics. China was seen as a threat for many of these years but, as Cold War attitudes moderated and the United States opened contacts with China, Australia was quick to develop its own sense of China's more positive role in the regional economy. Indeed, Australian foreign policy as a whole became more closely integrated with Asia/Pacific concerns, whether in regard to trade or even to cultural diplomacy.[2] Australia had long been aware that its links to Britain and Europe were fading, but it was not in favour of the United States simply replacing the Europeans. Australians grew more confident about their place in the world and, especially by the 1980s, were defining themselves far more in terms of their unique position in the booming Asia/Pacific region.[3]

Although China was never a major trading partner for Australia, Canberra has seen Peking as an important player in maintaining regional stability and as a power worth courting. The Peking massacre of June 1989 had a much greater impact on Australia's foreign policy than it did on Canada's, if only because of the nature of the more emotional prime minister, Bob Hawke.[4] But Australia remained concerned to limit the damage because it felt China was too important and therefore had to be woven into the web of regional politics.

Of course, Hong Kong, as a fast-growing NIC, was of more than passing interest to Australia. From Hong Kong's point of view in the early 1990s, Canada was more valuable as a destination for domestic exports, while Australia was just ahead, in ninth place, among destinations for Hong Kong's re-export trade. The two countries have roughly the same sort of trading stake in Hong Kong, but for an Australia anxious to build regional trade relations it is especially unsettling to see the fate of Hong Kong hanging in the balance. In earlier, more stable days, Australians were among some of the more flamboyant investors in Hong Kong. They were also some of the most committed to the idea of Pacific co-operation and saw Hong Kong as a vital base where they could weave their new overseas empires in the global market economy.[5] But the debates surrounding the seating of the Chinas in the Australian-inspired Asian Pacific Economic Co-operation Conference demonstrated the extent to which Australia was involved in the broader disagreements about defining the region.[6]

Like Canada, Australia had not been consulted in British negotiations about the colony and nor has it sought to be. Australia has also had its share of disagreement in the Commonwealth with Britain and would not wish to be seen as a defender of British colonialism. Indeed, with its special relationship with various former British colonies in the South Pacific, Australia holds up its own form of relations with former colonies as a more benevolent model. If anything, Australia has drifted further from closer relations with Britain than did Canada, and certainly there was nothing like the multilateral NATO or G-7 forum to set a new context for the relationship. The lingering connections through the Five-Power Defence Arrangements (FFDA) were not a major part of Australian or British defence policy.[7] After the end of the Cold War the FDPA took on added importance as a type of confidence-building measure in the region and Australia did join with Britain, the United States and other Western allies in the Gulf war of 1990/91. But in general it was still true that Australia felt itself to be more a part of Asia and certainly less connected with the European world. Hong Kong was seen primarily in the context of Asian politics and as a question more of relations with China than anything else. In typically blunt Australian fashion, the Hong Kong problem was judged one for Britain to manage, and alone. And yet, as the foreign minister Gareth Evans said on his trip to the colony in April 1991, Australia remained very concerned about how the transition to 1997 was handled, and thus implicitly was very interested in British policy.[8] Australian ambivalence about Hong Kong and its relations with Britain was obvious, and yet it was probably part of a more general Australian ambivalence about its relationship with Britain. This was evident yet again in February 1992, when Australia's new prime minister, Paul Keating, raised the issues of a new flag for Australia and Britain's alleged failure to defend Australia during the Second World War.

Although it is difficult to be precise about the changing nature of Australia's identity in the 1980s, the country was, as the Garnaut report in 1989 suggested, increasingly willing to accept its primary role as a player in the Pacific with a very special eye on East Asia. In contrast to Canada, which had good reason to maintain important transatlantic links, even while 'thinking Pacific', Australia became a player in the global economy, but with a much more obviously Pacific-based perspective. For that reason alone, Australian relations with Britain were likely to be cooler than in the Canadian case, and, not surprisingly, Australia seemed more willing to lean to the Chinese side when the matter of Hong Kong was raised. To some extent this Australian reaction was natural for a country less sure of its role than is Canada, but it also represented a degree of worry that Australia was simply becoming a less important place. With a long-standing tendency to blame Britain for such a position, long after it was even vaguely accurate, it was hardly surprising that Australia would be far less helpful on the Hong Kong problem than was Canada or the United States.

Of course, it was also true that Australia did not drain as many people from Hong Kong as Canada did, but the question of immigration into Australia was no less significant in domestic politics. Although the scale of the drain of people from the colony to Australia is not as large as it is to Canada, the essence of the problem remains the same. Precisely at the time when Britain wanted the people of Hong Kong to stay in place, Australia was drawing them away with a series of immigration schemes. Also like Canada, Australia had an ambiguous legacy in its immigration policy. In the last half of the nineteenth century there were four distinct phases in the development of a White Australia policy.[9] In the 1850s and 1860s there were minor and often temporary restrictive actions by individual colonies against Chinese immigrants. In the early 1880s there was an attempt at concerted restrictive action. In 1888 a fairly uniform restriction against Chinese immigration was adopted. And in 1901, well before Canada did so, an official White Australia policy was implemented.

The White Australia policy, or the Immigration Restriction Act, remained in place for seventy-two years, far longer than its equivalent in Canada. Between 1906 and 1914 White Australia received a considerable boost with the arrival of 393,048 British immigrants and by 1914 the Australian population reached nearly five million people. The inter-war years were an uncertain and then depressing time in both Canada and Australia. But as the societies evolved into more urban forms, the need for immigration became even more clear. The major programmes were designed to bring in Europeans and especially British immigrants. Empire settlement schemes involved incentives and direct collaboration with Britain. The inter-war years were clearly not tolerant years in the immigration policy of either Australia or Canada.[10]

The Second World War was a far more traumatic experience for Australia, which found its security threatened directly. But it was the Australian immigration minister, Arthur Calwell, who led the drive to a major immigration programme under the slogan 'populate or perish' but who reported also said 'two Wongs do not make a White'.[11] There was some diversification from British immigration, but there was still a focus on European immigrants. The official target was to increase the Australian population by one per cent per year, and this remained the target until the 1970s. Between 1947 and 1952 some 170,000 displaced Europeans were admitted. The 1961 census showed a population of 10.5 million, with 8 per cent European-born (228,000 Italians, 109,000 Germans, 77,000 Greeks, 60,000 Poles, 50,000 Yugoslavs). Between 1947 and 1971 some 991,431 British migrants arrived.

In December 1972 a Labour government under Gough Whitlam was elected and it brought in major changes in immigration policy in the following year. Although immigration policy had been changed in 1958, the 1973 legislation took a considerable act of leadership.[12] While the ban on non-Europeans was not total at that time (in 1971, 2,696 of 155,525 immigrants were non-European), only 185 immigrants in 1971 were Chinese. The new immigration package was sold by reducing overall numbers (50,000 in 1975), which allowed even a non-discriminatory policy to keep non-white numbers low. The Structured Selection Assessment System was introduced even though the far more fair Canadian point system had been considered. It would not be until 1979 that a Numerically-weighted Multi-factor Assessment System (NUMAS) was introduced, which was in turn amended in 1982 into the present Migrant Selection System. The Whitlam government began to shift to a multicultural policy and subsequent governments were to refine and entrench the principles.

By June 1982 the Australian population reached 15.2 million, of which 20 per cent were born overseas. In 1981/2 the immigration levels were back up to 118,700 and in 1978/9 a triennial rolling programme of immigration policy planning was introduced. The NUMAS system, which was closer to the Canadian point system, still put less weight on economic factors. The amendments later brought it closer into line with the Canadian system in its stress on family migration and the needs of the labour market.

The changes in the system allowed the gradual rise of non-white immigration. Of the 141,115 immigrants in 1989, only 26,987 were provided by Britain and Ireland, while Malaysia, Vietnam, Hong Kong, China and India provided 29,563. In 1988/9, of the 145,115 immigrants, 35.8 per cent (51,996) were from Asia and in the previous year the percentage was 32.4 per cent (46,469).[13] The number of people from Hong Kong had quintupled over the past seven years.[14] In 1988/9 Hong Kong contributed more people than any other location in Asia (9,975, or 6.9 per cent). In the fiscal year 1989/90 some 40 per cent of all immigrants and 57 per cent of all refugees to Australia came from Asia, although even in the early 1990s Asian migrants still accounted for under 4 per cent of the Australian population.[15] With 6.4 per cent of that total coming from Hong Kong (another 5.1 per cent from China) in 1990, the total inflow of 'Chinese' was still less than half the numbers coming from Britain and Ireland.[16] In early 1992 it was announced that, for the first time, quarterly immigration figures showed that Hong Kong had replaced Britain as the largest source of immigrants (14.4 per cent from Hong Kong and 13.1 per cent from Britain).[17] In early 1992 it was reported that the Chinese population in Australia had passed the 250,000 mark.[18]

Despite having only seventeen million people, race (apart from Aboriginal issues) has never become a violent public issue in Australia and the immigrants see the country as a relatively promising place which welcomes people with skills and talents. There have been controversial debates in the 1960s and 1970s, and briefly in the 1980s, but Australia has ranked with Canada among the most enlightened countries when it comes to keeping doors open. A detailed report on immigration, prepared by Dr Stephen Fitzgerald and delivered in June 1988, reported that immigration was, on balance, good for the economy.[19] But the debate surrounding the report suggested far more heat in the subject than was evident at any time in the recent history of Canada, where comparable percentages of immigrants were being absorbed. With a smaller population than Canada, Australia took in 140,000 immigrants in 1989, although the Fitzgerald reportedly urged 150,000 be taken. But the figure was down to 126,000 in 1990 and 110,000 in 1991, due to a reduction in the number of family reunions and the demand for skilled labour. In May 1992 Australia announced plans to cut immigration by 27 per cent, to about 80,000 people, in 1993. Stress would now be placed on skills, competence in English, and close relatives of earlier immigrants.[20] A study by the National Population Council in 1992 demonstrated that Australia had a system in place that could obtain the type of immigration that was of great benefit to the economy, but the recent stress on family reunions, rather than bringing in skilled people, was not making the best of the possibilities.[21] Thus the debate in Australia was often as much about what type of immigration as it was about absolute numbers.

In 1988/9, some 30 per cent of the Hong Kong immigrants were business migrants, 20 per cent family reunions and 40 per cent were described as 'independent migrants'. The pressure was so great that some 20,318 other people were refused immigration status from Hong Kong (21,425 from Vietnam were also refused). Total numbers of immigrants applying from Hong Kong rose sharply in the immediate aftermath of the Peking massacre in 1989 but in a matter of months the rates were back down to 500–1,000 per month.[22] The 1989 total number of visas issued was

10,477, an increase of 34 per cent over 1987 but slightly lower than the 10,600 in 1988. A minor uproar was caused in 1990 when Bob Hawke said a special migrant category would be created for the 20,000 Chinese students in Australia at the time of the Peking massacre.[23]

Asians alone could have taken up all the places in recent years but, like Canada, Australia operated an unofficial *de facto* system of country sub-quotas. The number of immigration officers in Hong Kong in 1985 has been increased from four to eleven, to cope with the particular demand from the colony, and yet even more people would come to Australia if even more officers were in place to process the applications at a faster pace. Vietnam furnished a regular supply of refugees – 112,000 by 1990, including almost 8,000 in 1989. The average migrant is twenty-seven years old, five years younger than the Australian average.

In 1989, of the 9,000 from all sources, there was a 35 per cent increase in business migrants from Hong Kong. In 1990 some 12,000 business migrants were estimated to produce $1.23 billion in capital investment per year.[24] By the early 1990s Australia had abandoned the idea of a specific minimum investment, in favour of specific criteria on the number of employees and export potential.[25]

Although there is much debate surrounding Australian immigration policy and the business migration scheme to boot, the aspect of the policy that so damages international relations (especially with Britain) has gone virtually unremarked. A cynic might suggest that Australia would actually be pleased if Britain were to make a major fuss over the issue, for it would be a useful diversion from the domestic Australian debate. Indeed, Australia, despite its smaller numbers of immigrants from Hong Kong, has been particularly tactless in pursuit of skilled migrants. When the Australian airline Qantas needed experienced airline technicians, it picked up 30 per cent of the staff of Cathay Pacific in Hong Kong by offering only half the pay but including passports.[26] This is, of course, part of a broader problem in Hong Kong of the haemorrhage of employees, but the Australian action was especially audacious at a time of particular sensitivity in the colony.

When the figures regarding the low take-up for the British right-of-abode scheme were published in March 1991, Australia, like Canada, felt that Britain would no longer press for a more helpful attitude to migration from Hong Kong. The people of Hong Kong who wanted to leave were clearly choosing North America and Australia as their prime destinations. Not until such action creates a real crisis of confidence in Hong Kong will there by any chance of halting the haemorrhage. Given continuing large flows to Australia and North America, and a lack of confidence in China, there can be no certainty that a major crisis still does not loom.

From the Australian point of view, such a risk of a major flow of immigrants or refugees touches on a number of concerns. Obviously, a major flood of people would challenge the delicate consensus on immigration and it is therefore not surprising that such risks are not discussed in the open. It is also felt that Britain would have the major problem and responsibility – and while Australia might help out, it would not have to take the lead. Australia prefers to focus on the Hong Kong problem in the context of its wider China policy and here there has been an evolution of policy after the events of 1989. As economic reform returned to the agenda in China, it was easier and more pleasant for Australia to focus on the possibility that, as Hong Kong and south China grew closer together, they would in effect create a new NIC in the region which would need Australian services and raw materials. Australia gradually came to have a stake in dealing with a more independent south China that was better integrated with the global market economy. This support for a version of convergence in Hong Kong was yet another reason for Australia to drift somewhat further from a concern with British policy and more towards a forward-looking strategy beyond 1997 that accepted and indeed welcomed a Hong Kong that was closely integrated with south China.

10

East Asia: Picking China Apart

Hong Kong has developed as a successful member of the Newly Industrialised Countries of East Asia and as a contributor to the booming regional economy of East Asia. But the success of these states has been based not only on their participation in the global market economy but also on the raw pragmatism in doing business. This very pragmatism will have a number of different effects with respect to the fate of Hong Kong. On the one hand, those who stand to benefit from business that Hong Kong might lose (e.g. Singapore) might not show much sympathy for the possible demise of Hong Kong. Others, such as Taiwan, might want to see the regime in Peking weaken, but because they might also benefit from the creation of a more independent south China Taiwan might also have a stake in helping Hong Kong converge with China. Still others in East Asia who might have hoped to pick up some of Hong Kong's business would worry more about their investment in Hong Kong and the general damage that might be done to business confidence in the region if Hong Kong should have a bumpy docking with China. Such countries (Japan or South Korea) might benefit if a more *de facto* independent south China means that other parts of China are also allowed to seek more natural connections to other neighbours. For many of China's neighbours, convergence leading to a south China strategy might well be the best option for the region.

Taiwan

Taiwan is roughly the size of Switzerland but has three times the population. It is geographically closer to Hong Kong than anywhere else except mainland China and has a larger stake in

151

the fate of Hong Kong than any other country. Despite being one of the most crowded countries in the world, Taiwan might have been expected to take a major interest in settling people wishing to leave Hong Kong. But Taiwan is not a country like any other – its government led by the Guomindang claims to be part of China and both it and the communist regime also claim to be rightful rulers of all of China. This legacy of the civil war which the communists won in 1949 ensures that, while Taiwan agrees with the mainland that Hong Kong is part of China and should return to the motherland, the people are not happy about Hong Kong being ruled by communists. Indeed, China has made such an explicit link between the fate of Hong Kong and the eventual fate of Taiwan that the Guomindang has deep misgivings about the fate of Hong Kong in 1997. If Hong Kong can be 'captured' by the slogan of 'one country, two systems', then can Taiwan hold out for much longer? If Hong Kong leads a more vibrant south China out of communism and into the international market economy as a powerful NIC, should Taiwan not be a part of the success story?

It would be wrong to treat Taiwan as just another Hong Kong. Taiwan has the size, population, distance from the mainland, and military power (including perhaps a nuclear potential) that Hong Kong lacked and the absence of which made it so vulnerable. Taiwan has nearly Hong Kong's level of prosperity and an even greater importance in the international trading system to make it a more than viable entity. Its sovereignty is challenged by the mainland, but it is not a colony as is Hong Kong. Taiwan is beholden to no power as a guarantor of its *de facto* independence. Indeed, it can be argued that all Taiwan lacks is general recognition as an independent state, for it has more than enough of all other attributes that most states might want and many official states lack.[1] Taiwan is unique, and so is its attitude to the Hong Kong problem.

The overall sense is that Taiwan is at a crossroads in its own self-definition, and many of the question marks about its own sovereignty are closely connected with key aspects of the Hong Kong problem. A confident Taiwan seeking recognition as an independent power might be glad to take immigrants from Hong Kong and it even might wish to lead a newly emerging unit in south China. But an uncertain Taiwan that fears a successful south China might stay aloof from the processes underway on the mainland alongside Hong Kong. The reality of modern Taiwan is a mixture of both emotions – a Taiwan increasingly integrated economically with China, but also growing less likely to accept its own political integration with the communist rulers of the mainland.

When the 1984 agreement between Britain and China was signed, Taiwan's official reaction was one of 'grave concern'. They officially offered help to those who wished to settle on Taiwan because it was claimed that the government on the mainland was a mere 'rebel group' and not the lawful rulers of China. They decried the violating of the human rights of the Hong Kong people who fled communism and did not want to be ruled by communists in 1997.[2] As it turns out, Taiwan actually held the documents signed by Britain and Imperial China that cover Hong Kong's present status. Britain, which had no diplomatic relations with Taiwan, apparently had no exchanges with the Taiwanese authorities on the subject of Hong Kong.[3] In August 1983 a task force of the Executive Yuan (Cabinet) in Taiwan was set up to monitor the negotiations on Hong Kong and after the 1984 deal it was upgraded to a co-ordinating panel under the vice-premier of the Executive Yuan.

One might have expected as much. But the real concern was apparently more to do with a fear that a successful integration of Hong Kong would make the attractions of 'one country, two systems' greater and thereby weaken Taiwan's own position. On the other hand, should there be a crisis regarding the integration of Hong Kong and China, the direction of the winds means that Taiwan is likely to receive more boat people from Hong Kong than anywhere else.[4] Lying only 360 miles away, Hong Kong is a three-day ride in a fishing boat in calm weather. Either way, Taiwan saw that it had something to lose.

The task force on Hong Kong and Macao affairs under the Executive Yuan decided on a three-point approach to Hong Kong. First, the Taiwanese government will work with 'democratic forces' in the colony. Second, they will use their existing institutions in the colony to foster the values desired by Taiwan. Third, they will counter the notion of 'one country, two systems' within the colony.[5] If this policy were taken seriously, it would have meant that Taiwanese officials would remain in Hong Kong to help undermine the 1984 accord and would do so after 1997. This would have been a serious test for the notion of two systems in Hong Kong and the mainland and Taiwanese authorities such as Vice-Premier Shih seemed to welcome the role as challenger.[6] But, in reality, Taiwan was far more cautious.

Taiwanese officials have made plain, even after the Peking massacre, that they really do not want to encourage large-scale immigration from Hong Kong. Foreign Minister Chien noted Taiwan is a crowded place with many mountainous areas unsuitable to large populations. 'I wish we could take more but our capacity is limited.' This line was at least more explicit than the one taken by the prime minister in 1984 when he said Taiwan will 'do its utmost' to help those who plan to move before the communists take over. The official government spokesman, Shaw Yu-ming, said (while he was an academic) that 'we should receive our compatriots warmly and with open arms for economic, political and humane reasons', but by 1990 and holding an official post he was far less welcoming.[7] Another Taiwanese official in 1989 said that, while entry procedures will be 'simplified' for those from Hong Kong wishing to come to Taiwan and contacts will be increased with the colony, 'the government will solve questions concerning Hong Kong taking into account our capability and the will of the Hong Kong people as two major considerations.'[8] In the region of 13,000 people in Hong Kong and Macao had apparently applied to settle in Taiwan by 1990 and no particular limit was placed on those who would be accepted as long as they were qualified.

The tougher line on taking in potential refugees from the mainland was at the same time as Taiwan was reporting a problem with a tide of alien workers who illegally entered the island. Rising wages and a strong currency had fed off a chronic shortage of labour in manufacturing and construction to attract tens of thousands of workers from Southeast Asia. Some 60,000 workers, mainly from the Philippines, Thailand, Malaysia and China, were said to be in the country illegally in 1990. Some estimates put the figure as high as 200,000.[9] Unlike South Korean industry, the smaller Taiwanese firms made it harder to keep track of people who seem to melt into the workforce. Obviously Taiwan could absorb a significant number of people from Hong Kong, but not necessarily the ones with money and skills who are now looking for safety in the developed world. Taiwan, which now searches for cheap labour in the mainland, might eventually find that if it is forced to take thousands of boat people from Hong Kong they can be found jobs in the manufacturing and construction sectors. In the meantime, Taiwan is happy enough to welcome investment from Hong Kong. In 1992 it was clear that large amounts were leaving Hong Kong for Taiwan, and just when other sources of investment in Taiwan were drying up.[10]

By the late 1980s Taiwan's *de facto* independence had become more clear and its interests were no longer that of a knee-jerk anti-communist. When the unrest took place in China in 1989 and Taiwan gradually became a more democratic country, many people in Taiwan questioned whether it was a good idea to persevere with the fiction of uniting with the mainland under Guomindang rule. Did Taiwan really want to give up its far better style of life for the poverty of the mainland? This is not to say that suddenly people wanted to be more independent, but that they recognised the advantages of relative independence which no longer needed the fiction of being the government of all China to sustain it.

What is more, economic prosperity also brought contacts with the mainland that gave economic benefits of closer co-operation without the liabilities of political union.[11] Thus Taiwan could assert a more sophisticated and a *de facto* more independent line on various issues, including the vital one of Hong Kong. The economic closeness between China and Taiwan had really only developed in the 1980s as the Chinese reforms opened up the mainland to pragmatic relations with all states. Taiwan was at first more cautious than the mainland, fearing that close contact would be a ploy to undermine Taiwanese defences. But increasing exchanges led Taiwanese to see just how dire was the state of the Chinese economy and the profits that could be made from contact. As Taiwanese labour grew more expensive, it was especially useful to be able to sub-contract work to the lower-waged people of the mainland and Taiwan began investing in China.[12] Increased contact with the mainland only made it clear how wide the gulf was between the two Chinas and basically reinforced the desire for *de facto* independence for Taiwan. In the meantime, China was interested in the trade and investment benefits and felt that just as convergence would bring Hong Kong into the motherland, so Taiwan would eventually succumb.

By the early 1990s the reality was that such a complex interdependence was growing up in south China that both Hong Kong and Taiwan could increasingly conceive of closer economic integration with a south China that was distinct from a Peking-ruled China. In 1990, Taiwan's indirect exports to China via Hong Kong totalled $3.3 billion. Exports to China were 6 per cent and imports were 2 per cent of Taiwan's total. By April 1990 Taiwan investment in China was said to total up to $3 billion, with 25 per cent going into Fujian (one third of the province's total foreign investment in 1990), with 42 per cent going to Guangdong and especially the Shantou SEZ. A Taipei trade centre was opened in Hong Kong in April 1991 as a conduit for investment in the mainland and in 1991 the Taiwanese government approved $200 million of investment in Hong Kong, a sharp increase on previous years.[13] By late 1991, Taiwan had 2,611 companies in Hong Kong, mostly for the China trade. By October 1991, 10 per cent of the investment on the Hong Kong Stock Exchange came from Taiwan.[14] In June 1992 the Bank of Taiwan was allowed to open an office in Hong Kong.[15] In January 1992 China and Taiwan began feasibility studies on establishing an economic zone grouping their countries as well as Hong Kong and Singapore. The zone was first proposed by Taiwanese and Hong Kong economists but then taken up by the Chinese as a way of getting greater convergence of the economies in the region.[16] China's agenda included a calculation that political unity would be gradually encouraged, but in both Hong Kong and Taiwan there was a hope that, as they were the economic powerhouses, this would serve to draw south China away from Peking and enhance their own freedom of manoeuvre. Similar variations in calculations had been evident when China allowed Hong Kong and Taiwan to join the Pacific Economic Co-operation Conference.[17]

By the early 1990s, Taiwan was coming to accept the notion of a south China integration strategy with far fewer misgivings. In March 1992 Taiwan even announced plans to encourage immigrants from Hong Kong who had special skills such as in engineering.[18] In general, Taiwan was growing far more relaxed about the movement of populations. Taiwan citizens will be able to visit Hong Kong after 1997 because it will be the Hong Kong authorities who will issue the visas, not China.[19] Indeed, Taiwanese officials promised that their representatives would stay in Hong Kong after 1997. The premier said in 1990 that the Republic of China 'would definitely support Hong Kong's political democratisation and economic liberalisation which will be the greatest threat to the Chinese communist regime'.[20] Mainland Chinese officials noted this determination and even publicly criticised the likely dislocation that would take place.[21] And yet to some extent this was all a bit of play-acting, for the pragmatic reality was that Taiwan was not manipulating politics in Hong Kong and was concentrating far more on enhancing economic co-operation in south China. It was increasingly recognised in Taipei that it was not sensible to pursue a strategy of overt independence, but that tacit independence could be best ensured by encouraging Hong Kong to help pull south China out of the grip of Peking and along a market economy route.

Needless to say, in all these increasingly close contacts in south China, Taiwan had little concern for British policy and the absence of official diplomatic relations made it somewhat more difficult for Britain and Taiwan to communicate. Of course, Taiwan knew that should the Anglo-Chinese agreement on Hong Kong break down and a rescue package be established, this might well include taking in many refugees from Hong Kong. But far more effort was being placed in Taiwan on ways of handling the fast-moving integration in south China. Taiwanese, like many people in Hong Kong and even China, were coming to realise that the fate of Hong Kong was increasingly being decided on factory floors in south China. Taiwan is likely to move to increasingly direct trade relations with south China in the hope that a more differentiated China will make fewer political demands on Taiwan and allow a more pragmatic approach to undefined sovereignty and booming economic prosperity. Direct links between Taiwan and parts of south China might lead to a diminution of the links between Taiwan and Hong Kong, but they would share a larger stake in a more independent south China and a more decentralized mainland China.

Singapore

Singapore, in keeping with its reputation for ruthless pragmatism, has adopted the cheekiest of policies towards the Hong Kong problem. In a strategy of betting on various options, it is prepared for most. Singapore has sought better relations with Hong Kong, Peking and Taiwan and placed itself in a position whereby, if business should bleed out of Hong Kong, some of it will think of moving to Singapore. A somewhat more attractive bet is on the emergence of a new south China economic unit that makes great play of the connections in the overseas Chinese world. Thus even if the transition of Hong Kong into China does not go particularly well, Singapore will hope that the south China strategy survives and it is well placed to benefit.

On one level it can be argued that, if there is a single rival for Hong Kong, it is the equally crowded and successful island state of Singapore. Both places have high savings rates, low taxation and high economic growth. As a rival NIC, Singapore might be expected to gain from business that flees Hong Kong and it even might profit from the exodus of people from the colony. But the two tiny NICs are also very different. Singapore has less than half the population and GDP of Hong Kong although per-capita rates of GDP are similar. Singapore may have built its success on a Chinese population just as Hong Kong did, but the method of government has been radically different. The light hand of authority in Hong Kong contrasts with the straight-laced and mild authoritarianism of Singapore. While both societies have lived, in part, in fear of the future, the security of Singapore has been far more assured and it has therefore been able to develop a remarkable regional and international role given the size of the state. Another contrast is that while Hong Kong has had to get on with its future owner in China, Singapore, until 1990, has had no official diplomatic relations with China but its leadership has maintained good relations with the government in Peking as part of a pragmatic approach to politics. Trade relations have existed but Singapore has managed to keep its distance from the communist authorities on the mainland.

But it would be misleading to make too much of the rivalry between the two tiny NICs. Singapore, although it offered permanent resident status to some 25,000 Hong Kong Chinese and their dependents (some 100,000 people) in 1990, is well aware that it is not as attractive to the people of Hong Kong as other developed parts of the Pacific rim in North America or Australia. Singapore itself reportedly loses some 16,000 Chinese a year to these other parts of the rim as many people find it difficult to live with the straight-laced style of life.[22] In 1988, when about 6,000 foreigners were granted citizenship, some 4,707 families – mostly skilled people, of which 78 per cent were Chinese – left Singapore. This drain was taking place along with the demographic shifts which projected a sharply reduced birth-rate. The offer to the Hong Kong people required that they had a recognised university degree or were assured of earning a base salary of more that S$1,500 a month. They would be granted an employment pass for some three years. Those wishing permanent residency and eventually citzenship must have secondary education, a minimum of S$1,500 per month in earnings and five years' work experience. Applicants can get approval in principle for five years, renewable for another five. Only if their families move to Singapore first do all of them need to apply for permanent residency immediately. A business investment scheme was amended to accept those applying for permanent residency who invest less than the previous minimum of S$1 million, so long as the investment is approved by the Economic Development Board.

The Singapore offer deepened a debate in the state as to why they were losing so many people and a discussion of the contrasts between the two societies. The debate also focused on whether Singapore really needed so many more people, who would add to the 76 per cent majority who are already ethnically Chinese and depress the high wages that local residents already receive. Concern was also expressed about the different business styles and, especially because the admixture of Hong Kong is Cantonese, the different qualities from those of the Hokkienese of Singapore.[23]

In the last years of the Lee Kuan Yew era in Singapore, there was a great soul-searching in the state about its true nature and the reasons why it had problems in keeping its own people. Singapore remains fascinated by what it sees as Hong Kong's glamour in the film industry and the music world.[24] The opportunity to import a bit of the Hong Kong spirit is both an opportunity for Singapore and a challenge to its conservative ways.

Yet this lack of confidence in Singapore has not prevented it from giving advice to Britain, China and Hong Kong on the best way to manage the transition to and beyond 1997. Lee Kuan Yew, on a visit to Hong Kong in January 1990, cautioned the people of Hong Kong not to see in democracy a real check on the behaviour of communist cadres. This was not a surprising judgement given the lack of parliamentary opposition in Singapore, but it was laced with a degree of *schadenfreude* when Lee added 'Hong Kong is subordinate to Beijing's overall sovereignty' and China only envisaged Hong Kong being governed in the same undemocratic ways that operated under British rule.[25] Lee argued that so long as that principle was accepted, then Hong Kong would prosper because China needed it as part of the open-door strategy. He had little time for those who sought to shun China after the Peking massacre. His view was that the region, and indeed Hong Kong, should not argue about politics. They should 'argue about economics' because that is what the prosperity of the region is built upon.[26]

This notion of economics in command has been at the root of Singapore's success, but it has also created the conservative climate that bothers some people and makes the city less attractive as a place of immigration for Hong-Kongers. Needless to say, from Britain's point of view this attitude on the part of Singapore is basically positive. The offer of 25,000 places was apparently made without a requirement for residency in Singapore, thus satisfying a British concern that the colony not be drained before it has a chance to stand on its own. Singapore has also been among the more constructive members of the Commonwealth and one that is concerned about the fate of Hong Kong. Although Britain is not the power it once was in Singapore, it is still an important trade partner and a provider of defence for Singapore through the Five-Power Defence Arrangements. As an NIC in the Pacific, Singapore has obviously been a major player in ASEAN (the Association of South East Asian Nations) and in the creation of APEC (Asia–Pacific Economic Co-operation), but it has also tried to ensure that bridges are built to the EC, so not to create exclusive trading blocs. As the quintessential middleman in international politics, Singapore has prospered in an open system.

It is precisely this desire to keep the international trading system open that has led some to believe that Singapore would not have a stake in seeing the fading of Hong Kong. Lee Kuan Yew has said that 'what Hong Kong loses, Singapore may also lose because she will lose Hong Kong's multiplier effect'.[27] This belief that there are mutually beneficial economic relations that stem from a generally booming region has apparently led Singapore to make major investments in Hong Kong, even after the knock to confidence in 1989. In keeping with his concern with the possible creation of trading blocs in the EC and the new confidence in Europe that may create new problems for the East Asian economy, Lee Kuan Yew has said that there are common interests among the NICs in making sure the international economy functions as a global system. To this end, a vibrant Hong Kong must be part of the strategy.[28] Singaporean officials have urged their firms to increase investments in Hong Kong in order to stabilise confidence in the colony and the region, although by 1992 there was little to show for the exhortations.[29] Indeed, some doubt must be cast on the notion of Singapore investing in Hong Kong. Singapore's strategy in 1991 was also to encourage Taiwan to leave Hong Kong and use Singapore as a conduit for investment in China.[30] Most probably Taiwan, like Singapore, was seeking to spread its risks. Clearly there were major rivalries in a wider south China that tried to include Singapore, Hong Kong, Taiwan and southern Chinese provinces.

Thus there continued to be more than a hint of suspicion that Singapore is more rival than friend of Hong Kong. Singapore's investment in Hong Kong is not negligible, but neither is it vital. Singapore has tended to export capital far more to low-wage neighbours, such as Malaysia or Thailand, in search of trading advantage. It has exported capital to more developed parts of the world such as North America and the EC in search of better advantage in local markets. But Hong Kong remains more of a rival. This relative lack of investment has not prevented a vibrant trading relationship with Hong Kong, but Singapore tends to run a clear trade surplus with Hong Kong.

In 1990, Hong Kong took 6.5 per cent of Singapore's exports, up from 6.1 per cent in 1984. In the same period, Hong Kong rose as a source of imports from 2 per cent to 3 per cent of Singapore's total imports. In the same period, Singapore's exports to China increased only from 1 per cent to 1.5 per cent and imports from China declined from 4.6 per cent to 3.4 per cent of Singapore's total. In 1990 Singapore ranked sixth among exporters to Hong Kong, with 4 per cent of the market. In 1989 Singapore took seventh place as a home for Hong Kong's domestic exports and the same place for Hong Kong's re-exports. Singapore clearly had a stake in Hong Kong as a re-export base for trade with China, but with the establishment of diplomatic relations between China and Singapore there could be confidence that Hong Kong will be needed far less as a place through which to channel trade with China.

Singapore might have had a chance earlier in the 1980s to pick up business from Hong Kong, especially in the financial sector, but that window has closed. Tokyo has taken up some of the slack and those who are more confident about the 1984 accord see people being reluctant to move from what is a far more comfortable base than Singapore.[31] But by 1989 there was far less confidence in Hong Kong's ability to compete, especially as people began leaving the colony in increasing numbers. Attention then turned to the matter of whether Singapore could take advantage of its new opportunity.

The main contest has been about whether Singapore can take over as the region's main financial centre. Some analysts have suggested Hong Kong is still ahead but Singapore is closing the gap.[32] Hong Kong's style is free-wheeling, in contrast with that of Singapore, where there are limits on the 'quality of financial advice' and speculation with the Singapore dollar. But businessmen are less worried about the press controls in Singapore and are far more worried about the potential for exchange controls as well as press controls in a future Hong Kong. Singapore already has a larger foreign-exchange market, a healthier financial futures exchange, and a banking system which, although smaller than that in Hong Kong, has avoided as many bankruptcies. More Asian dollar bonds are issued from Singapore than from Hong Kong. The British colony is the region's pre-eminent gold market but Singapore has an active market in rubber and a spot and futures market in oil. Hong Kong also leads in the provision of legal services, but Singapore boasts lower rental rates and executive wages in its business district. The infrastructure is somewhat better in Singapore, certainly when it comes to airport facilities. The container port in Singapore is now larger than that in Hong Kong. Singaporeans speak better English, the language of international commerce, and increasingly come out ahead on broader educational standards.

The Hong Kong dollar is pegged to the United States dollar, while that of Singapore 'tracks' the American dollar rate. Both are in the same time zone as Singapore adjusted its own position in 1982 to fall into line with Hong Kong. Both places make use of hinterlands nearby for lower-wage production bases. Service industries make up 70 per cent of both places' economy and provide by far the greater part of employment. Both places have adopted increasingly similar rules for their stock markets and financial regulation.[33] The financial sectors have focused on different niches, although Hong Kong's managers have ten times the funds to invest. Foreign lending out of Hong Kong tends to focus on China, Japan and South Korea, while in Singapore the focus is on Southeast Asia.

In sum, there is much to the argument that Singapore could pick up business from Hong Kong as the latter faded slowly. Only if the fading of Hong Kong was rapid would confidence be hit in the region as a whole, which eventuality would affect business in Singapore. Thus there is good sense in Singapore's present position of making no loud noises about wishing to see the demise of Hong Kong but also making it plain that it is ready to do business should the opportunity become available. Unlike Taiwan, Singapore does seem ready to take people who can make the business environment more effective and indeed solve some of the image problems that Singapore now has. Neither does Singapore plead over-crowdedness, as does Taiwan, for it is more far-sighted about what makes good business sense. Singapore can also not be accused of draining Hong Kong's main resource – its people – and in this way it avoids conflict with Britain. So far, Singapore is playing a pragmatic game in a pragmatic region. And even if Hong Kong should prosper as part of a south China strategy, Singapore is also well placed to benefit as part of the wider overseas Chinese community. It seems hard to believe that Singapore can lose with a betting strategy like this.

Japan

As the main economic power in the East Asian region, and indeed the world's second-largest economy, Japan is obviously a major actor in determining the fate of Hong Kong. Should the transition to Chinese rule in Hong Kong become problematic, Japan will be among the first to be affected. This is not merely a matter of Japan's growing investment in Hong Kong coming under threat; it is also because Japan puts a very high premium on keeping regional politics on an even keel in order to provide the best environment for economic growth. But unlike either Singapore or Taiwan, Japan will play virtually no role in matters concerning migration from Hong Kong. Japan has little interest in taking people from the colony and is among the toughest in the world about not wanting a refugee problem on its shores. Japan hopes that by using its major economic power it can help build confidence in Hong Kong and therefore avoid having to face either an economic or refugee crisis.

As befits its status as a major trading nation, Japan is a major player in the trade and investment picture in both China and Hong Kong. If one discounts the anomaly of China's trade with Hong Kong, Japan has been China's largest trade partner, accounting for 15 per cent of China's total trade in 1990 (down from 30 per cent in 1985, and compared with the 1990 figures for the USA, 19.2 per cent and the EC, 16.8 per cent).[34] Yet China's economic relationship with Japan remains far below its potential. China ranked eleventh among Japan's export markets in 1990, and fourth among sources of imports, accounting for only 2.1 per cent of Japan's exports (4.2 per cent in 1984) and 5.1 per cent of its imports (the largest source of Japanese imports in Asia, up from 4.3 per cent in 1984). Japan's investment in China was only $438 million or 5.3 per cent of the total for Asia and less than one per cent of Japan's total overseas private investment. Some 60 per cent of the total Japanese trade with China was controlled by the top five trading companies, suggesting an extraodinary ability on the part of China and Japan to manipulate the pattern of trade – and accounting, to some degree, for the relatively large fluctuations in the patterns of trade.[35]

In part because of the shifts in Sino-Japanese trade, and in part because the relationship was so important to Japan (even if it was underdeveloped), Japan was clearly anxious to avoid serious damage to its trade relations with China after the Peking massacre. Indeed, it has become a major feature of Japanese policy in East Asia to ensure that 'the China problem' does not become a major feature of regional instability. To that end, Japan was crucial in getting the G-7 meeting in Houston in 1990 to allow a resumption of contacts with China on an individual basis. Japan clearly perceives a stake in the stability of China and its continued connection to the regional and global trading economy.[36]

Japan is also a major investor and trader with Hong Kong. With more than 10,000 Japanese living in Hong Kong and 1,500 tourists per day visiting the colony (half that number of Hong Kong people visit Japan), there is clearly a Japanese stake in a stable Hong Kong.[37] Hong Kong ranks among the top five of Japan's trade patterns and the top ten of its destinations for investment.

By the mid-1980s some 1,000 Japanese firms had operations in Hong Kong. By 1990, Japan ranked second (behind China) as a source of imports, accounting for 16 per cent. Japan ranks fifth as a destination of domestic exports, accounting for 5.8 per cent, and third as a destination of re-exports (6.4 per cent). Therefore it is not surprising that Japan apparently offered its services to Britain and China when the talks on Hong Kong seemed to reach a difficult stage,[38] and Japan was pleased to see the 1984 accord on Hong Kong as the best way to preserve the economic prosperity that Japan so treasured.[39] As long as there was a relative degree of confidence in Hong Kong, Japan saw no need to take an especially high profile on the Hong Kong question. But by the later 1980s, as Japan's international role increased and the confidence in Hong Kong was sapped, so Japan increased its profile as a supporter of convergence between the colony and China and of confidence in its economic future.

Yet economic relations between Hong Kong and Japan have not always been smooth and to some extent Japan did stand to benefit from the fading of Hong Kong as a regional economic centre. Japanese have been the target of rioting in Hong Kong, as in China, concerning school textbooks and the general legacy of the Second World War, especially as Japan's economic profile seemed to grow so fast in the East Asian region.[40] Hong Kong traders used to complain about the difficulty of breaking into the Japanese market and it was only in the later 1980s, with the appreciation of the yen, that this issue began to fade as a focus of trade disputes.[41]

At the same time Japan sharply increased its stake in Hong Kong. The rising yen made Japanese investment far more viable and Japanese banks, manufacturers and retailers began arriving in droves. By 1987 there were more Japanese banks in the colony than banks from any other country. Investment in manufacturing industry from Japan in 1987 was $420 million, compared with $725 million for American companies. By the end of 1990, the Japanese figure had risen to $1.25 billion, just edging past the United States for the first time and accounting for 31.5 per cent of total investment in manufacturing in Hong Kong. But because of rising land and labour costs, Japanese investment in banking and insurance ($2 billion), services ($1.6 billion) and commercial groups ($1.5 billion) was far outstripping investment in manufacturing. In 1990 Hong Kong had come to rank second, behind Indonesia, as a location of Japanese investment in Asia.[42] When one considers that the rapid rise of Japanese banks also posed a threat to Hong Kong as Tokyo began to take on some of the international financial roles once held dearly by Hong Kong, it is clear that Japan was taking a pragmatic view of Hong Kong.[43] Japanese investment was sufficiently flexible and movable to lead to it being moved to other locations if a developing crisis in the colony made it economically sensible to do so.

After the 1989 crisis in confidence in Hong Kong, Japan was ready to make its views clear to China and Hong Kong. Japan wanted continued trade relations with China, and it also wanted confidence in Hong Kong. Japan had little interest in such issues as democracy and seemed entirely focused on the political economy questions of building business confidence.[44] Japan wished to see Hong Kong seated in Asia Pacific Economic Co-operation as an expression of confidence. As a result of concern over its investments – the second-largest location of Japanese FDI (Foreign Direct Investment) in Asia, Japanese firms were among the first to signify confidence in Hong Kong after June 1989 by announcing major investment programmes, and, by September, Japanese banks were backing major infrastructure investments. Japan was clearly concerned both about regional stability and its specific stake in Hong Kong. As a more confident regional economic power, Japan also felt able to take a more active role. By 1990 there were some 1,500 Japanese firms operating in Hong Kong. New manufacturing investment had outstripped that of the long-time leaders, the United States. Property purchases, new banks and 40 per cent of department stores were visible signs of the continuing Japanese commitment.

The Japanese stake in Hong Kong was a complex mix of factors. To some extent, Japan saw Hong Kong as an important NIC in its own right and therefore an important part of the regional and global market economy. But Japan also saw Hong Kong as the gateway to the China trade, although not nearly to the same degree as other Western investors. By the end of 1991 only some 100 Japanese firms were operating in Shenzhen.[45] Of course, Japanese investment in China was always more likely to focus on the more northern coastal sections closer to Japanese corporate bases. Just as Taiwanese and Hong Kong money saw south China as a natural economic territory (NET), so Japan and Korea saw NETs along the Yangtze river or in north China. To an important extent Japan therefore had a far smaller stake in the survival of Hong Kong as part of an integrated southern Chinese zone. What Japan was more concerned with was the general strategy of regionalizing Chinese economic policy and, to the extent that the creation of a NET in south China was conducive to the creation of a NET along the Yangtze or in north China, Japan had a stake in the convergence of China and Hong Kong. But clearly the Japanese view was different from that of many other Chinese trading partners.

Thus there are real limits to Japan serving as the filler of the vacuum that developed as confidence was lost after June 1989. Japanese investment appeared far more mobile and headquarters could be placed elsewhere if the business climate went bad. Japanese calculations seemed to be short term, but with little specific affection for Hong Kong. A large part of the recent surge may simply have been a function of the appreciation of the yen and not a specific calculation about Hong Kong's crisis of confidence. Japanese investment in Europe and North America was growing faster than investment in Asia, suggesting Japan really was operating as a global actor. It was Japanese banks more than any other players who could make or break such major investment projects as the new airport in Hong Kong, but these decisions would be made on the basis of global trends in interest rates and rates of return on investment around the globe. It is still notable that Japanese have by and large steered clear of big real-estate purchases, preferring more liquid investments, both in China and Hong Kong.[46]

Yet there is growing evidence that Japan does take the fate of Hong Kong seriously enough to raise the matter with the Chinese.[47] Japan's consul-general in Hong Kong said in 1990 that 'we talk frequently about the future of Hong Kong in our day-to-day contact in Peking'. Hong Kong has been included in high-level meetings between Japanese and Chinese leaders. In June 1991 Toshiki Kaifu, the Japanese prime minister, told the Chinese foreign minister that Japan attaches great importance to Hong Kong and wants to see it remain as a stable financial centre. Mr Kaifu also noted 'it is important for Hong Kong to maintain its economic freedom and vitality for the development of China's reform and Open Door policy, as well as for Sino-Japanese and Sino-British relations'.[48]

Similar messages were expressed by the Japanese foreign

minister to Zhou Nan, director of Xinhua in Hong Kong, in October 1991 and Zhou reiterated his appreciation of increased Japanese investment in Hong Kong.[49] As expected, Japan raises economic issues but steers clear of questions related to the political system in Hong Kong. Much like Singapore, it considers the two issues to be divisible and sees little reason to provoke the Chinese by discussion of democracy. Japanese businessmen are notably hard-nosed about calls for greater democracy in Hong Kong as a necessary condition of maintaining the freedoms of the colony after 1997. The decision of the G-7 summit at Houston in 1990 to allow Japan to reopen for business with China was not based on much affection for the Chinese, but on a sense that Japan needed to help maintain stability in its home region. Britain, with a common interest with Japan to reopen contacts with the Chinese over Hong Kong, joined with the United States, who had more strategic reasons for doing business with China.[50] The upshot was a coincidence of interests, all of which were hard-nosed and all of which supported the notion of convergence between the mainland and Hong Kong.

The tough Japanese approach is also seen clearly in its attitude to immigration. Japan is a remarkably homogenous country which takes a very dim view of any immigration.[51] The poor treatment of the 500,000 ethnic Koreans in Japan is a well-known story of Japanese ethnocentrism. But with a rising labour shortage, the number of foreigners living illegally in Japan rose sharply in the late 1980s. The largest number of illegal aliens in 1991 was from the Philippines (27,226), with a further 25,848 from Korea (out of a total of 159,828).[52] In 1989 when 1,600 Chinese tried to join the other thousands of illegal immigrants in Japan, this time posing as Vietnamese refugees, Japan was swift and summary in sending them back to China.[53] Some 2,400 boat people had landed in 1989, which compared with 219 in 1988 and 265 in 1987. Of the more than one million Vietnamese who fled since 1975, Japan took in only 6,400.[54] Japan prefers to offer money to places like Hong Kong to hang on to the refugees it has, rather than take any into the country.[55] While Britain and Hong Kong were sharply criticised by the United States for forcibly repatriating Vietnamese in 1989, Japan escaped without taint when, within months of the Peking massacre, it returned Chinese to the mainland.[56] On immigration issues the Japanese took a consistently tough line in defending their isolated island status.

Thus there can be little doubt that Japan would take a very dim view of large-scale immigration from Hong Kong and certainly would be unwilling to participate in an international effort to resettle Hong Kong people who wished to leave the colony. The maze of registration procedures in Japan is legendary. The necessity to apply for licences for a host of mundane tasks makes Japan a less than likely landing place, at least for any length of time.

From Britain and Hong Kong's point of view, in the short term Japan is one of the more constructive players in the East Asian relationship with the colony. As a major investor who places a high priority on relations with China, it supports the principles of the 1984 accord and the notion of convergence. It was seemingly not rattled by the events of 1989 and has remained consistent in support of building confidence. Indeed, from Britain's point of view, no country, except perhaps the United States, has been as constructive as Japan.

Yet there must be some doubt in the future about Japan's attitude. Japan is likely to be ruthless about economic calculations and is reasonably well placed to move much of its investment out of Hong Kong if necessary. Japan is not heavily tied in to investment in south China and sees the creation of NETs along the Yangtze and in north China as more vital to its interests. To an important extent Japan can be seen as a rival of Hong Kong and south China. And if there should be a crisis in Hong Kong, neither is Japan likely to help on the issue of refugees or immigration. In the short term this carefully ambiguous attitude in Japan about the fate of Hong Kong suits Britain. It certainly suits Britain and other interested market economies to suggest that Japan has a growing stake in a successful convergence between China and Hong Kong. But if a crisis should develop, it is likely that Japan will pull out what investment it can from south China and perhaps help in funding an Orderly Departure programme should one be organised for refugees from Hong Kong. But on balance Japan would not be among the leaders of efforts to defend the interests of the Hong Kong people. So far, Japan has been a force for stability in Hong Kong. But no one should be under any illusion that this is based on anything but pragmatism about contacts with China. Should Hong Kong fade, Japan knows enough about the region to take its business elsewhere.

East Asia and Beyond

Taiwan, Singapore and Japan are by far the three most important countries in the region with a stake in the fate of Hong Kong. But by virtue of the nature of the colony as an international trading centre, it has also developed relations with a range of countries and, indeed, a range of countries have developed a stake of some sort in the fate of the territory. None of these other countries (only some of which are in East Asia) are as important as those already discussed, but they are important enough to be assessed, albeit briefly.

If one begins with the fourth of the Newly Industrialised Countries, South Korea, one sees a relationship focused almost entirely on trade and some investment. South Korea, divided as it is from its brethren in the communist North, had a cautious attitude towards dealing with communist states. But in the second half of the 1980s there was a boom in Sino-South Korean trade and now official trade relations have been established. In the early days of the South Korean *détente* with China, much of the trade went through Hong Kong in the pragmatic way of regional politics. South Korea ranked fifth among exporters to Hong Kong, with 4.5 per cent of the market. But it was not even among the top ten on Hong Kong's chart of domestic export destinations, although it did rank fifth on the list of re-export destinations, with 3.8 per cent of the business. Yet this figure was falling as south Korean trade with China increasingly went the direct route.

Indeed, as Sino-South Korean trade relations were normalised, it was increasingly clear that an NET was being created in northern China that, as in the case of Japanese economic relations with China, meant that Hong Kong and south China could increasingly be seen as a rival for those investing in and developing northern coastal China. As China encouraged regionalism as a way of converging with Hong Kong, Korea and to some extent Japan were more able to develop their own NETs with China and therefore care less about the fate of Hong Kong.

To be sure, as an NIC, South Korea had good reason to do business with Hong Kong in its own right. In 1990 some 4,000 Koreans and 150 registered firms were based in the territory. Lucky Goldstar, Daewoo, Hyundai and other major Korean firms operate regional offices in Hong Kong as investment is spread around the East Asian rim. But Korean investment in the colony is only $25 million as the majority of Korean funds have gone directly into the mainland, and along the north coast closer to South Korea.[57]

South Korea, like Japan, is unlikely to be a place where immigrants from Hong Kong would be welcome as it too has a tough record on any kind of immigration except from the north of the divided country. Like Singapore it also to some degree sees Hong Kong as a rival and would not be very sad to see it fade from the map. Although South Korea has no particular warmth for the communists in China, it does have a stake in closer economic relations with the mainland and would make that its main priority. As in the case of Japan, that priority does not mean a major stake in Hong Kong is essential for improving economic relations with China. Also like Japan, South Korea is in favour of Hong Kong converging peacefully with the mainland, which means it has little interest in seeing democracy come to Hong Kong. It seems that the people of Hong Kong have few friends in the region.

Further down the East Asia rim are Southeast Asian neighbours of Hong Kong. They have long been said to covet the business that Hong Kong has, or directs, in its low-wage operations across the border in China. The Philippines and Malaysia in particular have expected a dividend from a gradual collapse of Hong Kong as a business hub.[58] In the later 1980s there has been increasing evidence that Southeast Asians have benefited from the outflow of capital from Hong Kong and the interconnections of the local overseas Chinese. Thailand in particular has been host to various FDI projects led by Hong Kong capital in search of low-wage production bases that do not carry the risks of investment in China.[59] As part of the growing interconnections of regional investments, Hong Kong has been a leading player, especially as concerns have grown about the sense of investing so much in the Chinese basket.[60]

Southeast Asians are also creating their own NETs, especially around Singapore, and therefore there is great interest in Hong Kong as a source of investment funds and concern about Hong Kong and south China as a potential rival for other people's investment. Southeast Asia has benefited from Japanese, Taiwanese and Singaporean investment and thus might well take

'Singapore's side' when it came to a gradual drift of business to the city-state of Southeast Asia. The Southeast Asians would certainly not be keen to take many people from Hong Kong, even if some should decide to try to stay within the region. Countries like Malaysia and Indonesia in particular are sensitive about the powers wielded by their Chinese minorities and would be unwilling to see an increase in Chinese immigration.

The ASEAN (Association of South East Asian Nations) states have shared a common concern with Hong Kong over the flow of refugees from Vietnam that should not be allowed to stay in their country of first asylum,[61] but that is quite another matter from co-operating with Hong Kong over potential refugees from Hong Kong itself. The ASEAN states might, as in the case of the Vietnamese, be the first place that refugees might land, but they would expect the international community to organise a relief effort to take the people from Hong Kong somewhere else. In this respect they might be participants in an international meeting on Hong Kong, perhaps even in anticipation of an international effort to provide a package of places for potential refugees. But ASEAN states would remain unwilling to take refugees on any significant scale, even if the people of Hong Kong should want to settle there in the first place.

Malaysia, like Singapore, is also a member of the Commonwealth of states once members of the British empire. So far there have only been sporadic attempts to involve the Commonwealth on the Hong Kong issue, and the first attempt to do so brought sharp criticism from China that the Hong Kong issue was being internationalized. Yet it is striking how so many of the key actors in the Hong Kong question are Commonwealth members – Britain, Canada, Australia, Singapore and Malaysia.

When the Commonwealth met in Kuala Lumpur, Malaysia, in October 1989, in the wake of the Peking massacre, Britain raised the matter of some Commonwealth action on Hong Kong. At that time Britain was looking for signs from the international community to China that there was a problem with confidence in the colony and China would have to take a more positive line towards the concerns of the Hong Kong people. As it turned out, Hong Kong was only discussed in the corridors of the Commonwealth meeting and an official statement was released giving Hong Kong qualified support. Concern was expressed about maintaining Hong Kong's special status as a trading and financial centre and 'those in a position to do so' were urged to take concrete action to establish confidence and prosperity. Britain had hoped for stronger language but, after British blocking tactics over sanctions against South Africa, there was little inclination to help Britain out over Hong Kong.[62]

Legco leaders lobbied the Commonwealth meeting but with little practical result. Hong Kong was not represented at the meeting, although it does participate as a separate member in the Commonwealth Games. There have been some suggestions that Hong Kong find a place in the Commonwealth after 1997, although the organisation would need to change its rules to include a non-sovereign state. Certainly as a sign of its special international status it would be a sensible idea, at least if Peking did not oppose such efforts to internationalise the Hong Kong question.

It seemed clear that the Commonwealth could not serve as a major forum for discussing the Hong Kong question. Although there was a great deal of accumulated expertise about matters of decolonisation, the Hong Kong question was always unique in that respect and did not mirror any of the previous cases. Nor was the Commonwealth united enough on such matters to take a clear stance, let alone one that would be in the teeth of opposition from China. In the case of some future discussion about co-ordinated policy regarding a nationality package, the Commonwealth might again be called upon to help organise a concerted policy. But so long as Canada, Australia and even Singapore took such different lines from Britain on the Hong Kong matter, there could be little more than the expression of concern that came out of the Kuala Lumpur meeting.

Finally, there have been a host of other countries, some of which are former British colonies, that have offered citizenship to the people of Hong Kong, sometimes much to the annoyance of Britain. Perhaps one of the more audacious offers has come from South Africa, which is concerned about its own drain of talent. South Africa was seeking such specific people as nuclear chemists, doctors, geologists and system analysts, but by March 1990 there were barely seventy applicants.[63] The South Africans said that those with the required skills would be able to obtain approval to immigrate from Hong Kong within a couple of weeks instead of the previous regulation whereby employment had to be obtained first. The South African business immigration package was also liberalised so that those with only a minimum of HK$600,000 could qualify and they need not actually transfer their money to South Africa. Citizenship would be granted after residence in South Africa for five years. In 1988 only four permanent residence permits were issued from the consul-general in Hong Kong and the total was two in 1989.[64] There are about 15,000 Chinese in South Africa and it looked like there were unlikely to be many more. But the South African scheme, like that of Singapore, at least had the virtue of not requiring immigration immediately. By offering a kind of insurance policy (according to some views, out of the frying pan and into the fire), there was a widening net of nationality packages, as Britain wanted. Although it was too impolitic in Britain to express any thanks for the South African offer, it was among the more constructive efforts to plan for the future.

Some of the less plausible bolt-holes included Belize, which offered a passport in exchange for an investment of $23,000 in a state-run investment fund for the benefit of the state. There was no need to live in Belize to benefit from such a scheme and there were still some twenty serious applicants a day in late 1989.[65] Gambia set a price of only $15,000 and other destinations included Tonga ($16,500 per person and $23,000 per family), Fiji (an annual income of $12,820), Iceland, Sri Lanka and Honduras. Not surprisingly, some opportunists were running a thriving trade in genuine and fake documents.[66] A crisis of sorts broke out in Tonga in 1991 after 'irregularities' were revealed in the sale of 400 passports to Hong Kong people.[67] Manuel Noriega's nephew allegedly sold Panamanian passports for $10–15,000 a piece and some 3,000 people reportedly took up the deal. The sum of $16,000 reportedly bought a passport to the Federal Republic of Corterra, an idyllic island in the South Pacific that never existed.[68]

It is hard to believe that many of the applicants to the less desirable countries actually intended to settle. The passport auction was simply symptomatic of the fear and uncertainty in Hong Kong and the range of countries that were ready to capitalise on those feelings. While it might also suggest the range of countries that might be involved in some international relief effort for those in Hong Kong who wanted to leave, it remained true that the overwhelming number of people wanted to go to Canada, Australia, the United States and Britain. Not surprisingly, wealthy people wanted to go to wealthy countries.

The fate of Hong Kong clearly did not depend on decisions made about immigration, but the evident pragmatism and self-interest suggested a great deal about how a crisis in Hong Kong might be handled. Far more important was the economic interests of Hong Kong's fellow Asians, for they demonstrated that, while they had an intrinsic interest in doing business with Hong Kong, they also had other options. While many favoured convergence between Hong Kong and south China, for some states this was merely part of a broader strategy of encouraging the creation of various NETs around China. For those such as Korea and Japan who might even see a south China NET as a rival, there were distinct limits to the support they might extend to saving Hong Kong.

11

Europe: Someone Else's Problem

Inasmuch as Hong Kong is still seen as a British problem, and Britain's foreign and even domestic policies are increasingly linked to its continental European partners, any consideration of the fate of Hong Kong needs to take into account the role of the Europeans. But unlike the other interested states discussed in previous chapters, the Europeans are distracted by the building of their own economic and military structures, the risks of war in Eastern Europe and the perils of mass migration from Eastern Europe, the former Soviet Union and North Africa. Europe has been interested in the economic prosperity of Hong Kong as a part of an increasingly important East Asian economy, but, other than in London, a gradual fading of Hong Kong would be of little concern in Europe.

Economic Issues

Most analysts make short shrift of the European relationship with China, let alone Hong Kong.[1] Certainly in comparison with the United States, Europe has been of far less strategic importance. In the late 1970s there was some talk of China as the sixteenth member of NATO, but China's shift to a more independent foreign-policy position in the 1980s made any such discussion obsolete.[2] For the Europeans, the relationship with the Soviet Union was always more important than the ties to China and thus even arms sales to China were constrained by the perception of the wider strategic interests. The East Europeans were also constrained by strategic factors, namely Soviet domination, from pursuing an independent relationship with China, at least until later in the 1980s when the Soviet Union decided to improve relations with China.[3] In the post-Cold War world both parts of Europe became far more inwardly focused as they dealt with the challenges of 1992, the disintegration of the Soviet Union, and democratic transition. China, let alone Hong Kong, was of far less importance than before 1989, which made Britain even more isolated on the subject.

For much of the Cold War period economic relations between China and Europe were focused on Western Europe, at least since the Sino-Soviet split and the normalisation of Western relations with China in the 1970s. In the 1970s Western Europe was the second-largest partner in trade with China (after Hong Kong), but by the late 1980s this trade seemed to be in decline and EC states constituted roughly 10 per cent of China's total.[4] Nevertheless, by 1990 the EC ranked just behind the United States as China's third-largest trade partner. If one discounted the anomalies of China–Hong Kong trade, the EC could be counted, along with Japan and the United States, as one of China's three primary trade partners. China saw Western Europe, as it did the United States, as a source of capital, technology and talent. As a Chinese scholar bluntly put it, 'Of particular interest to China is the fact that Western European countries have been more liberal than other Western countries in sales of technology.'[5] China understood that playing off one European against the other, let alone against other OECD states, was a good way to drive a harder bargain.

Although Britain was the first major European power to establish diplomatic relations with the communists in China, it was France (in 1978) that signed the first agreement on scientific and technological co-operation. In 1983–85, Germany, France, Italy and Holland signed nuclear co-operation agreements with China. In these senses China's relations with Europe were a priority of foreign policy.[6]

Nevertheless, the EC's portion of China's foreign trade has fluctuated as China widened its relations with OECD countries. EC trade with China totalled 20 per cent in the 1970s, in 1986 its share was 15.7 per cent and 12–14 per cent in the late 1980s and early 1990s. Of course, the volume of trade regularly increased in this period, but the relative weight of trade with Europe basically fluctuated as Japan and the United States altered their trade with China more substantially. What is more striking is that China's trade with EC members remains very uneven, with Germany taking 34 per cent of total EC trade with China in 1990, Italy 13 per cent, France 12 per cent and others even lower percentages. When considering the slightly rising East European trade with China in the 1980s before the revolutions of 1989, Europe's total share of trade with China was about one quarter. Perhaps most importantly from China's point of view, the EC, although not China's main lender, was still a major source of funds.[7] In 1987 the EC four (UK, Germany, France, Italy) provided nearly 20 per cent of all external loans for China and in the period 1979–87 Western Europe invested $1.75 billion in China, compared with the $1.93 billion from Japan and the $1.77 billion from the United States in the same period.

The record suggests there is a European stake in good relations with China and a Chinese stake in keeping open this other door to Western capital, technology and assistance. But the relationship has not been problem-free. The limits imposed by COCOM regulations have slowed down the transfer of technology. Although the EC signed a textile agreement with China in 1979 and in 1980 agreed to extend preferential trade terms, China still belongs to the fifth category of trade partners (state-controlled) and thus a relatively large number of trade restrictions remain in place. The EC can hardly be counted among the most forthright supporters of Chinese membership in the GATT.[8] Quotas – especially for textiles – anti-dumping measures and duties keep China's trade deficit with the EC high. In China, as elsewhere in the developing world, the challenge of the Single European Market in 1992 raises even more uncertainties about their ability to compete in the new marketplace as China remains a minor trade partner (one per cent of total EC trade).

The Peking massacre had a less than significant effect on these relations. The limited economic sanctions and the ban on high-level contacts did not affect the basic patterns of trade nearly as much as did the economic recession in China. Western technology, except in the military sector, continued to flow to China and that was the main Chinese interest in the relationship with the West Europeans. France was perhaps the most outspoken critic of China's human-rights policies and Paris provided a home for the dissidents who fled the Peking massacre. Britain, with its special concern for Hong Kong, was allowed to resume high-level contacts with the Chinese regime in July 1990, but the EC ban otherwise held longer than did that of the United States or Japan. Cynics suggested it was easier for the EC to do so largely because it had less invested in the Chinese reforms and could afford to be more moral, but the economic figures did not always bear out this judgement.

There certainly were no signs that the EC was especially worried about the impact on Hong Kong. This was perhaps not surprising considering that, of the largest EC trading states, only Britain and to some extent Holland did substantially more trade with Hong Kong than with China. Even Germany, which was the EC's second-largest trade partner with Hong Kong, sent 0.6 per cent of its exports to China in 1990 (0.4 per cent to Hong Kong) and took 1.4 per cent of its imports from China, compared with 0.9 per cent from Hong Kong. China was Germany's largest source of imports in Asia apart from Japan; and China was nearly its largest export market in Asia (also, apart from Japan).

But despite the greater importance of China for most EC members, the West European trading relationship with Hong Kong remained remarkably sound in recent decades, a testament to Hong Kong's leading role as an NIC in the international market economy. In 1982 total West European imports from Hong Kong were two-thirds of the American total and ranked second among Hong Kong's export markets. West European exports to Hong Kong were greater than the United States', and ranked third behind China and Japan. Britain and West Germany were by far the largest trading partners, although the British percentage had been decreasing in the years before. In 1990 the percentages were roughly the same, with West European imports from Hong Kong accounting for about 37 per cent of Hong Kong's exports to the developed world and one-fifth of its total. Hong Kong's imports from Western Europe were well above those from the United States, although still well behind those from China and Japan. United States trade with Hong Kong in 1982 was some 15 per cent larger than that of Western Europe; despite some fluctuations in the subsequent years, in 1990 the general pattern was roughly the same. Although Britain's percentage shrank in this period, major growth in trade with Germany, Italy, France and Holland more than compensated for this shortfall.

Thus if the United States can be considered to have an interest in Hong Kong by virtue of its major trade and investment in the colony, so can the EC states. But in comparison with the United States, the EC states (with the notable exception of Britain and Holland) have a relatively larger stake in doing business with

China. What is more, both the United States and the EC states have come to recognise that it is increasingly artificial to try to draw distinctions of this sort because so much of the trade with both China and Hong Kong is intertwined. An interest in an integrated Hong Kong and south China is shared by most of the developed market economies. But on balance it is probably fair to say that the EC states are less likely than the United States, at least for economic reasons, to bend over backwards to assist Hong Kong if it is seen to be in conflict with China. On the grounds of economic self-interest alone, EC states are thus more likely to be supporters of China's definition of the type of convergence it wants to see between Hong Kong and the mainland. In addition, not only is Hong Kong outside the sphere of European political and military influence, but there are also problems with the European attitude to trade relations with Hong Kong, not to mention the matter of immigration.

Whereas West European exports to Hong Kong constituted some 80 per cent of imports at the beginning of the 1980s, by 1990 the ratio had slumped to less than 60 per cent. It seemed that Hong Kong, like the other NICs, was increasingly successful in the West European market (as they were in the United States) and the deteriorating trade balance was cause for concern in Europe. The financial pages of newspapers in the past decade reported a series of trade disputes and concerns on both sides about the trade relationship. In 1985 there were serious worries about the textile and clothing export policies of Hong Kong and the easy penetration of the European market.[9] As the EC moved forward with its SEM (Single European Market) plan for 1992, Hong Kong's Governor expressed particular concern about trading blocs and the impact on the NICs. A specific attempt was made to distinguish Hong Kong from other NICs by virtue of its more open trading structure in order to avoid punitive restrictions being imposed from Brussels.[10]

On a swing through Germany, France and Belgium, Sir David Wilson bemoaned the limited nature of European investment in Hong Kong while noting the trade imbalance.[11] This was a recipe for trade problems rather than a coincidence of interests in the operation of the international trading system. The express purpose of Sir David's trip was to gain a better understanding of the SEM plan, at the same time seizing the opportunity to explain the nature of the 1984 accord. Since Sir David was the representative of a colony whose masters were members of the EC, this was a bizarre notion, but it was nevertheless indicative of Hong Kong's *de facto* independent interests in trade issues, and the potential for problems with the EC.

Also in 1988, the president of the European Community, Gaston Thorn, on a trip to Hong Kong expressed confidence in the 1984 agreement and Hong Kong's continuing role in the international trading system. The then usual expression of confidence in Chinese reforms was said to be the basis of a rosy attitude towards the future of Hong Kong.[12] But back in Brussels the EC Commission was investigating the problem of dumping of electrical goods on the European market as deep worries were expressed about the trading power of the NICs.[13] This was a time both of Euro-optimism about the 1992 programme and Euro-pessimism about the continuing competitive skills of the exporters in the NICs. Despite its size and problems with China, Hong Kong was seen as more of a threat than an opportunity.[14] And despite a brief period of quiet on these issues after the Peking massacre in 1989, by the early 1990s the EC resumed its statements of concern about Hong Kong's trading practices.[15]

In 1990 the EC announced that an office of the Commission would be set up in Hong Kong in order to improve trade and the level of mutual understanding. This was not so much an expression of confidence as a symbol of the depths of the trading disputes. Yet by 1990 the EC was also growing more confident about the SEM and it was recognised that there were real worries in the colony about its ability to penetrate the largest market economy being created in Europe. EC commissioner Frans Andriessen noted that the establishment of an office 'shows our confidence and positive attitude towards Hong Kong'. Stress was placed on the opportunities for Hong Kong to invest inside the Community and therefore take advantage of the larger market.[16]

Despite the upbeat rhetoric, the reality was still an uneasy relationship between two trading partners and rivals. There remained a limited degree of investment in Hong Kong and therefore in Hong Kong's future. But after the revolutions in Europe in 1989–91, Europeans were simply not paying much attention to Asian issues. This was true both in terms of economic problems and the more emotional question of migration.

Immigration

Although the economic relationship had its tensions and Europe stood far away from Hong Kong, there was some hope that in the immediate aftermath of the Peking massacre Europe would help with the question of immigration from Hong Kong and the possibility of international discussions about a co-ordinated rescue package for the colony. Of course, immigration issues were already a hot topic in Europe, but the nature of that debate suggested there was scant sympathy for the British problem in Hong Kong and little willingness to help. Despite the fact that the new Europe of 1992 and beyond was supposed to have a more co-ordinated European foreign policy,[17] there was little desire to help with what was seen as essentially a colonial hangover. Other Europeans had dealt with their own problems; Britain should deal with its own without expecting to be bailed out by Europe. Especially given Britain's cool attitude to European unity in the Thatcher years, it was considered more than a little cheeky of Britain to appeal to European unity on the Hong Kong issue.

Immigration was one of the more contentious issues on the European agenda; indeed, it has a long history in European politics. Some 1,000 years ago there were no Germans in Berlin or even Russians in Moscow and migration has clearly been a major part of the changing European map.[18] Passports did not exist until invented by Europeans in the sixteenth century and they were obligatory everywhere in Europe except England by the end of the eighteenth century. Europeans were used to major flows of population and sought methods to regulate the movement when an open territory was uncertainly being divided into territorial units. In the century since 1815 some 55 million Europeans left the continent entirely, for a variety of reasons. Some 15 million Germans moved elsewhere in Europe in the aftermath of the Second World War and a further 3.5 million East Germans (20 per cent of the population) left their new home in the years before August 1961 and the erection of the Berlin Wall. In the following twenty-five years a further 300,000 Germans moved from east to west. Nearly 200,000 Hungarians fled their country after the 1956 uprising and were scattered around the continent, with 'compassion fatigue' setting in by the summer of 1957.[19] There was a wide range of reasons for these flows, but the essential conclusion is that Europe has, in living memory, known more than its fair share of shifts of population.[20]

Indeed, recent work shows that Europe leads the OECD in taking registered immigrants, with Western Europe taking more than the United States/Canada and Oceania together in the 1980s.[21] Of the total migrants in the world in 1988 (80 million or 1.7 per cent of the world population), Western Europe had 25 million or 5 per cent of the total European population in this category. In 1991, over 8 per cent of Britain's population was foreign-born; in France, 11 per cent, and in the United States, 5 per cent.[22] These major shifts of people included both the migrant workers in Germany or Italy, or the masses of better-educated and trained people who increasingly moved about the EC in search of jobs in the increasingly integrated single European market.

Indeed it was the very attractions of the Single European Market that drew the poor North Africans or East Europeans. In the 1990s EC members were far more concerned with what Spanish civil servants called our 'southern flank' and their German counterparts saw as the need for a 'new Berlin wall' in the east. With the continuing collapse of, and chaos in, the Soviet Union, officials in the EC warned of millions of new immigrants. Some officials in the Soviet Union before the breakup of the Union spoke of 7 million people on the move in the 1990s, slightly more than the population of Hong Kong.[23] With the uncertainty after the disintegration of the Soviet Union and Yugoslavia, European concern about migration remained high, even though the actual numbers may not turn out to be nearly so dramatic.

European policy towards migration and border controls is clearly caught up in the broader discussions of the nature of the new market being created in Europe. Although there is still nothing that can be called an EC-wide agreement on harmonising visas or frontier procedures, some states have moved closer to sub-agreements. In general the pattern seems to suggest the need for a stronger perimeter to Europe while there is an abolition of internal barriers. Irregular meetings are held in a wide range of forums to deal with such issues, down to the mundane level of movements of aircraft and ships.[24]

One of the more vexed issues is how to consider the movement of refugees, because the fear is that if one country has lax policies, then, once inside the community, people will be able to move freely in search of jobs and a better life. With the former East European allies of the Soviet Union now outside the EC but no longer part of an alternative body, the question of controls of populations outside the frontiers of the community becomes a part of the difficult matter of making the EC wider before it becomes a deeper union. The fears, especially of millions of refugees from Eastern Europe, have led an increasing number of officials to speak, mostly unofficially, of the need for a new *de facto* Berlin wall to protect the new Europe.

It should be noted that EC members have also been generous to some refugees from outside their region or ethnic home base, most notably in the case of refugees from Vietnam. The 1979 agreement in Geneva on the Orderly Departure Program for refugees who had left Vietnam, and some of whom were in camps in Southeast Asia, was a major international effort in which European states played an important and constructive role. Between 1975 and 1988 France resettled more refugees from Indo-China than did any other European country – about 100,000, or about half the total number of refugees living in France.[25] Germany took 23,000, Britain 17,000, Switzerland 8,000, Holland and Norway each took 7,000, and Denmark, Sweden and Italy each took about 3,000.

But the problems, particularly in France, with a right-wing opposition to wider immigration, especially from North Africa, was making it very hard to reach a broad agreement on refugees and policy in general towards migration. The pattern so far has mostly been *ad hoc* consultation and national programmes.[26] Various intergovernmental groups had also been set up at various times to discuss such issues, including a working group on Iranian refugees. The Trevi group of EC justice and interior ministers met to discuss terrorism, but they also had an *ad hoc* sub-group on immigration and asylum. In May 1989 the EC agreed that applications for asylum should be processed on behalf of the whole Community by the country of first asylum. This scheme was more likely to encourage a trend to 'competitive toughness' in keeping people out than lead to a generous policy of allowing more in. The country of first asylum usually fears that people will simply stay where they first arrive.[27] Legislation in 1989 in Britain, Denmark, Germany, Belgium, Holland and Sweden required the airlines to check the documents of asylum-seekers before they boarded the plane or face a fine of £1,000 for carrying an asylum-seeker with the wrong documents.

Most importantly there was the Schengen agreement of 1985 between the Benelux countries, France and Germany gradually to abolish border controls between the members. A final agreement was reached in 1990 as the EC core moved ahead to 1992. Others, such as Britain, remained especially concerned about the problems of terrorism and refused to join in an agreement that lifted all internal border controls. Although there was some conflict between interpretations of the 'four freedoms' of the EC's Single European Market plan for 1992, it seemed that not all border control would be lifted in time for 1992, although the Schengen core would be more advanced in this respect.[28]

Nevertheless, it remained true that there would be a full movement for citizens of EC member states within the EC, thus allowing those from Hong Kong who obtain British passports, or Macanese who obtain Portuguese passports, to live and work anywhere within the EC. But the EC has so far not prevented individual countries from setting their own regulations for immigration or refugees from third countries. Of course, the EC countries have yet to harmonise their regulations on citizenship, and thus it is legally incorrect to identify 'a European' except as someone from an EC country. Europeans can still vote only in their own country. Members do not agree on whether citizenship is based primarily on blood or birthplace and thus for some time to come there still looks like being important variations in the ways in which immigration is handled in Europe.[29] Although many might argue that a wealthy Western Europe with a declining birth-rate should take in more people,[30] they will do so primarily on the basis of national policies and priorities.

In 1989 there were some 1,025,000 foreigners in Britain (1.8 per cent of the population), 464,000 in Holland (3.1 per cent), 332,000 in Belgium (3.3 per cent), 115,000 in Denmark (2.3 per cent), 3,500,000 in Germany (5.7 per cent), 236,000 in Italy (4 per cent) and 2,400,000 in France (4.4 per cent).[31] These figures included only non-EC foreigners and suggested the scale on which the EC member states were already dealing with major flows of population. The addition of several hundred thousand from Hong Kong (who would not be classed as foreigners) would still keep Britain's percentage well below the norm in the EC, as it would for a much smaller Portugal with its expected flow (65,000 or 0.9 per cent) from Macao. And countries such as France and Germany would certainly be unwilling to help Britain and

Portugal out with the Hong Kong problem, although under EC rules if Britain were to take in vast numbers of people from Hong Kong the other EC members could not prevent them from living and working elsewhere in the Community. With pressure building up outside the EC for entry into a better future, the 'Fortress Europe' slogan seems to apply more aptly to the attitude towards immigration than it does to trade issues. The so-called 'threshold of intolerance' is being reached, especially in countries like France.[32]

French Policy

French policy towards Hong Kong has perhaps been the most interesting of all the specific cases in Europe. As the only other European country that had a major Asian empire, France had a basic understanding of the kind of problems faced by Britain. As a fellow permanent member of the United Nations Security Council and the G-7, France would play a major role in any attempt to internationalize the Hong Kong problem. But with its major commitment to a united Europe and its own serious problem with immigration, France had very different priorities from those of Britain.

Persistent reports in the 1980s suggested that France was ready to grant passports or visas to employees of French companies in Hong Kong. This policy was intended to allow the employees to continue working in Hong Kong with the confidence of having a place to go if matters deteriorated in the colony. Some stories suggested that up to 3,000 such documents could be issued, but 1,000 seemed to be the number most often quoted. (It was also not clear whether, as in the British scheme, these were to be awarded to heads of household who could then bring their immediate family as well.[33]) A British foreign office minister, Francis Maude, gave the figure 1,500 in April 1990. This number, he said, would be part of a package of 50,000 people, which would complement the British scheme for a similar number of heads of households.[34]

Maude's embarrassingly premature revelations also included mention of Germany, Belgium and Luxembourg as other countries who would join the scheme, although national legislation would have to be amended in order to make such offers possible. Some reports suggested that only one or two countries were likely to respond favourably to a scheme to grant such places to residents of Hong Kong, most citing legal problems.[35] Few European countries were even prepared to respond favourably to recognising the new British Nationality Overseas passports which will replace the existing BDT passports which expire in 1997 when the colony reverts to Chinese sovereignty.[36]

Whatever specific details might eventually be agreed, the French *démarche* suggested the limited scale on which European countries might be willing to help Britain with the Hong Kong problem. Considering the numbers of people with uncertain immigrant status in Europe in the 1990s, the numbers being suggested for Hong Kong are tiny. France, like other EC states, seems to suggest that this is a British problem which only impinges on EC states in the sense that their companies operating in Hong Kong might be disadvantaged if they did not have a right-of-abode package similar to that which Britain and the United States have extended. Companies owned by other EC members will find themselves more vulnerable to a brain drain. By tacitly encouraging such self-interest, Britain is suggesting that those countries with the greater economic stake in Hong Kong will have to offer the greater amount of safeguards in order to keep business in operation. Thus countries like Germany will be expected to chip in with a larger passport (or visa) package, and even Switzerland will be expected to follow suit with some method for keeping their valued employees in place. Certainly the French-speaking Europeans doing business in Hong Kong were surprised to see the increasing popularity of French-language courses in the colony in the early 1990s, although this may have had more to do with the prospects of settling in Quebec than setting in Europe.[37]

The French reporting of the Hong Kong problem has suggested at least an implicit understanding of the hard-nosed rules of the Hong Kong question. For one thing, France has long been in the forefront of efforts to hit Hong Kong hard on trade disputes. As early as 1981 France was among the toughest in demanding EC efforts to limit what it perceived as Hong Kong's unfair trading practices.[38] Michel Jobert, minister of external trade in 1982, even took his case to Hong Kong to argue that France was determined to defend its interests and get the EC to help it do so.[39] Hong Kong chose to take France to the GATT committee in order to appeal against French quotas on quartz watches and eight other products. As we have seen, this was a pattern common to EC practices as a whole, but France was clearly out in front in treating Hong Kong as a trading rival to be fought.[40]

The GATT panel ruled in favour of Hong Kong but still France persisted in a complex game of setting up new and shifting quotas in order to deter Hong Kong from breaking into the French market. In 1984 France even received support from the EC, which allowed an extension of the ban on imports of products from Hong Kong that came via other EC members.[41] Hong Kong manufacturers retaliated with a campaign of their own against the drinking of French brandy – a major sacrifice for the heavy brandy drinkers of Hong Kong and a sign of the depths to which the dispute had fallen. French businessmen in Hong Kong tried to get their compatriots to moderate the tone of the dispute, but to little avail.[42]

French reporting of the 1984 accord on Hong Kong had none of the narrow, nationalist tones of the trade dispute, but neither did it suggest that the issue was anything but a matter for Britain.[43] Most French comment on the region, from officials or in the media, continued to be mainly concerned with trade issues.[44] It was not that the French were unaware of the problem of confidence in Hong Kong; it was simply that they felt it was a British problem – and one which concerned a colony that was strong enough to look after its own trading interests.[45] Indeed, the comments almost never made any reference to a French interest in Hong Kong apart from trade. There was certainly no sense that France had any part to play in building confidence in the colony.[46]

During a European tour in October 1988, Sir David Wilson paid what was the first visit to France by a Governor of Hong Kong. He focused first on trade issues and gave a robust defence of Hong Kong's position. He was looking for more investment from France and was critical of the tiny levels reached so far in comparison with the Americans. In the pre-1989 atmosphere, Sir David played up the prosperity and confidence in the future, and so it was not surprising that anyone in France might feel it necessary to propose anything to help keep confidence in Hong Kong's future. More time was spent on the question of Vietnamese refugees in Hong Kong than on the subject of any potential outflow of refugees from Hong Kong itself.[47]

In October 1990 Sir David Wilson was again in France to seek support and investment. He met trade officials as well as the prime minister, Laurent Fabius, but there were no special statements of support and no evidence that France was being anything but correct in its handling of Hong Kong.[48] Considering the rising importance of the immigration issue in France, there certainly could be little expectation that France would contemplate helping on the immigration issue. With some 15,000 Chinese (out of a resident Asian community of 300,000) in France the problems related to Vietnamese immigrants of Chinese descent were too recent to allow for a more liberal French approach to new immigration.[49] France, like the rest of its EC partners, had its eyes on other, far more pressing problems.

Portugal and Macao

No one would suggest that Portugal is a major player in Europe but, because of the colonial legacy in Macao, it is important to pause for a brief review of Portuguese policy. Portugal has held Macao for far longer than Britain has held Hong Kong, but with far less legal basis and far less political security. It has long been understood that the fate of Macao depended on the fate of Hong Kong – and to an important extent British handling of Hong Kong was far more important to Macao than policies made in Lisbon.

Macao, with its 17.5 square kilometres, has been more precarious than Hong Kong. It was first settled in 1557 and declared a free port in 1845. It was never ceded to Portugal and the treaty of 1 December 1887 with China only gave Portugal administrative powers.[50] Macao did not even control immigration from China until it was agreed in 1990 that Macao could establish a customs office on the frontier with Zhuhai. In contrast to the Hong Kong case, there is no popular mandate of any significant sort for Portugal to rule Macao. In 1987 Portugal agreed to return Macao to China after 20 December 1999.

Despite the official assurance in the 1987 agreement that the Portuguese administration was in control until the end of 1999, the reality has long been *de facto* Peking control. Brief attempts by Portuguese officials to give the territory more political autonomy have been swiftly stopped. Not even the Peking massacre and the demonstrations in Macao against the Peking regime changed this reality. Since the Governor of Macao visited China in May 1988 it became official policy to ensure that the Macao civil service was taken over by the local population. China has remained frustrated at the slow pace of this process, but the trend remains basically unchallenged.

There are some fears that Portugal will leave Macao in haste, much as it did its African colonies in the mid-1970s.[51] But the analogy is thin, if only because Portugal has already negotiated the basic outline of a process with China and has been particularly careful to maintain good relations with China. Peking has certainly been quick to suggest that Portugal has been much more amenable to its wishes than has Britain. What is more, there is little that can be called Macanese nationalism that is not part of a larger affinity with south China. Even those with some blood links to Europeans may well stay after Chinese control is reassumed, because the process of cultural interconnections with the local Chinese is far more advanced than in any previous Portuguese colony. Nevertheless, it is suggested that 65 per cent of the non-Chinese population is expected to leave for Europe by the year 2000.[52] While many residents of Macao will be able to live in Britain by virtue of the free movement of EC citizens in the Community, there will be many in Hong Kong with far stronger links to Europe who will not be so fortunate.

It is hard to imagine that Portugal sees Macao as a major issue and it certainly has far less expectation or pressure to do anything to help the people of its colony should something go wrong in the run-up to the hand-over of power. As in the past, Portugal will rely on Britain to hold a steady course. Portugal will also rely on China to keep a level head and allow the process of integration in south China to take its course. In some sense, Macao is already farther down this road than Hong Kong. Will Macao, with its far lower standard of living, be Hong Kong's future?

Europe Looks the Other Way

The people of Hong Kong are a practical lot and it is doubtful if many of them ever thought that Europeans would help them in time of need. There was never any reason for the people of Hong Kong to believe that continental Europeans would be any more generous than Britain about either trade practices or policies on immigration. Before 1989 it was common to hear such feelings expressed in the colony along with a sense that Europe was in any case in decline and mattered far less. Now that the European future looks more promising, the people of Hong Kong find it harder to dismiss Europe, but they still feel it unlikely that Europeans will care very much about their future. Europeans in general, to the extent that they even think about the Hong Kong problem, see little self-interest in preserving Hong Kong and, indeed, many might be pleased to see it fade as a trading rival. Although the levels of trade were high, the value of investment was low. Above all, the extent of immigration and refugee problems in Europe were such that most states and the EC itself had their minds on other things. The bizarre reports in 1990 of Hong Kong businessmen buying East German citizenship just before it was converted into a passport of the united Germany[53] said a great deal about where Hong Kong figured in the eyes of the continental European press.

As a result, Britain has little reason to expect much assistance from its European 'partners' should problems arise over Hong Kong. If Britain were to raise the issue of a rescue package for Hong Kong, there certainly exists the mechanisms for dealing with such issues. Britain might well find some support for a limited package of passports or visas in an extreme case, perhaps on something like the scale of the Orderly Departure Program for Vietnamese refugees, but matters would have to become particularly dire before such a scheme could be contemplated. Even so, France and Germany would be unlikely to be quite so generous as they were in 1979 and the attitude towards refugees in Europe in the 1990s has clearly been hardening.[54] But with its poor record as a 'good European', Britain seemed less than likely to rely on the EC to help it out of the Hong Kong problem, or indeed expect any such help. In the post-Cold War Europe most of Asia, and certainly Hong Kong, is off the agenda. Given the magnitude of the revolutionary changes in Europe, it should not be surprising if the Europeans continue to ignore Hong Kong well beyond 1997.

12

Getting to 1997

What will it be like at midnight on 30 June 1997 when the new rulers of Hong Kong move in from China? At 5 p.m. British summertime on 30 June, will Whitehall and 10 Downing Street be in crisis consultations? Will there be much concern at noon in Washington, DC, about how to handle tension in Hong Kong, China and East Asia? To be sure, nightmare scenarios have already been articulated, although as the earlier chapters have demonstrated a wide range of reasons for greater optimism can also be found.[1] The revolutionary events in 1989–91, in both China and Europe, should be sufficient warning that we are living through a period of an accelerated pace of change.

Perhaps British policy, and even the attitude of the Hong Kong people, might well have been different in 1984 if they had known how their confidence would be knocked in 1989. From a vantage point in the early 1990s, with so many uncertainties between now and 1997, it is obviously impossible to predict with any certainty Hong Kong's future. But the key variables that will shape that future can already be identified.

The Factors for Change

Hong Kong

The past success of Hong Kong has depended on the ability of its hard-working people to prosper in the international market economy. In recent decades that success has come to depend on an increasingly close connection with China, if only as the place for low-wage production managed by Hong Kong's service economy. The political system of the colony has never been democratic in the sense of its politics being decided by freely elected representatives. But Hong Kong's politics have benefited from a light touch of colonial rule, some representation at lower levels of politics, a free press and an independent judiciary. The specific mix of these features can be described as the 'secret' to Hong Kong's success, but the confidence that in reality makes the system run is impossible to define. Without confidence, Hong Kong seems likely to run down to a lesser sort of place. An often-discussed dimension of confidence is migration. While it is not clear what level of migration from Hong Kong will deal a decisive blow to the economy and hence political stability, it seems clear that present levels are damaging to Hong Kong's prospects. It is not so much the absolute numbers who emigrate as the quality of those that leave. When professionals and specialists depart, their place must be filled either by those less well qualified or by those who must be paid more to stay or to come in from outside. Inflation is a natural result of this process. Of course, failure to fill posts will damage Hong Kong's ability to keep up with the pace of growth and change in the regional and international economy.

Higher inflation is only one of the major uncertainties in the economic prospects of Hong Kong. Fading confidence, if manifest in lower rates of investment from inside or outside, will also stifle growth. A lack of confidence that takes corporate headquarters elsewhere in East Asia, or leads Hong Kong firms to move their domicile, will remove the seeds that often help this service-dominated economy to prosper. Although inflation rather than unemployment looks like being the larger risk for the economy, the government of the colony must be especially cautious in undertaking the usual remedy for an inflation-ridden market economy, for fear of driving more young professionals to the exit queues. Some of the more cynical supporters of the convergence argument for Hong Kong might well be pleased to see a slowdown in Hong Kong, if only to make for a smoother docking with the Chinese economy.

A smoother integration with China might also be better achieved if the level of corruption in Hong Kong were allowed to rise to mainland levels. It has become a notable feature of economic reform in a command economy that corruption has increased as a perverse sort of market indicator. While Hong Kong's market is far more free and therefore far less in need of corruption as a countermeasure against the failures of the constrained market, it is difficult to see how convergence with the mainland will not lead to an increase in corruption. Certainly the more that mainland companies become involved in the local economy, and the more that Hong Kong is seen as a playground for the well-connected élite of the mainland, the more the cancer of corruption will strangle the capitalism of Hong Kong. The business costs of the resulting inefficiency may well be yet another factor in the slowdown in the Hong Kong economy as it converges with the mainland.

There is also evidence that, in the political sphere at least, a degree of divergence rather than convergence is likely to be on the agenda. Politics, or their relative absence, have been a notable feature of pre-1997 Hong Kong. The Chinese would like to see it remain that way, at least in the sense that no one in Hong Kong should come to think that they can really rule themselves in a way that the communist rulers find unacceptable. So, the post-1989 evidence of more polarised politics in Hong Kong is a concern both to the authorities in Peking and even to sections of the business community in the colony.

So far, China has ensured that the level of representation in Hong Kong will not allow for self-rule. Nor is it likely that Britain will allow any substantial change to that reality, no matter what the provocation on the mainland (short of civil war, at least). One might then ask whether it matters if some elected officials in Hong Kong assume a higher profile in criticising Chinese rule if they lack any power to change it. And yet the risk must be that the rulers in Peking will view such radical politics, especially if they are accompanied by political parties that support dissident movements with connections on the mainland, as a basic threat deserving harsh treatment. Subsequent limits on free speech and the media, whether legal or self-imposed, must harm the business confidence in Hong Kong. Suppressive measures of this kind would certainly create a climate of fear and pessimism that might well become a self-fulfilling prophecy of collapse.

Some or even all of these problems need not arise in the years before 1997. But there is already worrying evidence of increased migration, a relative economic slowdown, increased corruption and political polarisation since 1984. The row over the Patten proposals in 1992–93 is further evidence of the political fragility of the system. However, most of all these trends can be reversed, given different policies in China, Britain and the wider world.

China

It has been a constant theme in the book so far that the fate of Hong Kong depends more on the policies of China than anything else. As the run-up to the succession of Deng Xiaoping coincides with the run-down of British rule in Hong Kong, there is no single more important factor shaping the fate of Hong Kong than the fate of Chinese reforms. Numerous learned articles and books have been published in the search for answers to questions whether and how the Chinese reform programme begun in 1978 might develop. Most observers would agree that until the death of the old leadership, the extent of real reform will not be fully tested. But it is an essential feature of all optimistic scenarios for Hong Kong that there be a regime in Peking committed to reform up to and well beyond 1997. If convergence is to work, not only must Hong Kong slow down to some extent but the mainland must speed up to the pace of the international economy. Without continuing and fundamental economic reforms, the Chinese economy is unlikely to be in shape for successful convergence. There are limited prospects that the Chinese dog can be wagged by the Hong Kong tail without a larger and more sustained commitment to reform.

Of course, there is a wide range of types of reform that might allow enough flexibility for a relatively safe convergence. There is reform in the regions which to some extent was being tested in the early 1990s. After the death of communism in Europe and the disintegration of the Soviet Union, Deng Xiaoping chose to allow regions, and especially Guangdong and south China, wide latitude in achieving growth through reform. This was done both for the good of the regions and as a way for Deng to deal with more conservative colleagues back in Peking. But as these reforms develop, the regions grow more distinct and with a greater stake in yet more reform, even if there should be a change of policy in Peking. The creation of NETs in the regions runs the risks of undermining central control in China and even the creation of types of independent foreign relations in the different regions. This is a kind of reform that could give Hong Kong greater leeway to prosper, but it also runs important risks in creating major struggles between centre and region in China, or even between competing regions as NETs are widened and developed.

A far less risky version of reform under which Hong Kong might also benefit would be one where reform is kept under tighter central control. Under these circumstances, Hong Kong would have to change more than if south China could become more effectively independent of Peking, but it still holds encouraging prospects. There is no necessity for such reform to be of the 'collapse-of-communism' type seen in Eastern Europe. Certainly the evidence of the decade of reform from 1978 was that there was much that could be done short of ending the command economy completely. There is no necessary and immediate link between political and economic reform, as the remarkable growth of the NICs in East Asia amply demonstrates. China, and to a much lesser extent Guangdong, have a long way to go before they reach the present standards of the NICs where some degree of political reform seems to be necessary. The NICs are also evidence of how elements of a command and market economy can be managed in a successful mix. Optimists would argue that a Hong Kong-type mix of pragmatic professionalism in politics and economics might be a 'Confucian'-type future for China that will benefit Hong Kong. It certainly seems that other booming economies in East Asia have prospered without the hand of democracy that many Americans and Europeans would recognize.

The more pessimistically inclined, while accepting that reform in China is both necessary and inevitable, might take some persuading that it is likely to come fast enough to save Hong Kong's economy and keep sufficient professionals in place. Even if there should be a succession to a reforming leadership before this edition is published, it would be unrealistic to expect a sudden and complete turn-round in confidence in Hong Kong. The more historically inclined will note that China's reforms have ebbed and flowed for decades (if not centuries) and certainly young professionals in Hong Kong would be rash to bet their entire working lives on a long-lived reform. The evidence from Eastern Europe is that transition to a genuinely reformed economy is painful and prolonged, and theirs have all been cases where communist parties have shrivelled. One can be an optimist about the eventual triumph of reform in China without being sure that it will happen soon or smoothly. If one is young, skilled and in search of prosperity, North America, Australia or Europe might be a better bet than expecting a politburo in Peking regularly to make the right decisions.

Nor would it necessarily make much sense for Hong Kong to run the risks of taking the lead in a reform of China that created a more independent southern NET with Hong Kong in the vanguard. In sum, given the level of risks involved in the uncertain politics of China, it seems inevitable that the people of Hong Kong and foreign investors will remain jittery. Moreover, it is hard to see why perceptions should become any calmer in the run up to 1997.

Britain

From Britain's point of view, there is little to be gained but irritation in holding on to Hong Kong. China gives it trouble over its handling of the transfer, most recently in the squabble over the airport and the Patten proposals of 1992–93. Some people in Hong Kong carp about what Britain might have done to get a better deal in 1984 and they regularly lobby for a tougher line with Peking. Outsiders grumble about Britain's fumbling on the future of Hong Kong and grumble even louder when London urges them to do something concrete to build confidence in the colony. Surely Britain must wish it could hand Hong Kong back earlier and breathe a sigh of relief.

Of course, it is unlikely that Britain would be allowed to shed the Hong Kong problem before 1997. China certainly has little interest in such a turn of events, and other countries are quietly pleased that Hong Kong is someone else's problem. But are there no circumstances in which Britain might get tough with China and at least threaten a premature withdrawal? Having survived the aftermath of the Peking massacre in 1989, Britain seems resigned to doing its unsavoury duty of handing over some six million people to communist-party rule. The task is only marginally less unsavoury with reform in China. Short of a major civil war in China, perhaps as a result of a catastrophic struggle for power after Deng Xiaoping goes to meet Marx, Britain is unlikely to try to undo or ignore the 1984 agreement. Even in 1989 the option of tearing up the 1984 agreement was never taken seriously in the corridors of Whitehall. Such a scenario seems far-fetched for the mid-1990s.

But are there any circumstances in which Britain might threaten to quit ahead of schedule? The ultimate reason for not doing so must be that Britain feels it can do better by the people of Hong Kong (and look better itself) if it stays to help manage the transition to Chinese rule. But what if the people of Hong Kong themselves demonstrate that they want to leave in even larger numbers than they have done already and, as a result, create a crisis? Under such circumstances, perhaps provoked by a prolonged succession crisis in China, Britain might well feel that Hong Kong is already damaged beyond repair and emergency measures are required. One might then imagine, for example, Britain calling an international conference as thousands of 'jumbo-jet' refugees begin landing in Western airports, seeking asylum. Just as an Orderly Departure Program (ODP) was organised with the co-operation of Vietnam for those wishing to leave Vietnam in the 1970s, so Britain might seek Chinese co-operation in organising the departure of those wishing to leave Hong Kong. Should China refuse to co-operate, Britain might well wash its hands of the problem. Such a scenario is far from likely. If Britain did not even come close to threatening non-co-operation with China in 1982–84, it is hard to imagine such a strategy being adopted in the 1990s. But assuming that the people of Hong Kong actually demonstrated they were so seriously concerned that they attempted to leave in large numbers – something they did not do in the early 1980s – Britain might possibly be more emboldened to try a different tack. But without wider international assistance, Britain would not contemplate anything so drastic.

Nor would Britain be likely to contemplate the other drastic scenario of not leaving in 1997. Even if there was major chaos in China, the only circumstances under which Britain might stay on would be if a China racked by civil war had a regional authority in Guangdong or southern China that asked Britain to stay. Short of full co-operation from the local authorities, Hong Kong cannot sustain its current 'independence'. For all the reasons identified in the run-up to the 1984 agreement, and including such prosaic ones as China's control of water and food supplies, Hong Kong cannot oppose the will of a China that wants the territory back.

The United States
Britain could not contemplate any such action without detailed negotiation with its primary ally, the United States. There are some circumstances under which the United States might urge Britain down such a road, but only if Sino-United States relations were already in serious trouble. As the only remaining superpower, the United States naturally has wider strategic interests than has Britain. With the disintegration of the Soviet Union and the emergence of a more multipolar world, China

seems set to become a major actor in a vital region of the world. The United States recognises that getting along with China is not only vital to ensuring the stability and security of East Asia, but that China is also a vital player in wider international events, as demonstrated by the 1990/91 crisis in the Persian Gulf.

The United States, like the developed market economies as a whole, has an interest in China returning to its reforming ways and playing a constructive role in closer international interdependence. The United States has already demonstrated after the Peking massacre in 1989 that, short of a total collapse of order in China, the United States will not isolate China. Thus if China forces the United States to choose between getting on with Peking or doing something significant to salvage Hong Kong, the United States will surely choose the pragmatism of great power politics. Of course, should Sino-American relations deteriorate because, for example, of trade disputes, then Hong Kong may well suffer. Increased convergence between Hong Kong and China could mean serious damage to the colony from American trade sanctions.

Should the fate of Hong Kong become tied up in a much more complex scenario where decentralization in China leads to the creations of NETs and more independent regional policies, the challenges for American policy will become all the greater. When, previously, China disintegrated, either into warlordism or civil war, the United States was a major player in the bloody international consequences. The United States would clearly have a large stake in the effective and peaceful management of decentralization in China and therefore would oppose deliberate efforts to divide China. The United States might see good reasons for encouraging some decentralization, if only as a way of making China as a whole into a more manageable partner. But the risks in encouraging NETs that might turn into more independent actors are high.

Even if the circumstances of the convergence between Hong Kong and China are less extreme, there is still a risk of a large exodus of people from the colony. If Britain should seek an ODP for Hong Kong, the United States might be called upon to help. But this is not very likely. What is far more likely is increased immigration from Hong Kong as the pressure gradually builds among the professional and middle classes for safe havens. As we have seen, the United States has already gone further than anyone else in meeting British desires for a larger number of deferred entry visas. Short of a massive collapse of confidence in Hong Kong, these extra places will probably be adequate. But it is also possible that the United States will find those places taken up earlier than they need be. What is more, even after 1997, under the framework of immigration to unite families, the United States may well find itself connected to a long line of Hong Kong people seeking refuge. If the fate of Vietnamese in the United States who fled communist rule at home is anything to go by, the United States will also find that the presence of former residents of Hong Kong will create additional pressure groups that might, if a crisis were to develop in Hong Kong, add to the call for a more interventionist United States policy regarding Hong Kong and Chinese policy.

If the United States is left merely to handle migration problems, then the fate of Hong Kong will not feature very high up the American policy agenda. If the fate of Hong Kong is part of a broader challenge arising from the decentralization or even the disintegration of China, then the focus will be on larger issues than the future of the colony. With so many other matters vying for space in policy-makers' in-trays, it should not be surprising if Hong Kong does not receive much attention. Of course, if the regionalization of China does develop apace, then American policy-makers will wish that they were better prepared and also better able to deal with Hong Kong as part of a more distinct southern China. Whether the challenge is about the narrower issues of migration, the middle-range problems of coping with regional NETs, or the far larger problem of a disintegrating China, the fate of Hong Kong warrants more attention in Washington.

Canada, Australia and Europe

Most people seeking refuge from Hong Kong now go to Canada. Significant numbers also leave for Australia as many people are unable to reach their first-choice destinations in North America. As we have already seen, Canada and to some extent Australia have been major players in the Hong Kong story after 1984 because their immigration policies have played a crucial part in draining the lifeblood from the colony. But are there circumstances under which their immigration policy might change?

Canada and Australia lack any power, unlike the United States or even to some extent Britain, to affect policies in Peking. Their main stake in the Hong Kong problem is their trade with China and Hong Kong, which is not of vital importance and is unlikely to change much in the years to 1997, and their desire to continue taking high-quality immigrants from Hong Kong. As long as Canada can count on keeping most of the people who have taken Canadian passports (and with them their money), then Canadian interest will be mainly satisfied. Much the same, only on a smaller scale, holds true for Australia. Of course, both countries are part of a wider Western community and have interests beyond their narrow immigration policies. But only in a case where the problem of Hong Kong becomes tied up with a wider discussion of the fate of China as a whole would Australia and Canada consider a major revision in their policies towards Hong Kong.

The balance of calculation about immigration in these two countries depends on an assessment of the economic and broader social benefit of large numbers of immigrants from Hong Kong. In harder economic times, Australia, in particular, seems prepared to reduce the number of immigrants. Canada appears to be less short-sighted, but the pressures to control the flow exist, especially if there are increasing demands from others, most notably from Eastern Europe, for scarce migration places. Canadian and Australian officials have expressed a willingness to take larger numbers under an ODP and Canadian immigration officials in particular have begun to think seriously about the possibility of having to take large numbers of what will then be refugees seeking family reunions with kin in Canada.

By contrast, it seems unlikely that Europeans will be much involved, even if an ODP should become necessary. Britain's EC partners have not so far shown anything that could be described as either compassion or even real self-interest regarding Hong Kong. Even after the Peking massacre there was little sign that many people in Hong Kong, even those employed by European firms, would be granted right of entry to the EC in any way other than through Britain or Portugal. The East European revolutions in 1989–91 turned the attention of EC members to the potentials and problems of their neighbours to the east and especially to the risks of large-scale immigration. EC members are likely to be far more interested in the potentials of trade with China and therefore less sympathetic to helping Britain and/or Portugal out of a bind with their soon-to-be-disposed-of colonies. Like Canada and Australia, the Europeans would not be very concerned to see a degree of regionalism in China that allowed Hong Kong to play an important role in leading a southern Chinese NET. Of course, if this process went much further and China began to disintegrate, the impact of East Asian unrest on international security would be so great that the issue would receive greater and perhaps different attention.

East Asia

If the Europeans can afford the luxury of closing their eyes to problems in Hong Kong, East Asian neighbours of the British colony have no such luck. And yet there is also likely to be a quiet ruthlessness about East Asian reaction if one of their number succumbs to power politics. The business can be shared around, so long as the circumstances of an opposed Chinese takeover do not involve large-scale instability in China itself. The primary interest of East Asia must be economic and political stability, and thus they have a major stake in a quiet and smooth transfer of power to Chinese rule. Certainly none of Hong Kong's neighbours want large-scale migration and most definitely not rafts of boat people.

For most East Asians, the best solution to the Hong Kong problem would be for the colony to emerge as a major force in a southern Chinese NET. Obviously, some states in East Asia would view such a NET as a rival and might therefore not be unhappy to see some problems in the convergence of Hong Kong and China. Most East Asians want there to be neither a major failure of the 1984 accord nor such a powerful NET that it poses a challenge to their own success. Nor do East Asians want to see such a degree of regionalization in China that the stability of the region is threatened. East Asians benefit from some regionalism in the sense that other NETs are created in their own region, but the risk is that unchecked regionalism will hurt not only Hong Kong but other East Asians on China's periphery.

It is hard to envisage circumstances under which East Asians would see the slow but peaceful fading of Hong Kong as a problem. Those with investments, most notably the Japanese, would move their mostly portable assets elsewhere in a region that is expected to be otherwise flourishing. If Singapore should pick up the business that does not have the confidence to operate out of Hong Kong, Japanese funds will follow quite happily. Taiwan has already indicated that it will shift to Singapore as the base for its indirect trade with China. South Korea and increasingly

Taiwan no longer needs indirect trade.

None of these trading states of East Asia will have illusions about the political system in either Hong Kong or the mainland. Few are democracies themselves and even fewer think China will be anything but ruthless, even when it is reforming. Short of a major breakdown in law and order in Hong Kong or China, East Asians are content to watch Hong Kong slowly integrate into south China.

The one major exception involved in these calculations must be Taiwan. As it is the main target of the 'one country, two systems' strategy, a successful transfer of Hong Kong to the mainland will add pressure on Taiwan to travel the same route. Indeed, the creation of a southern China NET depends to an important extent on integrating Taiwan into the regional economy but controlling the risks that Taiwan will help pull southern China away from Peking's control and thereby create a major crisis in the region. Some people in Taiwan wish to see a slow fading of Hong Kong that discredits the idea of reunification, but, on balance, far more advantage would be gained if Hong Kong converged with southern China and created good economic conditions for Taiwanese business. Any more radical regionalism would begin to increase sharply the risks for all concerned in southern China. Of course, some in Taiwan might wish to travel the route to reunification, just as others might wish for a catastrophic collapse that might justify intervention in a civil war on the mainland. But such dramatic outcomes are less than likely and even less attractive to the majority of the people of Taiwan. There is certainly little evidence that the people of Taiwan, as with other East Asians, would welcome thousands of immigrants from Hong Kong fleeing a rapidly collapsing system.

Paths to Follow?

Thus there is a range of factors shaping the future of Hong Kong, with no obvious, let alone a determined, path. But at this stage of a book titled 'The Fate of Hong Kong', the reader deserves to see the author stick his neck out with his view of the more probable outcomes.

Divergence I: *De facto* Independence

While it is most likely that Hong Kong will converge with China in the run-up to and beyond 1997, there is a school of thought that suggests that divergence is the only reliable way to guarantee Hong Kong's freedoms and life-style and that the people of Hong Kong should basically ignore China and try to carry on beyond 1997 as if nothing much apart from a new flag and a few Chinese troops has changed. It is assumed that Hong Kong has grown used to running itself as a near-perfect market economy and Britain has not really ruled here for decades. The light hand of government has allowed Hong Kong to evolve a new form of sovereignty where the meaning of legal sovereignty is inconsequential and therefore its transfer can be equally meaningless. Hong Kong prospers because its people operate in the international market economy without reference to frontiers or their government's policies.

This scenario depends, as do all optimistic scenarios for Hong Kong, on China moving forward with its reforms and allowing Hong Kong to make its own way. It assumes enlightened Chinese leadership that accepts it cannot and should not govern Hong Kong, and all it really wanted to change in 1997 was formal sovereignty. It assumes this Chinese government is also interested in wooing Taiwan back to the motherland and in taking a far greater role in the international economy. To both ends, China knows it must demonstrate that it is serious about tolerating two systems within one country and will use Hong Kong as evidence. These new Chinese rules will also recognise they have much to learn from Hong Kong and that, if they have any real hope of turning coastal China into the new NICs of the twenty-first century, they will have to allow Hong Kong to show them how it is done.

Under such blissful conditions, China and Hong Kong will be supported by a surprised and grateful world that welcomes such a co-operative and far-sighted China. Even Britain will admit that it had misjudged China and was far too suspicious about China's intentions. Outsiders will be happy to continue investing in, and trading with, Hong Kong as it continues to be the best entry point to the booming Chinese market. East Asians in particular will be pleased that they have a co-operative China in their regional economy. Those who fled Hong Kong in fear of the post-1997 world will return in large numbers, helping turn the former

British colony into an even more cosmopolitan place. Can this benign reading of the 1984 Anglo-Chinese agreement come to pass? In theory, yes. But the problem to date has been that none of the major actors seems to think – and, worse still, act as if – divergence rather than convergence is the road to travel. Certainly the behaviour of the Chinese has suggested that they want the convergence to begin well before 1997 and Britain seems prepared to drag its feet, but accept the reality. Most of the people of Hong Kong also seem relatively resigned to such convergence; those who are not choose to emigrate. Short of a major turn-round in the policies of the major players, success through divergence seems unlikely.

Divergence II: Independence Crushed

What would happen if China was not willing to accept the strategy of divergence and really did wish to carry on meddling in Hong Kong? Could Hong Kong, with or without British help, stand up to Peking and take itself down a separate road? This, of course, has been the policy urged by those most radically opposed to Chinese rule. It is the argument of those calling for *de facto* independence for Hong Kong. Some observers have labelled it the 'calling the Chinese bluff' scenario and many have attacked Britain for failing to do so in the 1982–84 negotiations and beyond. But what if it is tried in the final hours?

It seems risky for a number of reasons. First, do the people of Hong Kong want to try something that Britain has not attempted, the Chinese seem unlikely to accept and the international community would be reluctant to support? It is hard to imagine how a sufficiently representative group could now emerge in Hong Kong that could credibly issue a *de facto* unilateral declaration of independence. A combination of the business community and the pro-Chinese forces would certainly not have it. For such a politically apathetic population as that of Hong Kong, such tactics seem inconceivable and foolish. Only if there is near-complete chaos on the mainland, perhaps as part of a power struggle, might such an option offer any hope.

But short of such a civil war in China, the second major argument against a strategy of divergence must be the attitude of China. As Britain recognised throughout its rule in Hong Kong, and the international community has long accepted, China literally has its hands on the taps of Hong Kong's future. Even if one rashly assumed that China would not use force to oppose such a development, China could starve the people of Hong Kong sufficiently swiftly to cause the collapse of the colony well before even large numbers of people had a chance to flee in panic.

In large measure because of China's ability to pressure Hong Kong, and the evident determination of China's leaders to take a poorer Hong Kong rather than not take it all, Britain too has opposed, and would in the future oppose, such a strategy of divergence. In effect, the final decision on this matter was taken with the signature on the 1984 accord. The implications of that deal, although not always fully accepted by Britain since, are that Chinese rule gradually begins before 1997 and that it will strengthen beyond that date. With the possible exception of a few events after the Peking massacre in 1989, nearly everything Britain has done about Hong Kong in recent years has been based on the principle of convergence. Not even the Patten proposals in 1992 and sustained support from a large segment of the Hong Kong population in 1992–93 has changed the basic acceptance of convergence. Similarly, the players in the international community have accepted the logic of convergence, even if they too were horrified about the full meaning of the concept when watching the scenes from Peking in June 1989.

Convergence I: The Hong Kong-led NIC

Could it be that the optimists will be quite right – that Hong Kong can profitably converge with the mainland? The essence of this hope is that the people of Hong Kong are pragmatic enough to realise that they have to get on with China. Political dissent will quickly die and migration will drain the trouble-makers but not the deal-makers. The economy will readjust but prosper because China is also pragmatic and knows it must not scare off investment and skills from Hong Kong. Indeed, this entire scenario depends on a sensible China remaining on the path of reform and relying on Guangdong and other coastal zones to drag China into the Pacific Century. The Hong Kong tail will be encouraged to wag the Chinese dog and Peking will be in a mood to learn from the former British colony the best ways of living in the international market economy. As convergence develops and southern China prospers, perhaps as one of several NETs, the fate of Hong Kong becomes tied up with the general question of the fate of reforms and decentralization in China as a whole.

In such a world, the hand-over in 1997 may hardly be noticed except for the hordes of journalists who booked their rooms just after the 1984 Anglo-Chinese accord. The 'through train' will run straight on past 1997 and the rest of the world, perhaps with the exception of Taiwan, will breathe a sigh of relief that the Hong Kong crisis never arrived. Hong Kong will continue to be a place where a range of investors from the global market economy invest in their East Asian base and Japanese and Americans will continue to lead the way. Canadians and Australians of Hong Kong origin will return to make money in the Hong Kong SAR and even British conservatives might be pleased that Britain will not have to absorb anything except a handful of Chinese from the last significant colony.

A variation on this rosy scenario is possible and certainly not as unlikely as many pundits predicted in 1989. The key remains confidence in the colony – and the key to confidence remains the actions of the rulers of China. If one wants to bet on a rapid and smooth succession to a reforming government in Peking, then the odds for the positive version of the convergence scenario must be better than even. But what if convergence goes wrong? Reform and regionalism in China may merely be steps along a more dangerous road that threatens the breakup of China. With the fate of Taiwan so closely connected with the fate of Hong Kong, and the history of warlordism and civil war in China, it would be foolish to be too sanguine about the risks of decentralization. Experience in living memory of outside countries, most notably Japan, taking advantage of a divided China is an obvious warning about the need to be careful about managing the type of convergence that might merely be a prelude to civil war. By placing hope for Hong Kong on the wagon of convergence, there are serious risks of derailment as the process picks up speed.

Convergence II: Slowing to China's Pace

In the end we come to the most likely scenario of all, a strategy of convergence that sees Hong Kong slow down. This is not necessarily, as many have suggested, a scenario for sudden catastrophe, if only because the pace of southern China has picked up enough in recent years to give more cause for optimism. Nor is it a scenario that suggests malicious intent on the part of the rulers of China. It is based on the view that Hong Kong must converge with China, and because not enough objective conditions are suited to success it is likely that Hong Kong will suffer.

Significant numbers of skilled people continue to emigrate from Hong Kong. This vivid and fatal evidence of a lack of confidence in the future can, if it continues, virtually guarantee on its own that Hong Kong gradually slows on its way to convergence with China. The economy will therefore continue to stumble, especially as investment will also slow and be diverted elsewhere in East Asia. This is not to say that Hong Kong will cease to be the richest part of China, but it will certainly not grow as fast as most other states in East Asia. Hong Kong is not doomed to be another Shanghai, but nor will it be the uniquely vibrant and cosmpolitan city it now is. This is not a scenario for collapse but, rather, one for a loud grinding of gears as the cog of Hong Kong fits into the larger China.

Perhaps the most persuasive reason for thinking this scenario is the most likely one is the sense that China itself does not seem so worried about at least a degree of slowdown in Hong Kong if that is the price to pay for stability and a relatively secure transfer. Even in the headiest days of reform, Deng Xiaoping made it clear that Hong Kong would have to adapt to China far more than the other way round. Thus the principle of sovereignty dominates the self-interest of economic prosperity, at least as seen from Peking. China's reactions to the Patten proposals in 1992–93 is evidence of how Peking orders its priorities and can mismanage its policies.

The rulers of China seem to believe that they can have their sovereignty, and still retain a high degree of economic self-interest, while recognising that Hong Kong will not be quite as fat a golden goose as it once was. But better an undernourished goose than a plump but diseased one that infects all the others back in China. Even if China should remain on the path of reform after a swift succession to Deng, there is little reason to believe that the new rulers will want to take a large chance on trying to integrate a more dangerous Hong Kong. There is simply not enough time before 1997 for China to reform sufficiently fast to be in any state to take Hong Kong as it is. It seems that Hong Kong will have to converge with China, suffering a slowdown in the process, even though in the longer term the creation of a more dynamic NET may mean a decent future for those in Hong Kong who stayed behind to do business with the new rulers.

From Britain's point of view, at least unofficially, such a

scenario for convergence always seemed most likely. The difficulty for Britain was both how to manage this inherently unsavoury process and how to do it with some dignity. After the Peking massacre, the sense of the degree of decline became greater, as did the expectation that Britain itself would have to take more migrants from Hong Kong than first planned. Should there be a messy succession in China before 1997, Hong Kong's decline and its level of migration may well increase. In the worst of all possible versions of this convergence scenario, Britain will be faced with managing a major crisis, including a mass exodus from Hong Kong. Such a catastrophe seems unlikely, but is possible, and certainly deserves contingent planning in London and other Western capitals. If such a crisis were to be part of a broader disorder in a disintegrating China, then the Hong Kong issue would only be part of a much more important threat to international security.

Assuming a less disastrous version of the convergence scenario, Britain can anticipate enduring further criticism for its failure to do more for the people of Hong Kong. This will be unfair, if only because the people of Hong Kong have shown a remarkable lack of initiative about their own fate. The bedrock support for Chris Patten in 1992-93, despite vehement Chinese efforts to undermine the new Governor, came as a pleasant surprise. It suggested that a shrewd leader able to mobilize public support was able to tap a stream of democratic politics that had remained mostly covered before. And yet at the time of writing there were important doubts about the robustness of Patten's support in the medium and longer term.

Most of the million or so people who have, or will have, left Hong Kong in the 1984-97 period will not go to Britain. Canada looks set to take another 175,000 in the 1991-97 period, and that is in addition to a somewhat smaller number since 1984. The United States, with its increased quotas, will take a further 190,000 in the 1991-97 period and Australia will add a further 100,000 or so to its present total. Assuming the less-than-catastrophic version of the convergence scenario, there will be no boat people scattered around East Asia. Singapore may well take a few tens of thousands of people, especially if business in Hong Kong runs down gradually and companies can make their transfers in good time to Singapore. Taiwan will not be displeased at this outcome, if only because the notion of 'one country, two systems' will have been discredited without creating a major crisis in its pragmatic relations with China or for the regional economy as a whole. Indeed, pragmatism is the key to the fate of Hong Kong. If the people of Hong Kong continue in their pragmatic ways, most will be resigned to a fate within China. Life will not be as good as it once was, but it will be better than in the rest of China. As for the rulers in Peking, pragmatism will get them a rich and still respectably prosperous Hong Kong. Britain too will feel that its pragmatic approach to Hong Kong will have been vindicated, although no British government can take anything but the pride of a bureaucratically inclined manager in handing over so many people to a fate they did not choose. Finally, the world at large will accept that, in the pragmatic world of a booming East Asian economy, the relative decline of Hong Kong is no tragedy. Certainly there will be plenty of Hong Kong's competitors that will console themselves with a well-known saying in the region, 'it is good for business'.

Britain and China locked in their most acrimonious crisis about Hong Kong since the negotiations leading to the 1984 accord. The issues at stake are well known from the preceding course of Sino-British negotiations. Britain wishes to introduce a minimum level of democracy so as to give a civil society a chance of surviving in a relatively autonomous fashion after 1997. China opposes any change which has not received its prior blessing. As 1997 approaches, such debates become more frequent and important.

It seems increasingly clear that Hong Kong can only win its civil society and remain calm if its people remain resolute and Britain and Hong Kong are supported by a wider international effort. The United States and Japan, to name only the most prominent, have provided the kind of international support that Britain has wanted. But the key variable in the longer term remains China's policies. Will China's leadership succession produce the best sort of reforming leaders? Can Peking manage the problems of regionalism and the growing power of provinces such as Guangdong?

It is hard to imagine that Hong Kong will have any prolonged peace and quiet. Although it is probably true that in the last few months and even days before the handover in 1997, China will be anxious to avoid having demonstrations of active resistance on the streets. But certainly in the next few years to 1995 and 1996, there are too many basic uncertainties to expect calm to prevail.

As we look beyond the short-term fate of Hong Kong, it seems possibly that the two convergence scenarios may be part of a single, more protracted process. Even assuming a certain slowdown in Hong Kong, it is possible that as a southern Chinese NET takes shape, the region may indeed develop into the next economic powerhouse in East Asia. A southern Chinese NET might even be part of a process where several similar NETs are created around the Chinese periphery.

And yet, even this rosier type of convergence remains a risky strategy. Reform and decentralization in China are to be applauded, but can easily get out of hand. The result might be such serious fragmentation of China that regional and international security is threatened when outside forces try to take advantage of the chaos and vacuum of power. While it is usual practice for China-watchers to dismiss such a scenario for China, pundits should have learned a degree of humility after the revolutionary events of 1989–91. There are precedents for a disunited China, and if, in the dying years of the twentieth century, this disunity is mainly developed on the basis of creating NETs as part of a more integrated international economy, it may be a harder process for Peking to halt. With changing and possibly unstable international relations in East Asia in the post-Cold War world, there certainly are risks in trying to manage the loosening of the Chinese empire and the integration of its parts into the international system. If the fate of Hong Kong becomes tied up in these much larger processes, then it becomes all the more important to understand the international interests and conditions shaping the transition to Chinese rule in 1997.

Notes

Introduction

1 Various studies will be cited in later chapters but suffice it to mention here the most recent of the major surveys of the Hong Kong problem. Felix Patrikeeff, *Mouldering Pearl* (London: George Philip, 1989); Kevin Rafferty, *City of the Rocks* (London: Viking, 1989); Jan Morris, *Xianggang* (London: Penguin, 1989); Dick Wilson, *Hong Kong! Hong Kong!* (London: Unwin/Hyman, 1990); Jules Nadeau, *Hong Kong 1997* (Montreal: Éditions Québec/Amérique, 1990).

2 For an exception, see the excellent study of the 1982–84 negotiations by Philip Cottrell, *The End of Hong Kong* (London: John Murray, 1993) and Michael Yahuda, "Sino-British Negotiations," *International Affairs*, Vol 69 No. 2, April 1993.

1. Hong Kong to 1949

1 Gerald Segal, *Rethinking the Pacific* (Oxford: Oxford University Press, 1990), ch. 1.

2 Jack Gray, *Rebellions and Revolutions* (Oxford: Oxford University Press, 1990).

3 Details of this story are developed in Gray, *Rebellions and Revolutions*.

4 Nigel Cameron, *An Illustrated History of Hong Kong* (Oxford: Oxford University Press, 1991).

5 Jan Morris, *Hong Kong* (London: Penguin, 1989) p. 77.

6 Kevin Rafferty, *City on the Rocks* (London: Viking, 1989).

7 Evan Luard, *Britain and China* (London: Chatto and Windus, 1962) ch. 9.

8 Felix Patrikeeff, *Mouldering Pearl* (London: George Philip, 1989) p. 28.

9 Dennis Duncanson, 'Hong Kong as a Crown Colony' in Jurgen Domes and Yu-ming Shaw eds, *Hong Kong: A Chinese and International Concern* (London: Westview, 1988) p. 10.

10 Discussed more broadly in Jonathan Spence, *The Search for Modern China* (London: W.W. Norton, 1990) section 2.

11 Duncanson, 'Crown Colony' p. 12.

12 Cameron, *Hong Kong* p. 76.

13 Gray, *Rebellions and Revolutions*.

14 Discussed in Cameron, *Hong Kong* p. 161 and Segal *Rethinking* section 1.

15 Peter Wesley Smith, *Unequal Treaty, 1898–1997*. (Oxford: Oxford University Press, 1983).
16 Edward Hambro, *The Problem of Chinese Refugees in Hong Kong* (Leiden: A.W. Sijthoff, 1955) pp. 11–16.
17 Luard, *Britain and China* ch. 9.
18 Cameron, *Hong Kong* p. 237.
19 Rafferty, *City on the Rocks* ch. 6.
20 G.B. Endacott, *A History of Hong Kong* 2nd ed. (Oxford: Oxford University Press, 1973) p. 300.
21 Luard, *Britain and China* ch. 9.
22 Endacott, *A History of Hong Kong* p. 305.
23 Steve Yui-sang Tsang, *Democracy Shelved* (Oxford: Oxford University Press, 1988).
24 Tsang, *Democracy Shelved* p. 78.
25 Betty Peh-T'i Wei, *Shanghai* (Oxford: Oxford University Press, 1987).
26 See Marie-Claire Bergere, 'The Other China' in Christopher Howe ed, *Shanghai* (Cambridge: Cambridge University Press, 1981).
27 Richard Gaulton, 'Political Mobilization in Shanghai, 1949–1951' in Howe ed, *Shanghai*.

2. Thirty Years of Prosperity: 1950–80

1 Endacott, *Hong Kong*, ch. 27.
2 Tsang, *Democracy Shelved*, p. 172.
3 Cited in Endacott, *Hong Kong*, p. 316.
4 Endacott, *Hong Kong*, p. 317.
5 Dick Wilson, *Hong Kong! Hong Kong!* (London: Unwin/Hyman, 1990).
6 Ian Scott, *Political Change and the Crisis of Legitimacy in Hong Kong* (London: C. Hurst & Co., 1989), ch. 3.
7 Scott, *Political Change*, p. 97.
8 Wilson, *Hong Kong*, part 1.
9 Ezra Vogel, *One Step Ahead in China* (London: Harvard University Press, 1989), ch. 2.

3. Negotiating the End of Empire

1 Minorca was handed to Spain in 1802, the Ionian islands to Greece in 1863 and Heligoland to Germany in 1890. The better comparison is to Gibraltar, although it is closer in Europe; or to the Falkland Islands, which are further away in the South Atlantic but claimed by Argentina, a far less impressive military power. Of course, both Gibraltar and the Falklands are populated by whites. Perhaps the best comparison is to the former Portuguese colony of Goa (seized

in 1510), which was captured by Indian troops in December 1961.

2 The majority population in Singapore is Chinese, while the Chinese are a minority in the rest of Malaysia. As ever, nothing is quite like Hong Kong.

3 Noted in Chalmers Johnson, 'The Mousetrapping of Hong Kong', *Asian Survey* No. 9, 1984.

4 James Hsiung, 'The Hong Kong Settlement', *Asian Affairs* No. 2, 1985.

5 Not quite 'all other powers' in the sense that the problem of Macao had also not yet been resolved. Yet its fate was closely and explicitly linked to that of nearby Hong Kong.

6 Ezra Vogel, *One Step Ahead in China* (London: Harvard University Press, 1989).

7 David Bonavia, *Hong Kong, 1997* (Hong Kong: Columbus Books, 1985).

8 Joseph Cheng, *Hong Kong: In Search of a Future* (Hong Kong: Oxford University Press, 1984).

9 Frank Ching, *Hong Kong and China* (N.Y. Asia Society, 1985) p. 9.

10 See, for example, *Far Eastern Economic Review*, 5 February 1982.

11 Ian Scott, *Political Change and the Crisis of Legitimacy in Hong Kong* (London: C. Hurst & Co., 1989) p. 168.

12 *Far Eastern Economic Review*, 21 May 1982, p. 24.

13 Ching, *Hong Kong*, p. 11.

14 See a series of Chinese statements collated in Kevin Rafferty, *City on the Rocks* (London: Viking, 1989), ch. 12.

15 *Beijing Review*, No. 41, 1982.

16 Rafferty, *City on the Rocks*, p. 404.

17 Johnson, 'Mousetrapping', p. 901.

18 *Far Eastern Economic Review*, 21 July 1983, p. 12.

19 *Far Eastern Economic Review*, 20 August 1982.

20 Ching, *Hong Kong*, p. 16.

21 *Far Eastern Economic Review*, 6 October 1983.

22 See Sir Percy Cradock's comments noted in Peter Hennessy, 'Cradock's People', *New Society*, 11 October 1984.

23 Johnson, 'Mousetrapping', p. 899.

24 Y.C. Jao et al., 'The Monetary System and the Future of Hong Kong', *Hong Kong and 1997* (Hong Kong: Hong Kong University, 1985).

25 See some details in *Far Eastern Economic Review*, 20 January 1983.

26 See, for example, Lucian Pye, *Chinese Commercial Negotiating Style* (Cambridge: Oelgeschlager, Gunn & Hain, 1982).

27 Bonavia, *Hong Kong*, p. 110.

28 Ching, *Hong Kong*, p. 26, and Rafferty, *City on the Rocks*, p. 416.

29 Bonavia, *Hong Kong*, p. 112.

30 Until 1962 Hong Kong Chinese had the same rights as British-born passport holders. In response to anti-immigration campaigns at home, London changed the rules in 1962 to introduce the notion of

'right of abode'. Although the passports continued to look much alike, the Hong Kong documents did not say on p. 5 that the 'holder has the right of abode in the United Kingdom'. The 1981 Immigration Act, which came into force in 1983, actually changed the document more clearly, marking Hong Kong on the front of what became a BDT passport. Some countries, such as Japan, require visas for BDT holders, although not for those holding a full British passport. In the run-up to 1997, Hong Kong has begun issuing new documents called British National Overseas papers because after 1 July 1997 Hong Kong will no longer be a 'dependent territory'.

31 The remaining Chinese in Hong Kong, 2.3 million in 1989, are immigrants from China. For their first seven years in Hong Kong they carry Documents of Identity, after which they qualify for the right of abode and for a Certificate of Identity. A further small number of Hong Kong residents are people of Indian, Pakistani and Eurasian origin who have no right to passports from their country of origin and who also carry BDT documents. Some 12,000 of 20,000 Indians and Eurasians in Hong Kong are in this category.

32 Rafferty, *City on the Rocks*, p. 422.

33 Bonavia, *Hong Kong*, pp. 139–140.

34 Discussed in Vogel, *One Step Ahead*, p. 73.

4. On the Road to 1997

1 For the background of China's use of force see Gerald Segal, *Defending China* (Oxford: Oxford University Press, 1985).

2 Described in Jan Morris, *Xianggang* (London: Penguin, 1989), ch. 12.

3 The theme of Ezra Vogel, *One Step Ahead in China* (London: Harvard University Press, 1989).

4 Dick Wilson, *Hong Kong! Hong Kong!* (London: Unwin/Hyman, 1990).

5 Ken Davies, *Hong Kong to 1994* (London: Unwin/Hyman, 1990), p. 16.

6 Davies, *Hong Kong*, p. 16.

7 Davies, *Hong Kong*, pp. 18–19.

8 *The Economist*, 26 August 1989.

9 Kate Grosser and Brian Bridges, 'Economic Interdependence in East Asia', *The Pacific Review* No. 1, 1990.

10 Michéle Ledic, 'Hong Kong and China – Economic Interdependence', *The Pacific Review* No. 2, 1989.

11 Davies, *Hong Kong*, p. 53.

12 For details on the China crisis see David Goodman and Gerald Segal (eds), *China in the Nineties* (Oxford: Oxford University Press, 1991), and John Gittings, *China Changes Face* (Oxford: Oxford University Press, 1990).

13   *Financial Times*, 8 November 1989.
14   *Financial Times*, 15 November 1989.
15   *Financial Times*, 6 March 1991.
16   *Far Eastern Economic Review*, 21 March 1991, p. 62, and see generally Miron Mushkat, *The Economic Future of Hong Kong* (London: Lynne Reinner, 1990).
17   *The Economist*, 4 August 1990, p. 43.
18   *International Herald Tribune*, 21 March and 22–23 March 1991.
19   *The Economist*, 13 April 1991.
20   *Financial Times*, 12 October 1989.
21   *Far Eastern Economic Review*, 18 July 1991.
22   *Financial Times*, 5 March 1992.
23   *The Economist*, 5 October 1991, for a survey of the issue.
24   *South China Morning Post*, 4 September 1990, p. 3, and *International Herald Tribune*, 4 September 1990.
25   Cited in Ian Scott, *Political Change and the Crisis of Legitimacy in Hong Kong* (London: C. Hurst & Co., 1989), p. 318.
26   Ronald Skeldon, 'South China Pilgrims', *Far Eastern Economic Review*, 27 July 1989, pp. 24–25.
27   *Guardian*, 31 July 1988.
28   *Far Eastern Economic Review*, 27 July 1989.
29   Sir Garry Johnson, 'Hong Kong: Prospects for Stability', *RUSI Journal*, Spring 1990, p. 27.
30   *Financial Times*, 12 December 1989.
31   *International Herald Tribune*, 14 March 1990.
32   *Financial Times*, 16 January 1990.
33   *Financial times*, 18 December 1989.
34   *Asiaweek*, 13 April 1990, p. 28.
35   *Asiaweek*, 13 April 1990, p. 30.
36   *Newsweek*, 16 April 1990, p. 41.
37   *Dateline Hong Kong* No. 12, 1990.
38   *Hong Kong Standard*, 15 March 1991, and Xinhua on 14 March, both in FBIS-CHI-91-051-40.
39   *The Economist*, 16 December 1989.
40   Lawrence Lam, 'The Attitude of the Local Population Towards Vietnamese Boat People in Hong Kong', *Refuge*, Vol. 9, No. 3, February 1990.
41   *International Herald Tribune*, 1 September 1989, and *Financial Times*, 28 October 1989.
42   *Financial Times*, 11 October 1989.
43   *International Herald Tribune*, 4 May 1990.
44   *Far Eastern Economic Review*, 1 February 1990.
45   *Financial Times*, 15 February 1990, and *Far Eastern Economic Review*, 1 February 1990.
46   *Far Eastern Economic Review*, 26 September, 3 October and 7 November 1991.

47 BBC/SWB/FE/1197/i.
48 *Far Eastern Economic Review*, 1 February 1990, for a survey of this issue.
49 *South China Morning Post*, 25 February 1991, p. 2, *Far Eastern Economic Review*, 23 August 1990, pp. 22–23, and *The Economist*, 3 November 1990 and 9 March 1991.
50 *Far Eastern Economic Review*, 14 February 1991.
51 *Financial Times*, 6 June 1991, and *International Herald Tribune*, 16 October 1991.
52 *South China Morning Post*, 29 April 1991, and *The Economist*, 7 December 1991.
53 *International Herald Tribune*, 23 September 1991, 20 January 1992, *Far Eastern Economic Review*, 16 January 1992, and *The Economist*, 25 January 1992.
54 Roy Jenkins was reportedly offered the job in the 1970s by James Callaghan, the prime minister, while standing side by side in the urinal in the Grand Palais Kleber in Paris. *The Sunday Times*, 26 April 1992.
55 'Our Next Five Years', Address by the Governor, 7 October 1992.

5. China: Taking Charge

1 The options are best developed in Dick Wilson, *Hong Kong! Hong Kong!* (London: Unwin/Hyman, 1990).
2 The full text in *Beijing Review* No. 18, 30 April 1990.
3 Gerald Segal, *Defending China* (Oxford: Oxford University Press, 1985).
4 Wen Qing, 'One Country – Two Systems', *Beijing Review*, 13 August 1990.
5 For example, Zhongguo Xinwen She, 26 June 1990, FBIS-CHI-90-126-59-60.
6 Zhou Nan, cited in Hong Kong's Wen Wei Po, 1 July 1990, FBIS-CHI-90-127-67-68, and see also Xinhua, 1 July 1990, p. 68.
7 Zhongguo Xinwen She, 8 March 1991, FBIS-CHI-91-047-9.
8 Cited in Kuang Chiao Ching, 16 March 1991, FBIS-CHI-91-053.
9 Hong Kong's Wen Wei Po, 22 June 1990, FBIS-CHI-90-121-57.
10 *Financial Times*, 30 September 1989.
11 *Far Eastern Economic Review*, 13 February 1992.
12 *Wide Angle*, cited in *South China Morning Post*, 9 February 1991, p. 1.
13 On PLA mobility see Hong Kong's Liaowang, 24 July 1989, SWB/FE/0526/B2, 3–4, and generally Yitzhak Shichor, 'Defence Policy', Gerald Segal (ed), *Chinese Politics and Foreign Policy Reform* (London: Kegan Paul International for the RIIA, 1990).
14 Xinhua, 18 October 1989, SWB/FE/0592/A3/1.
15 Cited in Hong Kong's Ta Kung Pao, 2 May 1990, FE/0754/A3/1–2.

16 See earlier discussions, Zhongguo Xinwen She, 14 October 1989, FE/0590/A3/1.
17 *International Herald Tribune*, 10 November 1989, and generally, *Far Eastern Economic Review*, 24 August 1989, pp. 18–19.
18 Details from Yun-Wing Sung, *The China–Hong Kong Connection* (Cambridge: Cambridge University Press, 1991), p. 19.
19 Sung, *China–Hong Kong Connection*, pp. 144–5.
20 *Financial Times*, 2 August 1990.
21 *The Economist*, 10 August 1991.
22 Zhou Nan in Hong Kong's Wen Wei Po, 30 November 1990, SWB/FE/0936/A3/1.
23 Zongguo Tongxun She, 2 April 1990, FBIS-CHI-90-070-57-58.
24 *Financial Times*, 18 March 1992.
25 *International Herald Tribune*, 23 January 1992.
26 David Goodman, *Southern China in Transition* (Melbourne: Longman/Cheshire, 1992).
27 *Far Eastern Economic Review*, 4 July 1991.
28 Ezra Vogel, *One Step Ahead* (Cambridge: Harvard University Press, 1989).
29 Ming Pao, 21 January 1992, BBC/SW/FE/1286/B2/1–2.
30 Xinhua, 8 October 1989, FE/0583/A3/1.
31 Cited in Ta Kung Pao, 8 October, 1989, FE/0583/A3/12.
32 Reported in Hong Kong's Wen Wei Po, 19 October 1989, FE/0592/A3/1–12.
33 Xinhua, 10 June 1991, BBC/DSWB/FE/1096/A3/2–3, and Wen Wei Po, 11 April 1991, FE/1048/A3/1–2.
34 Kuang Chiao Ching, 16 February 1991, FBIS-CHI-91-030-81-5, and Wen Wei Po, 1 June 1991, BBC/SWB/FE/1088/A1/1, on US Republican Party efforts to monitor elections in Hong Kong.
35 BBC/SWB/FE/1327/A3/6.
36 Hong Kong's Wen Wei Po, 3 May 1990, FE/0755/A3/1–2.
37 Cited in Kuang Chiao Ching, 16 March 1991, FBIS-CHI-91-053-84-5.
38 *Far Eastern Economic Review*, 31 August 1989, p. 17.
39 For example, Zhonggou Xinwen She, 23 September 1989, FE/0571/A3/1.
40 *Financial Times*, 1 November 1989.
41 Xinhua, 26 April 1990, FE/0754/A3/2.
42 Lian Xishen, 'Hong Kong's Future Political Structure', *Beijing Review*, 16 April 1990.
43 Ji Pengfei, 28 October 1991, FE/1223/A3/6.
44 Xinhua, 11 March 1992, FE/1328/A3/1–2, and Wen Wei Po, 29 February 1992 in 1322/A3/3–4. See also *Observer*, 16 February 1992, and *Far Eastern Economic Review*, 6 February 1992.
45 *International Herald Tribune*, 26 June 1992.
46 *Far Eastern Economic Review*, 19 October and 2 November 1989.
47 Cited in Zhongguo Tongxun She, 22 August 1989, FE/0545/A3/1.

48 Hong Kong's Wen Wei Po, 21 December 1989, FE/0647/A3/1, and Chen Yang, 'UK's Decision a Violation of its Commitment', *Beijing Review*, 12 February 1990.

49 Xinhua, 28 July 1990, FE/0829/A1/1.

50 Wen Wei Po, citing Lu Ping, vice-director of the Hong Kong and Macao Affairs Office of the State Council, 12 March 1990, FE/0716/A3/2.

51 *Daily Telegraph*, 27 September 1984, and *Financial Times*, 5 April 1991.

52 Foreign ministry spokesman, 18 October 1989, FE/0591/i.

53 Peking Home Service, 25 October 1989, 0599/A3/1.

54 Reported in Xinhua, 25 October 1989, FE/0599/A3/2.

55 *People's Daily*, 21 November 1989, FE/0620/A3/2.

56 *International Herald Tribune*, 28 April 1990, and *Far Eastern Economic Review*, 1 January 1990.

57 Cited in Zhongguo Xinwen She, 8 March 1991, FBIS-CHI-91-047-80-3.

58 *Financial Post* (Toronto), 2 April 1991, p. 9, and Ziang Zemin quoted in Wen Wei Po, 11 April 1990, SWB/FE/0743/A3/1.

59 *Independent*, 19 December 1990.

60 *Independent*, 14 January 1991, and *Independent on Sunday*, 31 March 1991.

61 Financial Times, 26 March 1991.

62 *Far Eastern Economic Review*, 18 July 1991.

63 *Financial Times*, 5 and 6 March 1992.

64 *Financial Times*, 14 June and 31 October 1991.

65 *Financial Times*, 18 March 1992, 15 April 1992, and *Observer*, 24 May 1992.

6. Britain: Dignity in Retreat?

1 John Darwin, *Britain and Decolonisation* (London: Macmillan, 1988).

2 Department of Trade and Industry evidence to the House of Commons Foreign Affairs Committee, 1988–89, *The Sunday Times*, 11 August 1991, *Independent*, 17 September 1991, and *Far Eastern Economic Review*, 4 July 1991.

3 *Financial Times*, 25 May 1985.

4 When Hong Kong's re-exports are included, Britain slips down to eighth place.

5 *Independent*, 22 June 1990.

6 Gerald Segal, 'Britain and East Asia', Peter Bryd (ed) *British Foreign Policy in the Thatcher Years* (London: Philip Allan, 1988).

7 HMSO, *Population Trends* (London: HMSO, 1989).

8 William Wallace, *The Transformation of Western Europe* (London: Frances Pinter, 1990).

9 Colin Holmes, *John Bull's Island* (London: Macmillan, 1988), p. 3.

10   Michael Marrus, *The Unwanted* (Oxford: Oxford University Press, 1985).
11   Marrus, *The Unwanted*.
12   *The Economist*, 7 July 1990, p. 38.
13   This section is based on John Haskey, 'The Ethnic Minority Population of Great Britain', *Population Trends* No. 60, Summer 1990, Anthony Shang, *The Chinese in Britain* (London: Batsford, 1984), and Holmes, *John Bull's Island*.
14   *Financial Times*, 16 December 1989.
15   *The Economist*, 26 October 1991.
16   *The Economist*, 28 April 1990.
17   Some doubt the multiplier figure and suggest it should be considerably lower. See *Canada and Hong Kong Update* No. 3, Winter 1991, p. 10.
18   *The Economist*, 23 December 1989.
19   *Far Eastern Economic Review*, 19 April 1990.
20   Norman Tebbit suggested a criterion for judging immigrants might be which cricket team they would support.
21   *Independent*, 21 December 1989.
22   For an assessment of the role of Parliament on these issues, see Charles Carstairs and Richard Ware (eds), *Parliament and International Relations* (Milton Keynes: Open University Press, 1991), especially 'Behind the Scenes in the House of Commons' by Michael Lee.
23   The House of Commons, Foreign Affairs Committee, *Report on Hong Kong*, HC 281, 1988–89.
24   *Independent on Sunday*, 8 April 1990.
25   See, for example, Ralf Dahrendorf in *Independent*, 26 October 1989, Bernard Levin in *The Times*, 28 August 1989, and the strongly opposed David Blake in *Sunday Correspondent*, 15 October 1989.
26   *International Herald Tribune*, 1 December 1989, and *Financial Times*, 5 April 1990.
27   Details in *Financial Times*, 1 March 1991, *South China Morning Post*, 20 January 1991, p. 2, and 9 February 1991, p. 1. See also Gerald Segal, 'An offer they were able to refuse', *Guardian*, 5 March 1991.
28   *South China Morning Post*, 20 January 1991, p. 2.
29   *The Times*, 3 August 1990.
30   For the most notorious of these discussions, see Peter Hennessy, 'Cradock's People', *New Society*, 11 October 1984.
31   *Independent on Sunday*, 7 April 1991, *The Times*, 3 April 1991, *The Economist*, 13 April 1991, and *Far Eastern Economic Review*, 18 April 1991.

7. The United States: The Inactive Superpower

1 Harry Harding, *Sino-American Relations* (Washington: Brookings, 1992).
2 Gerald Segal, *Rethinking the Pacific* (Oxford: Oxford University Press, 1990), section 3.
3 Hungdah Chiu, 'The Hong Kong Agreement and US Foreign Policy', Jurgen Domes and Yu-ming Shaw (eds), *Hong Kong* (Boulder, Colorado: Westview Press, 1986).
4 Chiu, 'Hong Kong', p. 186.
5 *International Herald Tribune*, 9 July 1984.
6 Cited in Chiu, 'Hong Kong', p. 187.
7 On 26 September 1984, cited in Chiu, 'Hong Kong', p. 190.
8 *Daily Telegraph*, 22 March 1988.
9 *The Times*, 3 September 1988.
10 *International Herald Tribune*, 31 January 1988, and *Financial Times*, 30 January 1988.
11 *International Herald Tribune*, 1 February 1988.
12 *Financial Times*, 16 August 1988, and compare with *Financial Times*, 31 March 1987 and 26 June 1986.
13 *International Herald Tribune*, 16 May 1987, and *Financial Times*, 28 April 1987 and 21 December 1987.
14 *Far Eastern Economic Review*, 16 November 1989, p. 62.
15 *Financial Times*, 21 October 1985, for earlier cases but especially *Far Eastern Economic Review*, 24 October 1991.
16 *International Herald Tribune*, 10 May 1990.
17 *Far Eastern Economic Review*, 3 May 1990, pp. 42–3, and 24 May 1990, p. 66. Also *Financial Times*, 25 May 1991 and 20 December 1991.
18 Zhongguo Tongxun, 8 April 1990, FBIS-CHI-90-071-56-7.
19 William McGurn, 'Hong Kong needs a US Voice', *Far Eastern Economic Review*, 21 June 1990, p. 24.
20 *Far Eastern Economic Review*, 13 June 1991, and Wen Wei Po, 1 June 1991, FE/1088/A1/1, and 20 February 1992, FE/1312/A3/11. Xinhua, 26 May 1992, FE/1393/A2/1, and Zhongguo Tongxun She, 25 April 1992, FE/1368/A2/2.
21 Ta Kung Pao, 28 June 1992, FE/1422/A1/1–2.
22 For a general discussion of American priorities, see Harry Harding, *Sino-American Relations* (Washington: Brookings, 1992).
23 Andrew Brick, 'Hong Kong's Fate Concerns America', *International Herald Tribune*, 17 October 1989.
24 Alan Dowty, *Closed Borders* (New Haven: Yale University Press, 1987), p. 49, and R.A. Burchell, 'Recent Patterns and Policies in US Immigration', *The USA and Canada 1990* (London: Europa, 1991).
25 Charles Keely and Patricia Elwell, 'International Migration: Canada and the United States', Mary Kritz et al. (eds), *Global Trends in*

Migration (New York: Center for Migration Studies, 1983).

26   Hawkins, *Critical Year*, p. 259.
27   Robert Tucker, Charles Keely, Kinda Wrigley (eds), *Immigration and US Foreign Policy* (Boulder, Colorado: Westview Press, 1990).
28   Dowty, *Closed Borders*, p. 246.
29   Linda Gordon, 'Asian Immigration Since World War II', Robert Tucker, Charles Keely and Linda Wrigley (eds), *Immigration and US Foreign Policy* (Boulder, Colorado: Westview Press, 1990).
30   *International Herald Tribune*, 17 April 1984.
31   Myron Weiner, 'Asian Immigrants and US Foreign Policy', Tucker et al. (eds), *Immigration and Policy*.
32   Valerie O'Connor Sutter, *The Indo-Chinese Refugee Dilemma* (London: Louisiana State University Press, 1990), and *Washington Post*, 29 January 1990.
33   *Trends and Characteristics of International Migration Since 1950* (United Nations Demographic Studies, 64, 1979).
34   *Statistical Abstract of the United States, 1990*, p. 10.
35   *International Herald Tribune*, 13 June 1991, and *Far Eastern Economic Review*, 22 November 1990, p. 34, and 28 March 1991, p. 12.
36   The figures on the former Soviet Union were quoted by Tass, 29 January 1992, SU/1283/A1/2. See more generally *The Economist*, 16 March 1991, p. 80, and *Far Eastern Economic Review*, 26 March 1992.
37   Frank Bean, Barry Edmonston and Jeffrey Passel (eds), *Undocumented Migration to the United States* (Washington: The Urban Institute, 1990), and *Time*, 14 May 1990, p. 66.
38   *The Economist*, 9 September 1989, pp. 47–8.
39   *International Herald Tribune*, 4 January 1991.
40   *The Economist*, 16 March 1991, p. 11.
41   Details taken from USIS Wireless File, 30 October 1990.
42   Some figures suggested some people were returning from the United States to make money. See *International Herald Tribune*, 25 May 1991.
43   *Vancouver Sun*, 18 December 1990.
44   *South China Morning Post*, 11 September 1990, p. 7.
45   Wen Wei Po, 21 September 1990, FE/0876/A3/7.

8. Canada: Immigration Without Responsibility

1   *Canada and Hong Kong Update* No. 2, Fall 1990, p. 12.
2   *Canada and Hong Kong Update* No. 1, Spring 1990.
3   Canadian External Affairs Minister's speech in Hong Kong, 2 July 1980, External Affairs, Canada, *Statements and Speeches*, No. 14, 1980.
4   Gerald Segal, *Rethinking the Pacific* (Oxford: Oxford University Press, 1990), ch. 22.
5   Robert Bothwell, Ian Drummond and John English, *Canada Since*

1945 (Toronto: University of Toronto Press, 1989), and J.L. Granatstein and Robert Bothwell, *Pirouette: Pierre Trudeau and Canadian Foreign Policy* (Toronto: University of Toronto Press, 1990), ch. 7 and 13 especially.

6 Details from Canada's 'Background Information' brief for the London Economic Summit, 15–17 July 1991, p. 43.

7 Much of the non-attributed material in this chapter is based on interviews conducted in the Department of External Affairs and the Department of Immigration in Ottawa, in November 1990. For a recent survey of the Canadian debate about its character, see the Canada survey in *The Economist*, 29 June 1991.

8 Freda Hawkins, *Critical Years in Immigration* (Montreal: McGill–Queen's University Press, 1989), ch. 1.

9 Peter Li, *The Chinese in Canada* (Toronto: Oxford University Press, 1989), Ch. 6.

10 Hawkins, *Critical Years*, p. 63.

11 For basic statistics, see *Immigration to Canada*, Employment and Immigration Canada, 1989.

12 Li, *The Chinese*, ch. 6.

13 Li, *The Chinese*, ch. 7 and 8.

14 Margaret Cannon, *China Tide* (Toronto: Harper Collins, 1989).

15 *Financial Times*, 18 June, 1992.

16 *Canada and Hong Kong Update* No. 9, Spring 1993.

17 *Canada and Hong Kong Update* No. 2, Fall 1990.

18 *Vancouver Sun*, 31 January 1991.

19 Victor Malarek, *Heaven's Gate* (Toronto: Macmillan, 1987), ch. 13.

20 Malarek, *Haven's Gate*, pp. 226–7.

21 Statistics from *Immigration to Canada*, pp. 41–4, and 'Chinese Investment Exceeds Expectation', *Vancouver Sun*, 28 November 1990.

22 *International Herald Tribune*, 18 December 1987.

23 *International Herald Tribune*, 11 March 1986.

24 *Vancouver Sun*, 2 October 1991 and 27 May 1991, and *Canada and Hong Kong Update*, Spring 1991, p. 1.

25 *Canada and Hong Kong Update* No. 3, Winter 1991.

26 Cannon, *China Tide*, and John De Mont and Thomas Fennell, *Hong Kong Money* (Toronto: Key Porter Books, 1989).

27 Hong Kong Standard, 4 April 1990, FBIS-CHI-90-065-58-59, and *International Herald Tribune*, 14 May 1991.

28 *Immigration to Canada: Aspects of Public Opinion*, Employment and Immigration Canada, report prepared by Angus Reid Group Inc., October 1989, and De Mont and Fennell, *Hong Kong Money*, ch. 6.

29 *Independent on Sunday*, 28 January 1990, p. 12.

30 Reporting 900 members in 10–12 gangs of Triads, *Vancouver Sun*, 22 August 1990.

31 *Time Magazine*, 5 March 1990, p. 39.

32   *Far Eastern Economic Review*, 8 February 1990, pp. 34–5.
33   De Mont and Fennell, *Hong Kong Money*, ch. 5.
34   *Toronto Life*, November 1990, p. 76.
35   *The Economist*, 23 March 1991, p. 118.
36   *International Herald Tribune*, 10 February 1988.
37   *Far Eastern Economic Review*, 22 February 1990.
38   Official press release of the Department of External Affairs, 30 June 1989.
39   Press statement, 22 May 1990, issued by the Secretary of State for External Affairs.
40   *Canada and Hong Kong Update* No. 3, Winter 1991.
41   For a very different view of Canadian immigration policy from that presented here, see *Far Eastern Economic Review*, 31 January 1991, pp. 28–9.

9. Australia: Pragmatism in the Pacific

1   Segal, *Rethinking the Pacific* (Oxford: Oxford University Press, 1990), section 2.
2   Ross Garnaut, *Australia and the Northeast Asian Ascendancy* (Canberra: Australian Government Publishing Service, 1989), and regarding cultural diplomacy, see Michael Lee, 'The Projection of Australia Overseas', *Australian Journal of Public Administration* Vol. 50, No. 1, March 1991.
3   It is true that Australia has some important similarities to the position of New Zealand. See the report that some have called the equivalent of the Garnaut report for many of the commonalities, *Toward a Pacific Island Community*, Report of the South Pacific Policy Review Group (Wellington, 1990).
4   *Far Eastern Economic Review*, 28 June 1990, p. 16.
5   *International Herald Tribune*, 6 February 1987.
6   Garnaut, *Australia and Northeast Asia*, and see a discussion in Trevor Matthews and John Ravenhill, 'Australia's Economic Malaise', *The Pacific Review* No. 1, 1991.
7   Gerald Segal, 'Britain and East Asia'.
8   *Far Eastern Economic Review*, 13 June 1991.
9   Hawkins, *Critical Years*, p. 11.
10   Hawkins, *Critical Years*, p. 28.
11   Cited in *Spectator*, 7 April 1990, p. 12.
12   Hawkins, *Critical Years*, ch. 3.
13   *Far Eastern Economic Review*, 26 October 1989, p. 31.
14   *The Economist*, 10 March 1990, p. 80.
15   *Far Eastern Economic Review*, 1 November 1990, p. 39.
16   Interestingly, some 43% of migrants from Australia were of British and southern European origin. See *Far Eastern Economic Review*, 1

November 1990, p. 46.
17 Much of the jump was due to a sharp increase in applications after the Peking massacre in June 1989. Details in *Australian*, 4 February 1991.
18 *Australian*, 3 February 1992.
19 *Immigration: A Commitment to Australia*, A Report of the Committee to Advise on Australia's Immigration Policies (Canberra: AGPS, 1988).
20 *Financial Times*, 13 May 1992, and *The Economist*, 30 May 1992.
21 *Australian*, 3 February 1992.
22 South China Morning Post, 28 February 1990, FBIS-CHI-90-042-56.
23 *Far Eastern Economic Review*, 28 June 1990, pp. 16–17, 1 November, 1990, p. 45, and 20 June 1991.
24 *Far Eastern Economic Review*, 1 November 1990, p. 44.
25 *Asia Inc*, May 1993, pp. 50–51.
26 *Independent*, 22 December 1989.

10. East Asia: Picking China Apart

1 Lillian Craig Harris, 'Towards Taiwan's Independence', *Pacific Review* No. 1, 1988, and Simon Long, *Taiwan: China's Last Frontier* (London: Macmillan, 1991).
2 *Guardian*, 27 September 1984.
3 Richard Sorich, 'Realistic Barometer', *Free China Review* No. 3, March 1990.
4 *Financial Times*, 28 September 1984.
5 Interview with Vice-Premier Shih Chi-yang, *Free China Review* No. 3, March 1990.
6 Ibid., p. 17.
7 *The Economist*, 16 June 1990, p. 80.
8 Taipei Home Service, 12 August 1989, SWB/FE/0536/A3/3.
9 *Far Eastern Economic Review*, 5 April 1990, and *The Economist*, 2 March 1991, p. 62.
10 *Free China Journal*, 19 May and 16 June 1992.
11 Milton Yeh, 'The ROC's Policy Towards Hong Kong and Macao', *Issues and Studies*, December 1991.
12 Teh-pei Yu, 'Economic Links Among Hong Kong, PRC and ROC', Jurgen Domes and Yu-ming Shaw (eds), *Hong Kong* (Boulder, Colorado: Westview Press, 1988).
13 *Free China Review*, July 1992, p. 57.
14 Details from David Goodman, *Southern China in Transition* (Melbourne: Longman/Cheshire, 1992), and *Far Eastern Economic Review*, 6 June 1991.
15 *International Herald Tribune*, 26 June 1992.
16 *International Herald Tribune*, 31 December 1991, and *Free China*

Journal, 22 May and 6 June 1992.
17 Central News Agency, 27 May 1991, FE/1086/A3/2.
18 *International Herald Tribune*, 2 March 1992.
19 Taipei Home Service, 12 August 1989, SWB/FE/0536/A3/3.
20 China News Agency, 15 January 1990, SWB/FE/0667/A3/7. See also *Free China Journal*, 10 March 1992, opinion piece: 'Hong Kong should have democracy'.
21 Liaowang, 15 January 1990, SWB/FE/0669/A3/1.
22 *The Economist*, 10 March 1990, p. 75.
23 *Far Eastern Economic Review*, 7 September 1989, p. 35.
24 *The Economist*, 26 August 1989, p. 46.
25 *Far Eastern Economic Review*, 1 February 1990.
26 *Far Eastern Economic Review*, 31 May 1990, p. 13.
27 *Far Eastern Economic Review*, 1 February 1990, p. 23.
28 *Far Eastern Economic Review*, 31 May 1990, p. 12.
29 *Financial Times*, 30 July 1991.
30 *International Herald Tribune*, 27 and 29 April 1991.
31 *Financial Times*, survey of Hong Kong, 29 September 1986.
32 *Far Eastern Economic Review*, 7 December 1989, and *Billion*, March 1990.
33 *Far Eastern Economic Review*, 7 December 1989, p. 62.
34 *Far Eastern Economic Review*, 25 April 1991, p. 52.
35 *Far Eastern Economic Review*, 25 April 1991, pp. 53–5.
36 Laura Newby, 'Sino-Japanese Relations', Gerald Segal (ed), *Chinese Politics and Foreign Policy Reform* (London: Kegan Paul International for the RIIA, 1990).
37 Mineo Nakajima, 'The Hong Kong Agreement and Its Impact on the International Position of Japan', Jurgen Domes and Yu-ming Shaw (eds), *Hong Kong* (Boulder, Colorado: Westview Press, 1985).
38 *The Times*, 20 August 1984.
39 *The Times*, 27 September 1984.
40 *International Herald Tribune*, 1 September 1982.
41 *Straits Times*, 2 February 1982, *Japan Times*, 12 July 1982, and *Financial Times*, 21 May and 28 August 1987.
42 *International Herald Tribune*, 19 February 1987, and *Financial Times*, 28 November 1991. The *Financial Trimes* of 10 December 1991 reports that investment in Hong Kong in 1990 was the highest in Asia.
43 *Financial Times*, 17 March 1986.
44 *Far Eastern Economic Review*, 9 November 1989, p. 13.
45 *Financial Times*, 10 December 1991.
46 *International Herald Tribune*, 30 May 1990.
47 *Far Eastern Economic Review*, 28 June 1990, p. 72.
48 *Financial Times*, 28 June 1991.
49 Xinhua, 7 October 1991, FE/1203/A3/6.
50 *Financial Times*, 6 July 1990.
51 For a moving description of the impact of Japanese policy, see Rey

Ventura, *Underground in Japan* (London: Jonathan Cape, 1992).

52 *Financial Times*, 16 December 1991, 5 February 1992, and *Japan Times Weekly*, 1 July 1991.

53 *International Herald Tribune*, 31 August 1989.

54 *The Times*, 31 August 1989.

55 *Far Eastern Economic Review*, 16 November 1989, p. 26.

56 *International Herald Tribune*, 20 December 1989.

57 *International Herald Tribune*, 5 July 1990.

58 *International Herald Tribune*, 2 December 1982.

59 *Financial Times*, 29 December 1982, and *The Economist*, 8 December 1990, p. 80.

60 Kate Grosser and Brian Bridges, 'Economic Interdependence in East Asia', *Pacific Review* No. 1, 1990.

61 *The Economist*, 2 September 1989 and 27 January 1990.

62 *Far Eastern Economic Review*, 19 October 1989, p. 26, and *Independent*, 24 October 1989.

63 *Financial Times*, 10 March 1990.

64 South China Morning Post, 9 March 1990, FBIS-CHI-90-047-55-6.

65 *The Economist*, 23 September 1989.

66 *Far Eastern Economic Review*, 15 March 1990, p. 17.

67 *South China Morning Post*, 14 February 1991, p. 3, and Peter Lyon, 'Tonga: Two Contemporary·Tendencies', *Pacific Review* No. 3, 1991.

68 Cait Murphy, 'A Culture of Emigration', *Atlantic Monthly*, April 1991, p. 24.

11. Europe: Someone Else's Problem

1 Jean-Pierre Cabestan, 'Sino-European Relations', Gerald Segal (ed), *Chinese Politics and Foreign Policy Reform* (London: Kegan Paul International for the RIIA, 1990).

2 Lawrence Freedman, 'Western Europe and the Triangle', Gerald Segal (ed), *The China Factor* (London: Croom Helm, 1982).

3 Alyson Bailes, Sino-East European Relations (London: Royal Institute of International Affairs, 1990).

4 For details and analysis, see Harish Kapur, *Distant Neighbours: China and Europe* (London: Frances Pinter, 1990).

5 Shen Shouyuan, 'Sino-European Relations in the Global Context', *Asian Survey* No. 11, November 1986, p. 1173.

6 Cabestan, 'Sino-European', p. 225.

7 See report of Premier Zhao Ziyang's trip to Europe in 1984, *Financial Times*, 25 May 1984, and *The Times*, 30 May 1984.

8 Cabestan, 'Sino-European', p. 226.

9 *Financial Times*, 15 April 1985, 14 May 1985, and 13 August 1985.

10 *Financial Times*, 26 October 1988.

11 *International Herald Tribune*, 21 November 1988.

12 *International Herald Tribune*, 7 November 1988.
13 *Financial Times*, 11 and 16 November 1988, and 28 and 29 December 1988.
14 *Financial Times*, 26 January 1989, and *International Herald Tribune*, 12 January 1988. See also *Le Monde*, 21 May 1988, for a French perspective.
15 *Financial Times*, 15 May 1991, and *Dateline Hong Kong* No. 5, 1991.
16 Cited in *Dateline Hong Kong* No 4, 1990, p. 2.
17 For a general discussion of these issues, see William Wallace, *The Transformation of Western Europe* (London: Frances Pinter for the RIIA, 1990), and for Franco-British policies in general, see Françoise de la Serre, Jacques Leruez and Helen Wallace (eds), *French and British Foreign Policies in Transition* (Oxford: Berg Publishers for the RIIA, 1990).
18 Alan Dowty, *Closed Borders* (New Haven: Yale University Press, 1987), p. 21.
19 Louise Holborn et al., *Refugees: A Problem of Our Time* (Metuchen, New Jersey: Scarecrow Press, 1975) pp. 391–404.
20 Charles Tilly, 'Migration in Modern European History', William McNeill and Ruth S. Adams, *Human Migration* (Bloomington: Indiana University Press, 1978).
21 Jonas Widgren, 'Europe and International Migration in the Future', Gil Loescher and Laila Monahan (eds), *Refugees and International Relations* (Oxford: Oxford University Press, 1989).
22 *The Economist*, 16 March 1991, p. 11. The same source cites figures of 8% for the United States and Germany, 7% for France, 5% for Britain and 2% for Italy in 1989/90 in its issue of 17 August 1991. In its issue of 15 February 1992 it notes that, excluding American and EC nationals in each other's countries, only 2.3% of the EC population are foreign citizens. Equivalent figures for the United States, excluding Europeans and Canadians, is 3.7%.
23 *Financial Times*, 26 January 1991, and *Independent*, 7 October 1990.
24 Roy McDowell, 'Co-ordination of Refugee Policy in Europe', Loescher and Monahan (eds), *Refugees and International Relations*.
25 *Refugees*, June 1989, p. 34.
26 Johan Cels, 'Responses of European States to *de facto* Refugees', Loescher and Monahan (eds), *Refugees and International Relations*.
27 *The Times*, 30 August 1989.
28 Alan Butt Philip, *European Border Controls* (London: RIIA Discussion Papers No. 19, 1989).
29 *The Economist*, 17 August 1991.
30 Europe had a third of the world's population in 1900 and only 10% in 1990. For a general discussion, see William Wallace, 'Tide of Crisis', *New Statesman and Society*, 17 May 1991.
31 Eurostat figures cited in *The Economist*, 15 February 1992.
32 *Financial Times*, 12 March 1990.

33 *Sunday Times*, 15 October 1989, South China Morning Post, 4 March 1990, FBIS-CHI-90-043-56.
34 *Guardian*, 11 April 1990. This suggests that the 50,000 figure is a total number which would include families. Thus 1,500 from France would actually mean some 6,000 people, leaving the other Europeans and reportedly also Australia and Canada to chip in equivalent numbers per country.
35 *The Times*, 2 March 1990.
36 *The Times*, 11 December 1986.
37 *Canada and Hong Kong Update*, Fall 1990, p. 9.
38 *Financial Times*, 11 March 1981.
39 *Le Monde*, 4 June 1982.
40 *Daily Telegraph*, 31 January 1983.
41 *Financial times*, 10 February 1984.
42 *Le Monde*, 22 April 1984.
43 *Le Monde*, 27 September 1984.
44 See the interview with M.D. Bariani, 3 August 1987, issued by the French embassy in London.
45 *Le Monde*, 12 February 1988, 18 May 1988, and 24 July 1988.
46 See a serious analysis of the region by Philippe Lemaitre, *Le Monde*, 16 August 1988.
47 *Le Monde*, 22 October 1988.
48 *Le Monde*, 24 October 1990.
49 *The Economist*, 29 June 1991, and *Far Eastern Economic Review*, 15 November 1990, p. 62.
50 This section relies heavily on Herbert Yee and Sonny Lo, 'Macau in Transition', *Asian Survey* No. 10, October 1991.
51 Nalyn Newitt, *Portugal in Africa* (London: C. Hurst & Co., 1981).
52 Yee and Lo, 'Macau in Transition', p. 918.
53 *The Times*, 10 September 1990, and *International Herald Tribune*, 23 August 1990.
54 *Independent*, 4 October 1990.

12. Getting to 1997

1 The most nightmarish scenario can be found in Simon Winchester's *Pacific Nightmare* (London: Sidgwick and Jackson, 1992).

Index

Acheson, Dean, 96
Aden, 10
Afro-Caribbeans, 103
airport project, 62, 63, 93-4, 167, 197
Algeria, 13, 101
American war of independence, 9
Andriessen, Frans, 181
Anglo-Chinese agreement (1984), 32, 33, 47-53, 57-8, 59, 62, 71, 72, 74, 93, 94-5, 117, 153, 205, 207
Anglo-Chinese war, second, 14
Annex 3, 53
APEC *see* Asia-Pacific Economic Co-operation
Argentina, 38, 39
Arrow, 14
ASEAN *see* Association of South East Asian States
Ashdown, Paddy, 49
Asia-Pacific Economic Co-operation (APEC), 144, 156, 160, 166,
Association of South East Asian Nations (ASEAN), 160, 172
Atkins, Humphrey, 36
Atlantic charter (1943), 20
Australia, 1, 56, 67, 100, 101, 108-11, 120, 122, 124-7, 141, 143-50, 172, 173, 174, 196, 200, 201
Austria, 101

Balkans, 101
Bank of America, 65
Bank of China, 42
Bank of Taiwan, 156
Basic Law, 45, 50, 51, 53-4, 60, 69, 70, 74, 77, 82, 87, 89; Article 14, 53; Article 157, 54; Article 158, 54
Basic Law Drafting Committee (BLDC), 53, 89
BBC World Service, 44
BDT *see* British Dependent Territories
Belgium, 100, 101, 184, 185, 186
Belize, 174
Benelux countries, 185
Bermuda, 45, 57, 62, 65
Bill of Rights, 72, 135
Boxer rebellion (1900), 102
brain drain, 51, 64-5, 91, 107, 111
Britain, immigration to, 100-111
British Dependent Territories (BDT), 47, 49, 66, 106, 187
British East Indian Company, 9-10
British Nationality Act (1981), 48, 103-4, 107
Bush, George, 113-14, 119

Calwell, Arthur, 146

Canada, 1, 67, 100, 101, 108, 109, 111, 120, 121, 122, 124-30, 172, 173, 174, 200, 201; and Australia, 143-50; immigration policy, 130-38, 201; relations with China and Britain, 138-42
Canada Act (1982), 129
Canadian Association of Police Chiefs, 136
Canton, 8, 9, 11, 18, 19, 34
Cathay Pacific, 47, 58, 149
Chatham House Rules, 4
Chiang Kaishek, 113
Chien, Foreign Minister, 154
China International Trust and Investment Corporation, 58
Chinese constitution, 1982 (Article 31), 39-40
Chinese Exclusion Act, 122
Chinese Immigration Act (1923), 130, 131
Clark, Joe, 138, 139
COCOM (Coordinating Committee for Multilateral Export Controls), 118, 119, 178
Cold War, 23, 96, 97, 100, 111, 113, 118, 127, 143, 177
Commission for Racial Equality, 105
Commonwealth, 172-3; and British Nationality Act, 103-4; and HK problem, 93; and immigration to Britain, 102, 108
Commonwealth Games, 173
Commonwealth Immigration Act, 103
Congo, 101
Conservative government (Britain), 103
corruption, 28, 193-4
Court of Final Appeal, 72-3
Cradock, Sir Percy, 43, 44, 45
Crimean war, 13-14
Cuba, 123
Cultural Revolution (China), 26, 28, 29, 80, 115
Curzon, Lord, 101
Czechoslovakia, 101

Daya Bay nuclear power station, 55
decolonisation, 32, 33, 52, 200
democracy, 27, 70-72, 88-9, 90, 99
Deng Xiaoping, 35, 36, 40, 46, 66, 99, 109, 111, 195, 197, 208; on Chinese gradual participation, 80; effort to revive south China as a model for the whole country, 86; and greater 'participation' and 'changes' in HK, 89; and lease extension question, 37; on role of Britain in HK, 88; and stationing of PLA troops in HK, 45, 80, 81; takes control at phase two talks, 43; and Mrs Thatcher, 106; visits Guangdong, 63

230